Vocabulary for the COMMON CORE

Robert J. Marzano
Julia A. Simms

Marzano Research Laboratory

Copyright © 2013 by Marzano Research Laboratory

All rights reserved, including the right of reproduction of this book in whole or in part in any form.

555 North Morton Street

Bloomington, IN 47404

888.849.0851

FAX: 866.801.1447

email: info@marzanoresearch.com

marzanoresearch.com

Printed in the United States of America

Library of Congress Control Number: 2013906762

ISBN: 978-0-9858902-2-3 (paperback)

17 16 15 14 13   1 2 3 4 5

Editorial Director: Lesley Bolton

Managing Production Editor: Caroline Weiss

Copy Editor: Rachel Rosolina

Proofreader: Elisabeth Abrams

Text Designer: Amy Shock

Cover Designer: Rian Anderson

Marzano Research Laboratory Development Team

Director of Publications

Julia A. Simms

Marzano Research Laboratory Associates

Elliott Asp	Pam Livingston
Tina Boogren	Sonny Magaña
Bev Clemens	Beatrice McGarvey
Jane K. Doty Fischer	Margaret McInteer
Maria C. Foseid	Diane E. Paynter
Mark P. Foseid	Debra Pickering
Tammy Heflebower	Salle Quackenboss
Mitzi Hoback	Laurie Robinson
Jan K. Hoegh	Ainsley B. Rose
Russell Jenson	Tom Roy
Jessica Kanold-McIntyre	Gerry Varty
Sharon Kramer	Phil Warrick
David Livingston	Kenneth Williams

Table of Contents

About the Authors ix

About Marzano Research Laboratory xi

Introduction 1

PART I

Vocabulary Instruction for the Common Core State Standards 3

1 The Importance of Vocabulary 5

Vocabulary Development 5

Vocabulary Knowledge 7

The Effects of Vocabulary Instruction 9

2 A Six-Step Process for Vocabulary Instruction 13

Step 1: Provide a Description, Explanation, or Example of the New Term 14

Step 2: Ask Students to Restate the Description, Explanation, or Example in Their Own Words 19

Step 3: Ask Students to Construct a Picture, Symbol, or Graphic Representing the Term or Phrase 22

Step 4: Engage Students Periodically in Activities That Help Them Add to Their Knowledge of the Terms in Their Vocabulary Notebooks . . 24

Step 5: Periodically Ask Students to Discuss the Terms With One Another 34

Step 6: Involve Students Periodically in Games That Allow Them to Play With Terms 36

3 Vocabulary Terms From the Common Core State Standards 41

Tier 2 Vocabulary From the Common Core State Standards 42

Tier 3 Vocabulary From the Common Core State Standards 44

4 Building a Vocabulary Program 49

Selecting Terms to Teach 49

Creating Systems to Assess and Track Students' Vocabulary Knowledge 52

PART II

Tier 2 Vocabulary Terms From the Common Core State Standards.................55

Add To (ADD)...57

Arrange (ARR)...57

Collaborate (COLL)...58

Compare/Contrast (C/C)...59

Create (CRE)...61

Decide (DEC)...63

Define (DEF)...63

Elaborate (ELAB)...65

Evaluate (EVAL)...66

Execute (EXEC)...67

Explain (EXP)...68

Hypothesize (HYP)...70

Infer (INF)...72

Measure (MEAS)...72

Problem Solve (PS)...73

Prove/Argue (P/A)...74

Pull Apart (PULL)...76

Redo (REDO)...77

Reference (REF)...78

Seek Information (SI)...79

See the Big Picture (SBP)...81

Symbolize (SYM)...82

Think Metacognitively (TM)...84

Transform (TRANS)...85

PART III

Tier 3 Vocabulary Terms From the Common Core State Standards......89

English Language Arts 91

    Reading 91

    Reading Foundations..113

    Writing..115

    Speaking and Listening...127

    Language 134

Mathematics 145

    Number and Quantity...145

    Operations and Algebra..159

    Functions 177

    Geometry 183

    Measurement, Data, Statistics, and Probability.............................199

Appendix: Master List of Terms 215

    Part II Categories 215

    Part III Measurement Topics..215

    Terms 219

References and Resources 253

Index 263

About the Authors

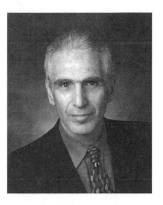

Robert J. Marzano, PhD, is the cofounder and CEO of Marzano Research Laboratory in Denver, Colorado. Throughout his forty years in the field of education, he has become a speaker, trainer, and author of more than thirty books and 150 articles on topics such as instruction, assessment, writing and implementing standards, cognition, effective leadership, and school intervention. His books include *The Art and Science of Teaching*, *Leaders of Learning*, *On Excellence in Teaching*, *Effective Supervision*, the *Classroom Strategies* series, and *Using Common Core Standards to Enhance Classroom Instruction and Assessment*. His practical translations of the most current research and theory into classroom strategies are known internationally and are widely practiced by both teachers and administrators. He received a bachelor's degree from Iona College in New York, a master's degree from Seattle University, and a doctorate from the University of Washington.

Julia A. Simms, EdM, MA, is director of publications for Marzano Research Laboratory in Denver, Colorado. She has worked in K–12 education as a classroom teacher, gifted education specialist, teacher leader, and coach. She is coauthor of *Coaching Classroom Instruction* and *Using Common Core Standards to Enhance Classroom Instruction and Assessment* and has led school- and district-level professional development on a variety of topics, including literacy instruction and intervention, classroom and schoolwide differentiation, and instructional technology. She received her bachelor's degree from Wheaton College in Wheaton, Illinois, and her master's degrees in educational administration and K–12 literacy from Colorado State University and the University of Northern Colorado, respectively.

About Marzano Research Laboratory

Marzano Research Laboratory (MRL) is a joint venture between Solution Tree and Dr. Robert J. Marzano. MRL combines Dr. Marzano's forty years of educational research with continuous action research in all major areas of schooling in order to provide effective and accessible instructional strategies, leadership strategies, and classroom assessment strategies that are always at the forefront of best practice. By providing such an all-inclusive research-into-practice resource center, MRL provides teachers and principals with the tools they need to effect profound and immediate improvement in student achievement.

Introduction

In 2009, the National Governors Association Center for Best Practices (NGA) and the Council of Chief State School Officers formed the Common Core State Standards Initiative. Their goal was to create a set of statements about what students should know and be able to do as a result of schooling that would be common to all states. Shortly after the Common Core State Standards (CCSS) were released in 2010, forty-five of the fifty states adopted them.

The advent of the CCSS presents educators in the United States with new resources and opportunities, but also with significant challenges. Teachers need to understand the ideas behind the new standards, how they differ from their state's previous standards, and how to implement them in their classrooms. To help educators address these challenges, researchers at Marzano Research Laboratory sought to develop tools and strategies that educators could use to successfully implement the CCSS in their classrooms and schools. As they analyzed the CCSS and talked to teachers across the United States, they realized that vocabulary instruction was an important area of need. The CCSS prioritize students' acquisition of a wide range of academic and domain-specific vocabulary, and educators needed research-based strategies and processes that would help them implement CCSS-aligned vocabulary instruction in their classrooms and schools. This book was written to meet that need. Other tools and resources for the CCSS are available in the book *Using Common Core Standards to Enhance Classroom Instruction and Assessment* (Marzano, Yanoski, Hoegh, & Simms, 2013) and online at **marzanoresearch.com/commoncore**.

A book that focuses exclusively on vocabulary is not common among the many (otherwise very useful) books that have already been written about how to implement the CCSS. Previous books have focused on the history and organization of the CCSS (Kendall, 2011; Reeves et al., 2011; Rothman, 2011), thinking skills within the CCSS (Bellanca, Fogarty, & Pete, 2012), assessments and the CCSS (Daggett, Gendron, & Heller, 2010), using the CCSS within existing instructional frameworks (Burris & Garrity, 2012; Crawford, 2012), and leading implementation of the CCSS (Dunkle, 2012). Others have offered curriculum maps for the CCSS (Common Core, 2012a, 2012b, 2012c) and strategies for achieving success with the CCSS (Silver, Dewing, & Perini, 2012). This omission is unfortunate, since the CCSS present unique demands on the breadth and depth of students' vocabulary knowledge and, in turn, on the instructional techniques teachers must employ in their classrooms. For instance, while students must acquire an attitude of exploration and curiosity toward new words, teachers must identify a manageable number of CCSS vocabulary terms for direct instruction; help students understand, internalize, remember, and use those terms; and assess and track students' progress with the terms. This book was written to address those challenges.

The book includes three parts. Part I contains chapters 1–4. In chapter 1, we explain the importance of vocabulary knowledge and instruction, factors that affect students' vocabulary development, how vocabulary influences students' reading ability and achievement in school, and the research supporting direct vocabulary instruction as an effective strategy for increasing students' vocabulary knowledge. Chapter 2 presents a six-step, research-based process for vocabulary instruction that guides teachers as they introduce and explain new terms and prompt students to create descriptions and graphic representations for terms, interact and play with terms, and refine their understanding of terms. In chapter 3, we describe the process we used to identify and organize two types of vocabulary terms from the CCSS: academic terms and domain-specific terms. Finally, chapter 4 explains how to build a classroom, school, or district vocabulary program and how to assess and track students' vocabulary knowledge.

Part II contains the academic terms (in this case, cognitive verbs) that we identified from the CCSS, organized into twenty-four categories. These verbs describe how students should interact with the knowledge and skills they learn in class.

Part III contains the domain-specific English language arts (ELA) and math terms that we identified from the CCSS, organized into 116 measurement topics (groups of related words that can be taught together).

The appendix lists all academic and domain-specific terms alphabetically with identifiers so readers can easily find specific words.

PART I

Vocabulary Instruction for the Common Core State Standards

1

The Importance of Vocabulary

Students' vocabulary knowledge is directly tied to their success in school. This is partly because vocabulary is an important aspect of reading comprehension (Cunningham & Stanovich, 1997; Hattie, 2009; National Reading Panel, 2000; Petty, Herold, & Stoll, 1967; Scarborough, 2001; Stahl, 1999; Stahl & Nagy, 2006) and reading is an important part of learning in school. However, vocabulary knowledge helps students in other ways as well. Knowing what words mean and how they interconnect creates networks of knowledge that allow students to connect new information to previously learned information. These networks of knowledge are commonly referred to as *prior knowledge* or *background knowledge* (Marzano, 2004). Studies have shown that students with greater background knowledge about a topic learn more, remember more, and are more interested when that topic is taught than those who have less initial background knowledge (Alexander, Kulikowich, & Schulze, 1994; Dochy, Segers, & Buehl, 1999; Tobias, 1994). For example, a student learning to measure temperatures would benefit greatly from previous experience with terms such as *Fahrenheit, Celsius, degree, positive number, negative number,* or *number line.* A student learning to write argumentative pieces would probably understand the task and purpose better if he or she had even a rudimentary understanding of terms such as *claim* and *support.* Conversely, a student who has never heard these terms and has no experiences associated with them may require more time and effort to understand their meanings and the concepts they signify.

Vocabulary Development

The creators of the Common Core State Standards (CCSS) explained that children initially develop their vocabularies through oral conversations, wherein context clues and background knowledge can help them determine word meanings:

> Such conversations are context rich in ways that aid in vocabulary acquisition: in discussions, a small set of words (accompanied by gesture and intonation) is used with great frequency to talk about a narrow range of situations children are exposed to on a day-to-day basis. (NGA & CCSSO, 2010a, p. 32)

For example, most children can easily identify different parts of their face and body at a young age because their parents spend lots of time asking them where their nose, mouth, ears, hands, and feet are, using gestures to help them associate words with parts, and praising them ("That's right! Good for you!") when the child identifies the correct part. However, not all children have equal exposure to the same quantity and kinds of rich oral conversations necessary for early vocabulary development.

The critical role of oral conversation in the development of vocabulary was brought into sharp relief by the research of Betty Hart and Todd Risley (1995). In the late 1980s and early 1990s, they conducted a study designed to observe forty-two young children and their families in their homes at regular intervals over the course of two and a half years (beginning at age one and concluding when the children were three or four). They concluded that "what parents said and did with their children in the first 3 years of language learning had an enormous impact on how much language their children learned and used" (Hart & Risley, 1995, p. 159). Although they found that the quality of the talk that went on in households at all socioeconomic status (SES) levels was about the same, children in higher socioeconomic families simply experienced *more* talk, as shown in table 1.1. Hart and Risley also found a correlation between children's vocabulary size and their IQ scores.

Table 1.1: Correlations Between Socioeconomic Status, Talk, Vocabulary Size, and IQ Score

	Professional Families	Working-Class Families	Welfare Families
Parent Utterances Per Hour	487	301	176
Child's Recorded Vocabulary Size	1,116	749	525
IQ Score at Age 3	117	107	79

Source: Adapted from Hart & Risley, 1995, p. 176.

As shown in table 1.1, children whose parents talked to them more began preschool and kindergarten with larger vocabularies and higher IQ scores than children whose parents talked to them less. In 2003, Hart and Risley published "The Early Catastrophe: The 30 Million Word Gap by Age 3." In that article, they used their 1995 data, along with further data collected on the same children in the years since the original study, to extrapolate that in the first four years of life, "an average child in a professional family would accumulate experience with almost 45 million words, an average child in a working-class family 26 million words, and an average child in a welfare family 13 million words" (p. 9). The eponymous 30 million word gap between children in professional families and children in welfare families highlights the powerful role that socioeconomic status plays in vocabulary development.

Although not as extensive as Hart and Risley's work, Erika Hoff's 2003 study of over sixty high- and middle-SES children's interactions with their mothers found similar results. However, she also highlighted the fact that children in higher SES families not only hear more words, but they also have more language-learning experiences around which to interact. She stated that "aspects of experience that support vocabulary acquisition are not equally available to children across socioeconomic strata" (p. 1375). When considered together, Hart and Risley's (1995, 2003) and Hoff's (2003) research paint a worrying picture of the vocabulary challenges that lower-SES students face.

Vocabulary progresses in rather predictable ways beyond oral conversation. For example, students develop vocabulary associated with their interests. Jill Castek, Bridget Dalton, and Dana Grisham (2012) explained that in addition to learning vocabulary through interactions with parents, siblings, and other important people in their lives, children learn new vocabulary "as a result of socialization into various communities of practice" (p. 305). A student interested in Greek and Roman mythology will probably develop a larger vocabulary of terms related to that topic than a student interested primarily in cars and motorcycles (who would probably develop rich vocabulary knowledge in that field).

One of the biggest challenges in developing academic vocabulary, like the terms important to the CCSS, is that it might not initially seem related to students' interests. Additionally, many CCSS terms tend to be intangible and not commonly used in everyday interactions. Castek and her colleagues (2012) observed that "learning to use academic language is one of the greatest challenges of schooling because this register tends to be abstract and distant from spoken vocabulary" (p. 305). Explicit descriptions and examples are necessary to help students understand and use many of the academic vocabulary terms critical to their success in school.

Vocabulary Knowledge

In addition to their findings about socioeconomic status and vocabulary, Hart and Risley (1995) found that children with larger vocabularies acquired new words at a faster rate than other children. Andrew Biemiller and Naomi Slonim (Biemiller, 2005, 2012; Biemiller & Slonim, 2001) reported similar research:

> By the end of grade 2, children in the lowest vocabulary quartile had acquired slightly more than 1.5 root words a day over 7 years, for a total of about 4,000 root word meanings. In contrast, children in the highest quartile had acquired more than 3 root words a day, for a total of about 8,000 root word meanings. (Biemiller, 2012, p. 34)

According to Loren Marulis and Susan Neuman (2010), a slower rate of learning new words leads to a "cumulative disadvantage over time" (p. 301). Here we review three areas affected by this disadvantage: (1) reading ability, (2) independent reading, and (3) mental processes.

Vocabulary and Reading Ability

The nature of the cumulative disadvantage described by Marulis and Neuman (2010) becomes clear when one considers vocabulary's effects on learning to read and reading comprehension. Michael Kamil and Elfrieda Hiebert (2005) described the process of learning to read as follows:

> Beginning reading instruction is typically accomplished by teaching children a set of rules to decode printed words to speech. If the words are present in the child's oral vocabulary, comprehension should occur as the child decodes and monitors the oral representations. However, if the print vocabulary is more complex than the child's oral vocabulary, comprehension will *not* occur. (p. 3)

Students who have large oral vocabularies will recognize and understand more of the words they are asked to decode, which in turn allows them to more fully comprehend the passages they read. The importance of vocabulary knowledge in learning to read was emphasized by the National Reading Panel's (NRP) 2000 report, *Teaching Children to Read: An Evidence-Based Assessment of the Scientific Research Literature on Reading and Its Implications for Reading Instruction*. Concerning vocabulary, the NRP (2000) reported:

> Benefits in understanding text by applying letter-sound correspondences to printed material come about only if the target word is in the learner's oral vocabulary. When the word is not in the learner's oral vocabulary, it will not be understood when it occurs in print. *Vocabulary occupies an important middle ground in learning to read. Oral vocabulary is a key to learning to make the transition from oral to written forms* (ch. 4, p. 3, italics added)

As seen in the NRP's report and echoed by the authors of the CCSS, "the importance of students acquiring a rich and varied vocabulary cannot be overstated" (NGA & CCSSO, 2010a, p. 32).

Vocabulary and Independent Reading

A large vocabulary helps children learn to read; because of the connections between vocabulary and reading comprehension, students with large vocabularies are more successful readers and therefore more likely to read independently than students with smaller vocabularies. Steven Stahl (1999) described how this relationship affects the amount of reading that students do as they progress through school:

> Because poor readers tend to read less than better readers, the gap between good and poor readers in absolute numbers of words read becomes progressively greater as the child advances through school. . . . Children who are good readers become better readers because they read more and also more challenging texts, but poor readers get relatively worse because they read less and also less challenging texts. Indeed, researchers have found large differences in the amount of free reading that good and poor readers do in and out of the school. (p. 12)

In other words, students who read well tend to read more, thus improving their vocabularies and reading skills, while students who have trouble reading tend to read less, thus missing opportunities to augment their vocabularies and improve their reading skills through practice. Much additional research supports the correlation between vocabulary level and reading comprehension (for example, Coyne, Capozzoli-Oldham, & Simmons, 2012; Cromley & Azevedo, 2007; Lesaux & Kieffer, 2010; Stahl & Nagy, 2006). In sum, the effects of vocabulary knowledge on reading comprehension and skill are significant and long lasting.

Vocabulary and Mental Processes

Vocabulary is also related to basic mental processes and skills that affect students' overall academic achievement. Katherine Stahl and Steven Stahl (2012) explained that "children's ability to name things establishes their ability to form categories" (p. 72). For example, a student who learns the word *shake* can subsequently attach other words and concepts to it, such as *shiver, vibrate, wiggle, flutter, jitter,* and so on. As students develop more complex categorization systems for new words, they are better able to summarize (Kintsch, 1998; Kintsch & van Dijk, 1978) and make inferences (Anderson & Pearson, 1984) about new information. Stahl and Stahl (2012) concluded that "to expand a child's vocabulary is to teach that child to think about the world, and in a reciprocal fashion, [a] more refined vocabulary indicates that child's degree of knowledge about his or her world" (p. 73). Essentially, knowing more words allows students to think about more concepts in more ways.

Researchers have also found that there is a significant correlation between vocabulary and intelligence. Joseph Jenkins, Marcy Stein, and Katherine Wysocki (1984) cited correlations as high as 0.80 between vocabulary and intelligence, and Marzano (2004) summarized similarly high correlations between vocabulary knowledge and intelligence, as shown in table 1.2.

Table 1.2: Correlations Between Vocabulary and Intelligence in Various Studies

Study	Correlation
Terman (1918)	0.91
Mahan and Whitmer (1936)	0.87
Spache (1943)	0.92

Study	Correlation
Elwood (1939)	0.98
McNemar (1942)	0.86
Lewinski (1948)	0.82
Wechsler (1949)	0.78
Raven (1948)	0.93

Source: Marzano, 2004, p. 32.

To interpret the correlations in table 1.2, keep in mind that a perfect positive relationship between two variables is indicated by a correlation of 1.00. As one variable increases, so does the other. Therefore, correlations approaching 1.00 (such as those shown in table 1.2) are considered quite strong.

There are several possible reasons for the correlation between vocabulary and intelligence. First, Stahl (1999) suggested that students who have higher general ability (or intelligence) are simply better at more things, including learning new vocabulary words. Alternatively, Sternberg (1987) postulated that students with higher intelligence learn better from context, and so soak up more words as they encounter various situations. However, it is also possible that students with larger vocabularies can understand more information and therefore analyze information more effectively, thus allowing them to perform better on intelligence tests. A study by Brent Berlin and Paul Kay (1999) illustrates this principle. Berlin and Kay investigated different cultures' perceptions of color. They discovered that some cultures had fewer terms for colors than others. For example, some cultures only had color terms for light and dark; others for light, dark, and red; others for light, dark, red, and green; and so on. The vocabulary for color in a culture's language affected their ability to talk and think about the concept of color. In the same way, it is difficult for a student to think about a concept if he or she doesn't know the word for it. One final explanation for the correlation between vocabulary knowledge and intelligence may have to do with the use of vocabulary-based tasks on intelligence tests. If an intelligence test asks a student to select the appropriate use of a specific word, the student's success with that task is directly related to his or her knowledge of that word. Whatever the reason for the correlation between vocabulary and intelligence, Stahl and Nagy's (2006) statement holds true: "Words divide the world; the more words we have, the more complex ways we can think about the world" (p. 5).

The Effects of Vocabulary Instruction

Given the importance of vocabulary knowledge to academic success, one might assume that vocabulary instruction is of primary importance in most schools. However, Marzano (2004) reported that "uniform and systematic vocabulary instruction is scarce in U.S. schools" (p. 62), citing previous researchers (Durkin, 1979; Roser & Juel, 1982) who found that vocabulary instruction consumed less than one-half of one percent of instructional time in schools. The authors of the CCSS bemoaned the fact that "vocabulary instruction has been neither frequent nor systematic in most schools" (NGA & CCSSO, 2010a, p. 32) and cited a number of research studies (Biemiller, 2001; Durkin, 1979; Lesaux, Kieffer, Faller, & Kelley, 2010; Scott & Nagy, 1997) to support their assertion.

A number of meta-analyses have examined the effects of vocabulary instruction and intervention on students' comprehension, oral language, and print knowledge. A meta-analysis is a statistical technique that compiles a large number of studies on a specific topic or instructional strategy (such as direct vocabulary instruction) in order to compute the average effect for that strategy. In other words, a meta-analysis seeks to quantify the overall effectiveness of a given strategy across a number of studies. This effectiveness is often reported using a number called an effect size. In educational research, effect sizes around 0.15–0.20 are considered small, 0.45–0.50 are considered medium, and 0.80–0.90 are considered large (Cohen, 1988; Lipsey, 1990). The higher the effect size, the more effective the strategy.

Effect sizes are interpreted differently from correlations (discussed previously) because effect sizes commonly represent a student's expected improvement if they are exposed to a specific strategy. Correlations simply describe the relationship between two variables. So, as illustrated previously in table 1.2 (page 8), intelligence and vocabulary are highly correlated. That is, as one increases, so does the other. For correlations, the closer the decimal number is to 1.00, the stronger the relationship. Although effect sizes are also expressed using a decimal number, they are commonly interpreted in terms of how many standard deviations a student can be expected to improve as the result of a strategy's use. So, an effect size of .40 might be interpreted to mean that a student's performance would be expected to improve four-tenths of a standard deviation when a specific strategy is used.

Effect sizes are often translated into expected percentile gains. For example, Steven Stahl and Marilyn Fairbanks's (1986) meta-analysis found that if a teacher used direct vocabulary instruction, a student at the 50th percentile would be expected to improve to the 83rd percentile. In comparison, a student who didn't receive direct vocabulary instruction would be expected to remain at the 50th percentile. Table 1.3 shows effect sizes from various meta-analyses on direct vocabulary instruction with their corresponding percentile gains, including the Stahl and Fairbanks example.

Table 1.3: Meta-Analyses on the Effects of Direct Vocabulary Instruction

Meta-Analysis	Focus	Effect Size	Percentile Gain
Elleman, Lindo, Morphy, & Compton, 2009[a]	Effects of vocabulary instruction on comprehension	0.50 for words taught directly	19
		0.10 for all words	4
Haystead & Marzano, 2009	Effects of building vocabulary on academic achievement	0.51	19
Klesius & Searls, 1990[b]	Vocabulary interventions	0.50	19
Marmolejo, 1990[b]	Vocabulary interventions	0.69	25
Marulis & Neuman, 2010	Effects of vocabulary training on word learning	0.88 overall	31
		0.85 for preK	30
		0.94 for kindergarten	33
Mol, Bus, & de Jong, 2009[a]	Effects of interactive book reading on oral language	0.28	11
	Effects of interactive book reading on print knowledge	0.25	10

Meta-Analysis	Focus	Effect Size	Percentile Gain
Mol, Bus, de Jong, & Smeets, 2008[a]	Effects of dialogic reading on oral language	0.50 for preK 0.14 for kindergarten	19 6
National Early Literacy Panel, 2008[a]	Interactive book reading	0.75 for preK 0.66 for kindergarten	27 25
Nye, Foster, & Seaman, 1987[b]	Language intervention	1.04	35
Poirier, 1989[b]	Language intervention	0.50	19
Stahl & Fairbanks, 1986[a]	Effects of vocabulary instruction on comprehension	0.97 for words taught directly 0.30 for all words	33 12

[a] *As reported in Marulis & Neuman, 2010.*
[b] *As reported in Hattie, 2009.*

Stahl (1999) pointed out that direct vocabulary instruction can have a significant impact on students whose vocabularies are small or whose vocabulary growth is slower than their peers'.

> If one can teach 300 words per year, this will be a larger percentage of words for a child who might ordinarily learn 1000 words a year . . . than it would be for a child who would ordinarily learn 3000 or 5000 words. (p. 13)

Over the past three decades, Isabel Beck, Margaret McKeown, and their colleagues (Beck & McKeown, 1991, 2001, 2007; Beck, McKeown, & Kucan, 2002, 2008; Beck, Perfetti, & McKeown, 1982; McKeown, Beck, & Apthorp, 2010; McKeown, Beck, Omanson, & Perfetti, 1983; McKeown, Beck, Omanson, & Pople, 1985) have researched direct vocabulary instruction and concluded that the characteristics of effective direct vocabulary instruction are "frequent exposures to the words, encounters in multiple contexts, and deep or active processing of the words" (McKeown et al., 2010, p. 1). To summarize, the research on the effectiveness of direct vocabulary instruction is strong. Direct instruction about a targeted set of vocabulary terms helps students learn new words and gain the vocabulary knowledge they need for success in school.

As shown in this chapter, vocabulary development and knowledge are crucial for students' success. Vocabulary is a fundamental aspect of reading and literacy, and it also allows students to think about information and experiences in broader and deeper ways. However, students from lower-SES families often enter school with smaller vocabularies than their higher-SES counterparts. This disadvantage can affect their literacy abilities, their interest in reading, and their development of important mental processes. The good news is that direct vocabulary instruction can increase students' vocabularies and help them gain the vocabulary knowledge they need for success in school. Research provides support for the effectiveness of direct vocabulary instruction and guidance about the characteristics of that instruction. In the next chapter, we present a six-step process based on those characteristics that teachers can use to develop their students' knowledge and familiarity with terms from the CCSS.

2

A Six-Step Process for Vocabulary Instruction

Vocabulary knowledge develops gradually over time. Therefore, vocabulary instruction should be thought of as a process—not a singular event. The following depiction is a useful way of thinking about vocabulary development.

The first few times we encounter an unknown word, we create a container for that word in our brains. As we encounter the word more and more, we gradually fill up that container with bits of knowledge about the word: what it means, how to pronounce it, how to spell it, how it is used in sentences, what other words are normally used with it, its role in sentences, how often it is used, and how it is related to other words (Nation, 1990), among other things. Words whose containers are mostly full are generally the ones we use in our speech and writing. Words whose containers are half full or less are those we understand but don't use. Mostly empty containers contain words we profess not to know but are still able to answer questions about or distinguish between their correct and incorrect usage. Francis Durso and Wendelyn Shore (1991) and Mary Curtis (1987) found that even when people reported that a word was unknown, they were able to identify sentences in which it was used correctly, correctly identify its synonyms, and correctly answer questions about it.

The metaphor of words as containers is useful because it highlights the fact that direct vocabulary instruction does not necessarily have to produce in-depth understanding of vocabulary terms to be useful. Marzano (2004) stated that "the goal of direct vocabulary instruction is to provide students with a surface-level, not an in-depth, understanding of vocabulary terms" (p. 120). Similarly, Nagy and Herman (1987) wrote:

> Although a strong case can be made for rich, knowledge-based vocabulary instruction, one should not underestimate the possible benefits of less intensive instruction. . . . One should not underestimate the value of any meaningful encounter with a word, even if the information gained from the one encounter is relatively small. (pp. 31–32)

Useful guidelines for vocabulary instruction are implicit in these findings. If time is available to provide an in-depth understanding of vocabulary words to students, teachers should by all means encourage as much learning as possible. However, if only a limited amount of time is available, teachers should not neglect direct vocabulary instruction because they are only able to provide a surface-level understanding of the terms. Even brief instructional activities aimed at providing an initial surface-level understanding might help students form a "cup" or container for a word that allows them to connect future learning to that word.

Chapter 1 described elements of effective vocabulary instruction from research and theory. In this chapter, we describe a six-step process for vocabulary instruction based on that research and theory. This process has its own unique body of research supporting its effectiveness (Dunn, Bonner, & Huske, 2007; Gifford & Gore, 2008; Haystead & Marzano, 2009; Marzano, 2005, 2006). The first study supporting the utility of the six-step process (called "Building Academic Vocabulary" or BAV) was completed in 2005 (Marzano, 2005). During the 2004–2005 school year, 11 schools, 118 teachers, and 2,683 students participated in an evaluation study of the BAV process for vocabulary instruction. The study found that "students who participated in the BAV program exhibited greater ability to read and understand grade-appropriate materials in mathematics, science, and general literacy than their counterparts who did not participate in the program" (Marzano, 2006, p. 1). Furthermore, the study found that the BAV program was particularly effective for students who were English learners or who qualified for free and reduced lunch (indicating low socioeconomic status). Given Hart and Risley's (1995, 2003) previously reviewed conclusion that students from low SES families typically have smaller vocabularies than other students, these findings are particularly compelling.

Additionally, Haystead and Marzano (2009) synthesized the results of a number of studies conducted by classroom teachers on the effectiveness of the six-step process for vocabulary instruction. They found that the process was associated with an effect size of 0.51, which is associated with a gain of 20 percentile points. In other words, a student at the 50th percentile whose teacher used the six-step process for vocabulary instruction would be expected to improve to the 70th percentile, compared to a student whose teacher did not use the process. These findings indicate that the process can be effective in increasing vocabulary knowledge and reading comprehension for a variety of students in a variety of school situations.

The six steps of the vocabulary instruction process are as follows:

1. Provide a description, explanation, or example of the new term.

2. Ask students to restate the description, explanation, or example in their own words.

3. Ask students to construct a picture, symbol, or graphic representing the term or phrase.

4. Engage students periodically in activities that help them add to their knowledge of the terms in their vocabulary notebooks.

5. Periodically ask students to discuss the terms with one another.

6. Involve students periodically in games that allow them to play with terms.

The process is designed to be used with students of all ages and works equally well in self-contained classrooms (usually at the elementary level where one teacher teaches every subject) or in content-specific classes (as are usually used at the middle and high school levels). Teachers can devote as much or as little time to each step as they have available. As described previously, even surface-level knowledge of words is useful to students. Here, we describe and exemplify each step.

Step 1: Provide a Description, Explanation, or Example of the New Term

The first step involves providing a description, explanation, or example of the term for students. Before you can do that, however, you must determine what students already know. To verify this information, a teacher can simply ask, "What do you think you know about this term?" For example, an eighth-grade mathematics teacher asks students what they know about the term *function*. The students offer the following comments:

- A function is a kind of event. My mom organizes social functions for her ladies' club.

- People often say that something "is a function of" something else. My dad says that "the quality of a meal is a function of how hungry you are."

- A function is what a person does. My uncle functions as the president of our HOA.

- A function is arch-shaped. My brother graphs them on his calculator.

As students reply, the teacher listens for accurate knowledge as well as misconceptions. Accurate knowledge that students already have about a term can be incorporated into the teacher's subsequent description and explanation of the term. If students have misconceptions about a term, the teacher can correct and clarify these in her explanation of the term. From the student comments, the teacher determines that students have accurate knowledge about different meanings attached to the term *function* (an event, a relationship, a role) and realizes that she needs to help them focus on the mathematical meaning of "a relationship between two measurements." She also notes that some students understand that functions can be expressed visually by graphing them but recognizes the misconception that all functions' graphs are arch-shaped. She decides to refer back to the second comment about "the quality of a meal being a function of how hungry you are" and build on it when she gives examples of different real-world situations expressed by functions.

Once the baseline for student understanding is set, the teacher can begin the six-step process by providing a description for the term.

Definition vs. Description

Providing students with information about a word's meaning is an integral part of direct vocabulary instruction. Unfortunately, many teachers rely on dictionary definitions for this purpose. This practice is ineffective because the main goal of a dictionary definition is not necessarily to provide the clearest possible explanation for a word. In fact, Sidney Landau (1984) pointed out that one of the most important considerations when writing dictionary definitions is space. Definitions in dictionaries are typically designed to take up as little space as possible, in order to accommodate the large number of words that need to be included.

Additionally, dictionary definitions are designed using a classical structure that classifies, rather than explains, each concept. Stahl (1999) wrote, "There is a form for a definition, dating back to Aristotle, in which the definition first identifies which class (*genus*) the word belongs to, and then how that word differs from other members of its class (*differentia*)" (p. 17). For example, the *DK Merriam-Webster Children's Dictionary* (2008) defines *jeans* as "pants [class] made of denim [differentiation]" (p. 450) and *countdown* as "the process [class] of subtracting the time remaining before an event [differentiation]" (p. 202). Because of this structure, Snow (1990) found that students' ability to define words depended more on their understanding of the structure of a definition than on their actual understanding of a word.

Isabel Beck, Margaret McKeown, and Linda Kucan (2002) suggested that *descriptions* are more effective than definitions. Descriptions explain and exemplify words, often by using the words in sentences or explaining the contexts in which a word commonly appears. The *Collins COBUILD Illustrated Basic Dictionary* (Roehr & Carroll, 2010) represents one effort to supply students with descriptions rather than

1 illustrates the difference between descriptions found in the COBUILD dictionary n the DK children's dictionary (2008).

vs. Definitions

	Definition in *DK Merriam-Webster Children's Dictionary* (2008)	Description in *Collins COBUILD Illustrated Basic Dictionary* (Roehr & Carroll, 2010)
abrupt	Happening without warning	An **abrupt** change or action is very sudden, often in a way that is unpleasant.
dignity	The quality or state of being worthy of honor and respect	If someone behaves or moves with **dignity**, they are serious, calm, and controlled.
inclined	Having a desire	If you say that you are **inclined** to have a particular opinion, you mean that you have this opinion, but you do not feel strongly about it.
overlook	To fail to see	If you **overlook** a fact or a problem, you do not notice it.
threat	The act of showing an intention to do harm	If you make a **threat** against someone, you say that something bad will happen to them if they do not do what you want.

Descriptions, such as those shown in the right column of table 2.1, help students gain a clear understanding of what a word means and how it is generally used. Definitions, on the other hand, can often be confusing or lead students to infer incorrect meanings for words. For example, based solely on the dictionary definition for *abrupt* (from table 2.1) a student might compose sentences such as the following:

- Ben's surprise party was **abrupt**.

- The clown jumped out of the cake **abruptly**.

- Ben's **abrupt** gift of an Xbox 360 made all the children crowd around excitedly.

Technically, these sentences use the word *abrupt* to mean "happening without warning," but they also show that this student has failed to capture the usually negative connotations associated with the word. The description in table 2.1 highlights that aspect of the word, explaining that abrupt actions or events can often be unpleasant.

Explaining Features of Words

Effective description and explanation of a term involve helping students understand the important features of a word. For example, a word's part of speech (noun, verb, adverb, adjective, and so on) is one of its important features. Other important features may depend on who or what the word refers to. For example, words that refer to *people* have different key features than words that refer to *events*. Table 2.2 shows seven types of words with accompanying questions that teachers can ask students to draw out key features for each word type; these types are not meant to be definitive but rather to help teachers and students think about words in various ways. This list is a simplified version of Marzano's (2004) synthesis of vocabulary research (Marzano & Marzano, 1988; Stahl, 1999) and artificial intelligence research (Fellbaum, 1998; Miller, 1995) on various types of words.

Table 2.2: Features of Different Types of Words

Types	Questions About Key Features
People (for example, *author, character, villain, narrator, guest speaker, host, hostess, film director, political cartoonist*)	1. What actions does this kind of person perform? 2. What is required to become this kind of person? 3. What physical or psychological characteristics does this kind of person have?
Events (for example, *play, interview, simulation, chance event*)	1. What people are associated with this kind of event? 2. What process or actions are associated with this kind of event? 3. What equipment, materials, resources, or contexts are associated with this kind of event? 4. What setting is associated with this kind of event? 5. What causes and consequences are associated with this kind of event?
Intellectual, artistic, or cognitive products (for example, *essay, argument, tessellation, proof, model*)	1. What process is associated with this kind of product? 2. What purpose is associated with this kind of product? 3. What people are associated with this kind of product? 4. What equipment is associated with this kind of product?
Mental actions (for example, *revise, edit, reflect, problem solve, prove*)	1. What process is associated with this kind of mental action? 2. What people are associated with this kind of mental action? 3. What location is associated with this kind of mental action? 4. What causes or consequences are associated with this kind of mental action?
Social/societal groups, institutions, or organizations (for example, *audience, Modern Language Association, American Psychological Association, control group, representative sample, population*)	1. What purpose is associated with this kind of group, institution, or organization? 2. What people are associated with this kind of group, institution, or organization? 3. What setting is associated with this kind of group, institution, or organization?
Shapes/direction/position (for example, *order of events, introduction, conclusion, polygon, coordinate plane, circumference, data distribution*)	1. What physical features are associated with this kind of shape, direction, or position? 2. What uses are associated with this kind of shape, direction, or position? 3. What reference points are associated with this kind of shape, direction, or position?
Quantities/amounts/measurements (for example, *time frame, pacing, Roman numeral, cardinal number, greater than [>], function*)	1. What relationships are associated with this kind of quantity, amount, or measurement? 2. What referents are associated with this kind of quantity, amount, or measurement?

Source: Adapted from Marzano, 2004, pp. 81–84.

If a teacher was trying to explain the term *function* to her students, she might decide that the term fits best in the type *quantities/amounts/measurements*. In table 2.2, there are two questions for quantities/amounts/measurements:

1.   What relationships are associated with this kind of quantity, amount, or measurement?

2.   What referents are associated with this kind of quantity, amount, or measurement?

A teacher could use these questions to frame the class discussion of the term *function*. The teacher begins by explaining that a function expresses a relationship between two measurements. As one measurement changes, it affects the other measurement. The teacher then explains that different functions express different types of relationships: for example, linear functions refer to different kinds of relationships than quadratic functions.

Providing Examples

Description and explanation of a term must be accompanied by examples, such as the following:

- Experiences (field trips or guest speakers)

- Stories (personal experiences with the term)

- Images (videos, descriptions of mental pictures, or drawings)

- Drama (skits or pantomimes)

- Current events related to the term (news stories or magazine articles)

These techniques involve both linguistic and nonlinguistic ways of interacting with a term. Depending on the amount of time a teacher has, each of these types of examples can be extensive or brief. For instance, to highlight the first feature of *function* that the teacher identified (a function expresses a relationship between two measurements), the teacher tells students a story about how her mom taught her to cook rice. She explains that for every cup of rice, she had to add two cups of water, so two cups of rice needed four cups of water, three cups of rice needed six cups of water, and so on. She could visually graph the relationship between how many cups of water are needed for a specific number of cups of rice, as in figure 2.1, explaining that it is called a linear function because it creates a line on the graph.

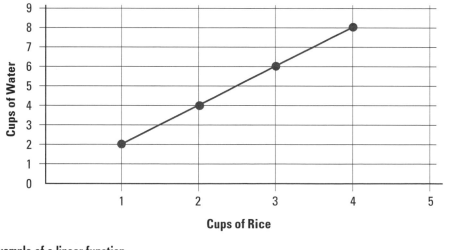

Figure 2.1: Example of a linear function.

To highlight the other feature of *function* that she identified as important (different functions express different types of relationships), the teacher first reminds students of the phrase "the quality of the food is a function of how hungry you are" from their previous discussion and points out that the phrase means that the hungrier you are, the better food tastes. This approach requires relatively little time. If the teacher has more time, she could play a video that shows the frequency of sound waves at different pitches, pointing out that as the frequency increases, so does the pitch. Finally, she might ask students to mentally picture a group of basketball players lined up according to height and ask them to guess which ones weigh the most.

In summary, step 1 involves describing and explaining the important features of a term to students after determining what students already know about the term. Description and explanation of each important feature should be accompanied by examples of that feature. Depending on the amount of time a teacher wishes to spend in this first step, the examples can be abbreviated or more in depth.

Step 2: Ask Students to Restate the Description, Explanation, or Example in Their Own Words

Steps 2 and 3 of the process ask students to respond to the teacher's description, explanation, or example of a new term by expressing it in their own way, both linguistically (step 2) and nonlinguistically (step 3). These steps are crucial to vocabulary learning because they ask students to actively process the new information provided by the teacher in step 1.

In step 2, the teacher asks students to record their own descriptions, explanations, or examples in their vocabulary notebooks. It is important that students do not simply copy the teacher's description but instead think about how they would describe the new term and consider situations or circumstances in their own lives that exemplify the term. For example, a student defining the term *function* might write, "A function tells how one group of numbers is matched up with another group of numbers." Another student might write, "Functions tell what happens to a measurement when another measurement changes." At this stage, students' descriptions and explanations may be rudimentary. This initial simplicity is to be expected and, as long as major errors or misconceptions are avoided, is acceptable during this step. As students explore a word and learn more about it, they can return to their initial explanations to refine, clarify, and add to them (this revision process is further explained in step 4).

Linguistic and Nonlinguistic Representations

Within their framework of dual coding theory, Mark Sadoski and Allan Paivio (2001) suggested that information is stored in the brain in two forms: *logogens* and *imagens*. Logogens are storage packages that use language; imagens are storage packets that use pictures or images. For example, information about the vocabulary word *narrator* could be stored in both ways. A logogen might contain sentences that use the word, other words related to the word, titles of stories or plays that feature a prominent narrator, or other language-based information, such as that shown in figure 2.2 (page 20).

In contrast, a student's imagens would contain image-based information about the word *narrator*. These images are often very rich and might include sounds and smells associated with a concept, in addition to mental pictures. Imagens will be discussed more fully in step 3.

Notice that in figure 2.2, each bit of information is connected to other bits of information. This is referred to by linguists as a *propositional* or *semantic network* (Clark & Clark, 1977; Kintsch, 1974, 1979;

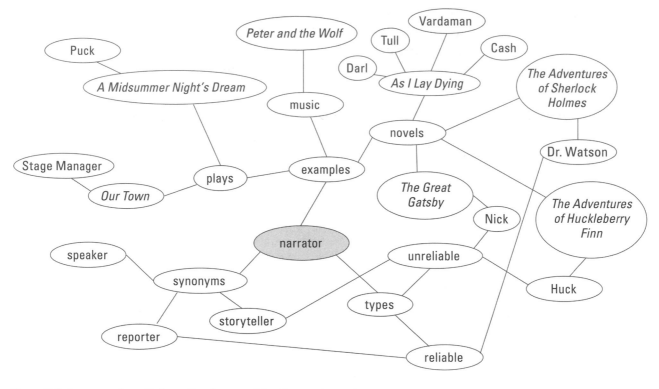

Figure 2.2: Language-based information (logogens) for the word *narrator.*

Tulving, 1972; van Dijk, 1977, 1980; van Dijk & Kintsch, 1983). Over time, as students accumulate experiences and store them in propositional networks, the networks become increasingly generalized (Tulving, 1972). For example, a student who has seen *Our Town* performed might associate the word *narrator* with that particular experience until he or she sees *A Midsummer Night's Dream*, which also features a narrator figure. Then, the same student might hear or see a musical piece with narration such as Benjamin Britten's *Young Person's Guide to the Orchestra* or Camille Saint-Saëns' *The Carnival of the Animals*. As his or her experience broadens, the information that the student attaches to the idea of *narrator* becomes more generalized.

As noted previously, step 2 focuses on the linguistic side of description and explanation; students create logogens for a term by describing, explaining, and exemplifying it in their own words. If students have trouble formulating their own descriptions, explanations, or examples of a term, the teacher can help in several ways. Perhaps the simplest is to offer further description and explanation to the students. The teacher might ask questions that prompt the student to think of examples from his or her own life that exemplify the term. Additionally, the teacher could ask students to form pairs or small groups to discuss the term and share examples of it in their own lives. If a student is still stuck, the teacher might ask him or her to complete step 3 (creating a nonlinguistic representation for the term) before returning to write a linguistic description of the word.

Vocabulary Notebooks

Vocabulary notebooks are a place where students can record and revise information about vocabulary terms. Many teachers and schools ask students to keep academic notebooks in which they record information related not only to vocabulary but to all the information presented in their classes. Whether

students keep academic notebooks or vocabulary notebooks (or a combination of bot[h]
the same: students record new information using words and images and return to re[view]
that information as their knowledge about a topic or term grows and deepens. Resear[ch]
the use of notebooks positively affects student achievement (Dunn et al., 2007; Giff[ord &]
Marzano, 2005, 2006).

Vocabulary notebooks can be created and organized in various ways. We recommend that the area (which may be a quarter-page, a third of a page, a half-page, or a whole page) for each vocabulary term include a place to record the following elements:

- The term

- The academic subject the term is associated with, if applicable (for example, ELA or mathematics)

- The category or measurement topic (discussed in chapter 3) the term is associated with (for example, *Transform*, *Themes and Central Ideas*, or *Shapes*)

- The student's current level of understanding of the term (for example, 4, 3, 2, 1)

- The student's linguistic description of the term

- The student's nonlinguistic representation of the term

- Words related to the term, such as synonyms or antonyms

Figure 2.3 shows one example of a vocabulary notebook page. Visit **marzanoresearch.com/common core** for a reproducible version of this figure.

Term:		
Subject:	Topic/Category:	Level of understanding: 1 2 3 4
Description in words:		Synonyms:
		Antonyms:
Picture:		

Figure 2.3: Sample vocabulary notebook page.

The level of understanding indicator for each term is based on Marzano and Pickering's (2005) four-point scale for self-evaluation of knowledge of vocabulary terms:

4   I understand even more about the term than I was taught.

3   I understand the term, and I'm not confused about any part of what it means.

2   I'm a little uncertain about what the term means, but I have a general idea.

1   I'm very uncertain about the term. I really don't understand what it means. (p. 32)

We discuss other methods for tracking students' vocabulary knowledge in chapter 4. As described here, vocabulary notebooks are designed to capture students' thinking about each term so they can revise and refine their understandings during steps 4, 5, and 6 of the six-step process.

Step 3: Ask Students to Construct a Picture, Symbol, or Graphic Representing the Term or Phrase

As explained previously, nonlinguistic processing deepens students' understanding of terms and creates image-based information packets (imagens) in their brains. For example, consider a student who remembers seeing a live performance of *Peter and the Wolf*, an orchestral composition of a children's tale that is typically narrated. The student has a mental picture of the concert hall with the orchestra fanned out on stage and the narrator of the piece standing next to the conductor, facing the audience, telling the story of Peter and his animal friends defeating the wolf. The student connects that image of a narrator with other narrators he has encountered. He remembers the voice of Nick in a movie version of *The Great Gatsby* that he saw. If his grandfather told him stories when he was little, he includes the sound of his grandfather's voice, the smell of his pipe, and an image of the room or chair he sat in when telling stories. These are all examples of imagens, which should be recorded in some form in the student's vocabulary notebook.

Teachers and students should recognize that different words may require different types of representations. Table 2.3 depicts five different ways terms can be represented nonlinguistically.

Table 2.3: Methods for Nonlinguistic Representation

Method	Term	Picture
Sketch the actual object. **If a term is concrete and easy to depict, simply sketch a picture of it.**	*résumé*	*Annie J. Lee* *Objective:* *Education:* *Work Experience:*

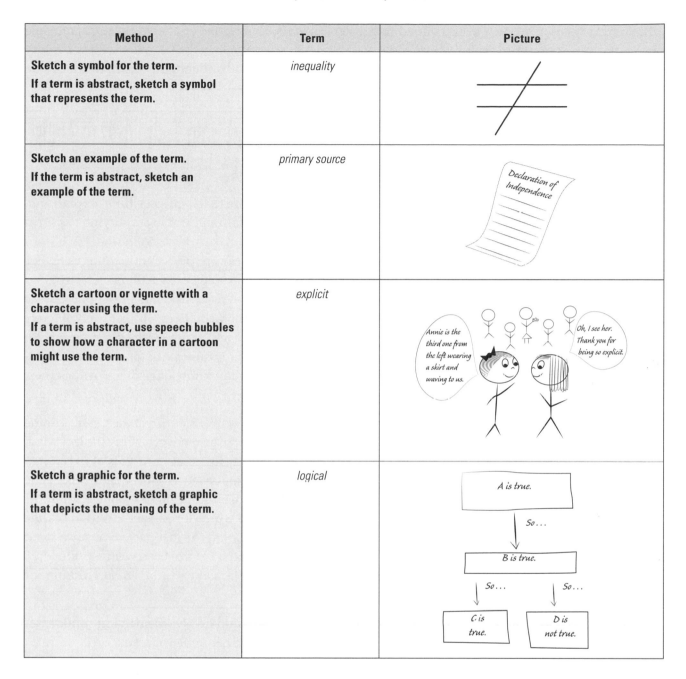

Method	Term	Picture
Sketch a symbol for the term. **If a term is abstract, sketch a symbol that represents the term.**	*inequality*	
Sketch an example of the term. **If the term is abstract, sketch an example of the term.**	*primary source*	
Sketch a cartoon or vignette with a character using the term. **If a term is abstract, use speech bubbles to show how a character in a cartoon might use the term.**	*explicit*	
Sketch a graphic for the term. **If a term is abstract, sketch a graphic that depicts the meaning of the term.**	*logical*	

Even with these five methods, some students may still have trouble creating nonlinguistic representations for terms, saying that they don't know how to sketch or aren't good at drawing. Others may try to overdraw terms, creating such detailed pictures that they lose sight of the term itself. Still others may feel like a description is enough and they don't need a picture. Teachers can use several techniques to help these students. First, teachers can model appropriate sketches for vocabulary terms. This will help students see the appropriate level of detail to include in their pictures and also provide an opportunity for the teacher to explain the differences between drawing and sketching. Second, the teacher can provide examples of past students' nonlinguistic representations for terms. Third, the teacher can allow students to discuss their ideas for nonlinguistic representations in groups before they work individually on their pictures. Finally, the teacher can help students look for images on the Internet that represent the terms. For instance, a student depicting the term *time zone* might print out a picture of the United States and color the states to represent the different time zones.

In summary, steps 2 and 3 are designed to deepen students' knowledge of a term through multiple exposures. Students record their linguistic and nonlinguistic descriptions of the term in their vocabulary notebooks, where they can revisit them to clarify or add to their initial understandings as they become more familiar with the term.

Step 4: Engage Students Periodically in Activities That Help Them Add to Their Knowledge of the Terms in Their Vocabulary Notebooks

Steps 1, 2, and 3 are designed to be implemented in order, with the teacher describing, explaining, and exemplifying a term and students subsequently describing, explaining, and exemplifying the term on their own, both linguistically and nonlinguistically. Steps 4, 5, and 6 are less sequential. Each is an important element of the process described here, but it is not necessary to perform them in order. For example, step 4 involves activities that help students add to their knowledge of vocabulary terms, and step 6 involves games that allow students to play with terms. In some cases, students might play games with a word (step 6) before completing comparison activities with the word (step 4). This is completely acceptable. In fact, a teacher might use steps 4, 5, or 6 only once per week or once every two weeks. No matter how frequently or infrequently steps 4, 5, and 6 are employed, it is important for students to continue revising and adding to their vocabulary notebook entries as their knowledge of a word deepens and grows.

There are many activities that help students add to their knowledge of terms as directed in step 4. Some are very simple. For example, a teacher might ask students to say or write any words they think of when they hear a target word. When used orally, this is an excellent activity for small intervals of time, such as when students are waiting in line to go to lunch or recess or during the last minutes before it is time for students to change classes. Students can complete this activity as a class, in small groups, in pairs, or individually. The teacher should allow students to brainstorm related words for a specific period of time and then ask students to stop. If students have been saying words aloud, the last person to say a word then briefly explains how that word is related to the target word. If students have been writing individual lists of words, students could trade lists and ask their partners to explain any words that are unfamiliar or don't make sense.

Other activities for augmenting students' vocabulary knowledge could involve identifying similarities and differences or examining affixes and root words. Here we provide a number of activities for each.

Identifying Similarities and Differences

Marzano, Pickering, and Pollock (2001) identified four strategies that students can use to identify similarities and differences: (1) comparing and contrasting, (2) classifying, (3) creating metaphors, and (4) creating analogies. *Comparing and contrasting* involves identifying attributes that are the same or different between two or more items or concepts. *Classifying* involves grouping like items or concepts into categories based on their attributes or characteristics. *Creating metaphors* involves finding connections between ideas or concepts that do not seem connected at a surface level. Finally, *creating analogies* involves describing the relationship between a pair of items or concepts by comparing the pair to another pair.

Comparing and Contrasting

When comparing and contrasting terms, students can think about ways that terms are similar and different by using sentence stems provided by the teacher. This sort of structure helps students both make substantive comparisons and compare terms logically. Following are a few examples:

_____ and _____ are similar because they both:

- _____

- _____

_____ and _____ are different because:

- _____ is _____, while _____ is _____.

- _____ is _____, while _____ is _____.

These stems help students structure their thinking and clearly express their thoughts. Thus, a student might compare _circle_ and _sphere_ as follows:

Circles and spheres are similar because they both:

- Have circumferences, radii, diameters, and surface areas

- Have perfect symmetry

Circles and spheres are different because:

- A circle is two-dimensional, while a sphere is three-dimensional

- A circle does not have volume, while a sphere does have volume

In this case, the student found similarities between the measurements and symmetries and differences between the dimensions and volume.

Venn diagrams are another structure that can help students compare and contrast characteristics of two to three terms. For example, a student might compare _adage_ to _idiom_ as shown in figure 2.4.

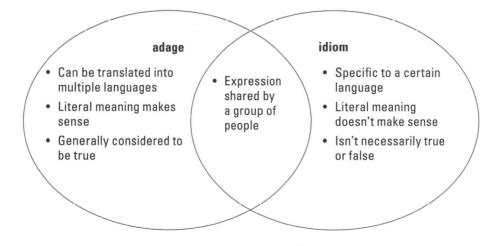

Figure 2.4: Venn diagram comparing _adage_ and _idiom_.

Note that in the Venn diagram, each characteristic under *adage* corresponds to a characteristic beneath *idiom*. So, the first characteristic involves the term's specificity to a certain language, the second involves literal meaning, and the third involves veracity.

Similar to the Venn diagram is the double bubble diagram. Here, students compare two terms by identifying their shared and unique characteristics. For example, if a student was comparing the terms *base 10* and *base 60*, he or she might create a double bubble diagram like the one shown in figure 2.5. Each term is placed in a bubble, one on the right and one on the left. Characteristics of each are written in the surrounding bubbles. Shared characteristics are placed between the two terms; unique characteristics are placed around the outside of each term. Then, lines are drawn to show which characteristics are unique and shared. The double bubble diagram in figure 2.5 indicates that both the base 10 and base 60 systems used finger counting methods and were used in ancient cultures.

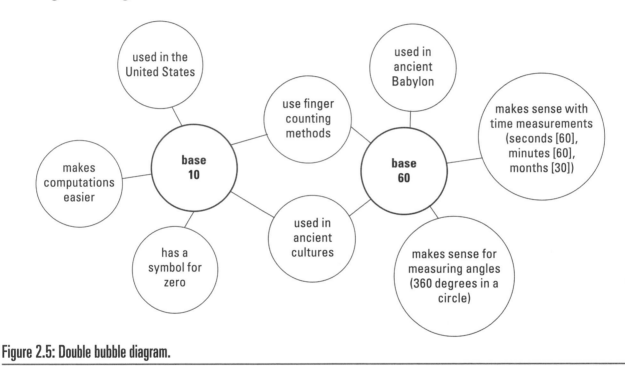

Figure 2.5: Double bubble diagram.

Like the diagrams presented previously, the double bubble diagram is a structure that can help students make and organize substantive comparisons between two terms.

Sometimes students need to compare and contrast more than two terms at a time, however. In these cases, students can use a comparison matrix, which examines several items according to several attributes. Like the Venn and double bubble diagrams, the matrix structures students' comparisons and helps them identify meaningful similarities and differences between terms. The matrix, however, has the added advantage of accommodating a larger number of terms for comparison. For example, the comparison matrix in table 2.4 shows how a student might compare the three terms *argumentative*, *informative/ explanatory*, and *narrative*.

The student first fills in his or her observations about each term relative to each attribute in the matrix. For example, the student observed that the purpose of argumentative writing is to convince someone of something. Once each cell has been filled in, the student examines the matrix and draws conclusions about similarities and differences between the terms, which are recorded at the bottom of the chart.

Table 2.4: Comparison Matrix for *Argumentative, Informative/Explanatory,* and *Narrative*

	Argumentative	**Informative/Explanatory**	**Narrative**
Purpose	To convince someone of something	To explain or inform about a topic	To entertain or tell a story
Important Elements	Opinion, evidence, opposing viewpoints	Topic, facts, pictures/diagrams, step-by-step instructions	Plot, characters, setting, problem, themes
Structure	State an opinion, defend it logically with evidence, anticipate opposing opinions, provide a conclusion	State the topic; explain the structure; illustrate points with pictures, diagrams, and step-by-step instructions; provide a conclusion	Introduce characters and setting, describe the problem, solve the problem, provide a conclusion
Types	Persuasive, analytical, personal opinion	Essay, report, research	Fictional, factual, fantasy, mystery, science fiction, fables, myths, personal experience

Conclusions: Argumentative and informative/explanatory are similar because they are both focused on facts and evidence about a topic and because they both begin by stating the subject of the writing. However, their purposes are different. All three are similar because they can be inspired by personal experiences. Narrative and informative/explanatory can be similar if the narrative is about an actual event or person's life. Although all three are alike because they all *can* be entertaining, it is not the primary purpose of informative/explanatory and argumentative.

Classifying

Classification activities help students group like terms or concepts into categories. For example, an ELA teacher asks her students to classify the following terms based on their characteristics: *adage, foreshadowing, hyperbole, idiom, metaphor, personification, proverb, simile, stanza, tone,* and *verse.* While the teacher could ask students to create their own categories, she decides to provide categories such as Figurative Language, Structural Features, and Literary Techniques. One student sorts the words as follows.

Figurative Language: *hyperbole, idiom, metaphor, personification, simile*

Structural Features: *stanza, verse*

Literary Techniques: *adage, foreshadowing, proverb, tone*

Classification activities can fall anywhere on a continuum from structured to open-ended. If the teacher provides both the words to sort and the categories, then the task is fairly structured. If the teacher provides only the words, the task will be more open-ended. The most open-ended version of a classification activity would involve students identifying both the words to sort and the categories in which to sort them. For example, a high-school math teacher whose students have been studying functions might ask students to look at all the words they had recorded in their vocabulary notebooks, select the ones they thought were most important for the study of functions, and create a classification scheme for those words. This exercise could allow students to think about words in new ways. A student might select the math words he thought most directly applied to functions and then flip to the ELA or cognitive verbs section of his notebook and identify words from those subject areas (such as *relationship* or *derive*) as well. Including those words would influence the student's choices about which classification categories were most appropriate. Whether structured or open-ended, the key to successful classification activities is prompting students to group words into categories.

Creating Metaphors

Creating metaphors involves identifying similarities and connections between words at a figurative, abstract, or nonliteral level. For example, the phrase "he is the light of my life" uses a metaphor to describe one who is beloved. While people often associate light with joy, happiness, and security, a person cannot literally be luminescent. Consider a fifth-grade math teacher who asks her students to create metaphors using the term *common denominator*. One student says, "Common denominators are the dating websites of math," and explains that in the same way that common denominators make it easier to add fractions, dating websites make it easier for couples to pair up. Students should not only create metaphors but also explain why they grouped the two terms together. To prompt and facilitate this explanation, a teacher might use the following sentence stem:

_____ is/are _____ because _____.

For more complex metaphors, students can fill in a matrix. First, they identify specific characteristics of a term in the left column; then they state those characteristics more generally in the center column. In the right column, students look for a different term that also fits with the general characteristics described in the center column. For example, a student wants to create a metaphor using *source*. He completes the left and center columns of the matrix as shown in table 2.5. Then, he looks for a term that could be equated with *source* at an abstract level. The student decides to use the term *character* as the second term in the metaphor and fills in the right column of the matrix to explain his reasoning.

Table 2.5: Metaphor Matrix for Source

Term *source*	General Description	Term *character*
Provides evidence to support an argument	Provides important support for the text	Moves the story along as he or she encounters and solves problems
Usually a person or organization	Has an identity	Has a personality and physical characteristics
Usually only a little bit of the source text is used	Excerpt or summary	Most characters are not fully described; only glimpses of their lives

After completing a matrix like the one in table 2.5, the student decides to phrase his metaphor as follows: Characters are the sources of stories. To explain the abstract relationship, the student uses the general descriptions listed in his matrix.

Because metaphor activities ask students to examine the abstract or nonliteral elements of a term, they are an excellent way to help students deepen their vocabulary knowledge about words they know at a surface level.

Creating Analogies

To create an analogy, students must identify and describe a relationship between two items or concepts. For example, "Betty is to Jeff as oil is to water" implies that in the same way that oil repels water, Betty repels Jeff. This sort of analysis requires in-depth examination of the nuances of relationships between terms. There are several ways in which a teacher can prompt students to generate analogies. For example, an ELA teacher could provide the first term of each analogy pair and ask students to fill in the second term in each pair, as follows:

An adjective is to a _____ as an adverb is to a _____.

A student responds by saying, "An adjective is to a noun as an adverb is to a verb." He might extend his answer by explaining that *adjectival phrase* and *adverbial phrase* could be substituted for *adjective* and *adverb* in the analogy.

Alternatively, the teacher could provide both terms in the first pair and ask students to create the second pair, as follows:

Prefix is to suffix as _____ is to _____.

A student responds by saying, "Prefix is to suffix as first names are to last names because first names come at the beginning of your full name and last names come at the end of your full name." She then extends it by comparing a root word to a person's middle name.

Another useful strategy is to ask students to label the relationship between two sets of terms. Visual analogy diagrams are useful for this purpose, as shown in figure 2.6.

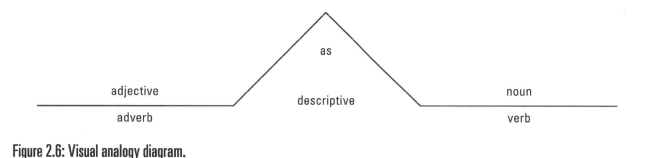

Figure 2.6: Visual analogy diagram.

In figure 2.6, the student labeled the relationship described by the analogy "an adjective is to a noun as an adverb is to a verb" as *descriptive*. Another student might label the same relationship *modifying* or *adding information.*

Examining Affixes and Root Words

Understanding word parts and how words are constructed has been shown to have a correlation of 0.83 with vocabulary knowledge (Nagy, Berninger, Abbott, Vaughan, & Vermeulen, 2003). As explained in chapter 1, correlations that are close to 1.00 indicate strong relationships between two variables. So, as students' understanding of word parts and word construction increases, so does their vocabulary knowledge. Some (Adams, 1990) have cautioned against teaching word parts to students learning to read, because the segmentation of a word into syllables does not always match the segmentation of a word into word parts. For example, a student learning to read would probably try to segment the word *information* into syllables (in-for-ma-tion) to decode it. However, its morphological segmentation is different (in-form-ation), and this difference could be confusing to an immature reader. For confident readers who have reached a level of automaticity with decoding longer words, however, understanding roots and affixes can help them remember words they have learned and figure out the meaning of unfamiliar terms. Stahl (2005) explained,

A discussion of word parts should become an integral part of word-learning instruction. Discussions that include stories about word origins and derivations can stir interest in learning more about language—that is, build word consciousness. Stories that help children to see and understand how similarities in word spellings may show similarities in meaning, may solidify and expand their word knowledge. For example, the seemingly dissimilar words *loquacious*, *colloquium*, and *elocution* all come from the root word *loq*, meaning "to talk." Knowing this connection may make it easier for children to remember the words. (p. 111)

There are three distinct types of word parts: prefixes, suffixes, and root words. Prefixes, which come at the beginning of a word, typically add to or change the meaning of the root word to which they are attached. Suffixes, which come at the end of a word, typically affect the root word's part of speech. Collectively, prefixes and suffixes are referred to as *affixes*. Root words are often based on Greek or Latin and carry specific meanings.

Affixes

In 1989, Thomas White, Joanne Sowell, and Alice Yanagihara examined the words in *The American Heritage Word Frequency Book* (Carroll, Davies, & Richman, 1971) to identify the most frequently used prefixes and suffixes in English. They found that the top twenty prefixes and suffixes accounted for 97–99 percent of all words with affixes (as shown in table 2.6). It is interesting to note that the three most frequently occurring prefixes are used in 51 percent of all prefixed words and the three most frequently occurring suffixes account for 65 percent of all words with suffixes.

Table 2.6: Frequently Occurring Prefixes and Suffixes

Prefix	% of All Prefixed Words	Suffix	% of All Suffixed Words
un-	26	-s, -es	31
re-	14	-ed	20
in-, im-, ir-, il- (meaning "not")	11	-ing	14
dis-	7	-ly	7
en-, em-	4	-er, -or (indicating agency)	4
non-	4	-ion, -tion, -ation, -ition	4
in-, im- (meaning "in" or "into")	4	-ible, -able	2
over- (meaning "too much")	3	-al, -ial	1
mis-	3	-y	1
sub-	3	-ness	1
pre-	3	-ity, -ty	1
inter-	3	-ment	1
fore-	3	-ic	1

Prefix	% of All Prefixed Words	Suffix	% of All Suffixed Words
de-	2	*-ous, -eous, -ious*	1
trans-	2	*-en*	1
super-	1	*-er* (indicating comparison)	1
semi-	1	*-ive, -ative, -itive*	1
anti-	1	*-ful*	1
mid-	1	*-less*	1
under- (meaning "too little")	1	*-est*	1

Source: Adapted from White et al., 1989, pp. 303–304.

White and colleagues (1989) reasoned that since such a small number of affixes were used in the majority of affixed words, it would be best to focus word-part instruction on those. They designed two series of lessons, one for prefixes and one for suffixes. Each series of lessons is summarized in table 2.7.

Table 2.7: White et al.'s (1989) Recommended Sequences for Teaching Affixes

Teaching Prefixes	Teaching Suffixes
Lesson 1: Present examples and nonexamples of words with prefixes (*unkind* and *refill* have prefixes [*un-* and *re-*]; *uncle* and *reason* do not have prefixes).	**Lesson 1:** Present examples and nonexamples of words with suffixes (*employee* and *natural* have suffixes [*-ee* and *-al*]; *bee* and *charcoal* do not).
Lesson 2: Explain and give examples of the negative meanings of *un-* and *dis-* ("not" as in *unlike* and *disagree*).	**Lesson 2:** Present words with suffixes whose spellings do not change when the suffix is added (such as *monkeys, foxes, walking, higher, jumped, softly, laughable, comical,* and *windy*).
Lesson 3: Explain and give examples of the negative meanings of *in-, im-,* and *non-* ("not" as in *incompetent, impossible,* and *nonconforming*).	**Lesson 3:** Illustrate each of the three major spelling changes that can occur with suffixes:
Lesson 4: Explain and give examples of both meanings of *re-* ("again" as in *rebuild* or *revise* and "back" as in *recover* or *relapse*).	• Consonant blending (*bigger, running, skipped, sunny*)
Lesson 5: Address the less common meanings of *un-* and *dis-* ("do the opposite" as in *unbutton* or *disown*) and *in-* and *im-* ("in" or "into" as in *inquire* or *implant*).	• Change from *y* to *i* (*married, skies, happily, classifiable, filthiness*)
Lesson 6: Explain and give examples of *en-* and *em-* ("in" or "into" as in *encircle* and *embrace*), *over-* ("above" or "beyond" as in *overreact*), and *mis-* ("bad" or "wrong" as in *mistrust* or *mistrial*).	• Deleted silent *e* (*riding, gated, baker, advisable, natural, wheezy*)
	Lesson 4: Provide many examples of inflectional endings (*-s, -es, -ed, -ing*) and derivational suffixes (*-ly, -er, -ion, -able, -al, -y, -ness*) so that students can understand the differences between them.

Source: White et al., 1989, pp. 304–306.

Note that the lessons outlined on the left side of table 2.7 focus on the most frequently used prefixes: *un-, re-, in-, im-, dis-, en-, em-, non-, over-,* and *mis-*. The lessons on the right side of table 2.7 focus initially on how to add derivational suffixes to words and conclude by focusing on the most frequent suffixes: *-s, -es, -ed, -ing, -ly, -er, -ion, -able, -al, -y,* and *-ness*.

Root Words

Many words in English have Greek or Latin roots. Knowing what these root words mean can help students discern the meaning of an unknown word, but root words are extremely numerous, and no rigorous studies have been done to identify which roots are most frequent or most useful for students. Several authors have compiled lists of common Greek and Latin roots (Fry, Kress, & Fountoukidis, 2000; Marzano, 2004; Stahl, 1999), and Timothy Rasinski and his colleagues (Padak, Newton, Rasinski, & Newton, 2008; Rasinski, Padak, Newton, & Newton, 2007) created a sequence of Greek and Latin roots useful for teaching. We present a selection of root words in table 2.8.

Table 2.8: Common Greek and Latin Roots

Root	Meaning	Origin	Examples
act	do	Latin	react, transact
ang	bend	Latin	angle, angular
ast	star	Greek	astronomy, disaster, asterisk
aud	hear	Latin	audible, auditorium, audition, audience
bio	life	Greek	biology, biography, biochemistry
chron	time	Greek	chronological, synchronize, chronicle
cosm	universe	Greek	cosmonaut, cosmos, cosmopolitan, microcosm
cred	believe	Latin	credit, discredit, incredible, credential, credulous
cycl	circle, ring	Greek	cyclone, cycle
dict	speak	Latin	dictate, predict, contradict, verdict, diction
duc	lead	Latin	duct, conduct, educate, aqueduct
fac, fic	make, do	Latin	factory, manufacture, benefactor, facsimile
gen	birth, race	Greek	generation, progeny, genealogy
geo	earth	Greek	geology, geography
gram	letter, written	Greek	telegram, diagram, grammar, epigram, monogram
graph	write	Greek	photograph, autograph, biography, graphite
loc	place	Latin	location, allocate
man	hand	Latin	manuscript, manipulate
meter	measure	Greek	thermometer, centimeter, diameter, barometer
min	little, small	Latin	minimum, minimal
miss, mit	send	Latin	missile, dismiss, mission, remiss, submit, remit, admit, transmit
morph	shape	Greek	amorphous, metamorphosis, morphology, anthropomorphic

Root	Meaning	Origin	Examples
ped	foot	Latin	pedestrian, pedal, pedestal
phon	sound	Greek	symphony, telephone, microphone, phonics
photo	light	Greek	photograph, photosynthesis
poli	city	Greek	metropolis, cosmopolitan, police, political
pop	people	Latin	population, popular
port	carry	Latin	portable, transport, import, export, porter
rupt	break	Latin	rupture, erupt, interrupt, abrupt, bankrupt
scop	see	Greek	microscope, periscope
scribe, script	write	Latin	scribe, inscribe, describe, prescribe, script, transcript, scripture
sign	mark	Latin	signature, signal
spec	see	Latin	inspect, suspect, respect, spectator, spectacle
struct	build, form	Latin	structure, construct, instruct, destruction
tact	touch	Latin	tactile, intact, contact, tact
therm	heat	Greek	thermometer, thermal
vid	see	Latin	video, evidence

Source: Adapted from Fry et al., 2000, pp. 106–108.

Additionally, the Internet offers many resources for exploring word roots and affixes. The following websites are particularly useful:

- **Online Etymology Dictionary** (www.etymonline.com)—Type in any part of a word (affix, root, or word) and see its origin, root words, and other words related to it.

- **English-Word Information** (wordinfo.info)—Type in a word and see information about its language of origin, what family of root words it belongs to, and how it is commonly used.

- **Merriam-Webster Online** (www.youtube.com/user/MerriamWebsterOnline)—These two-minute videos feature editors from Merriam-Webster talking about the etymology and roots of various English words (for example, octopuses vs. octopi, healthy vs. healthful, irregardless vs. regardless, and many more).

Stahl (1999) cautions that instruction about morphology (that is, how words are formed) should also create an awareness of its weaknesses. He explained:

> The modern meanings of words (especially the most common derived words) often do not reflect the meanings of their historical roots, and . . . readers might be misled by a literal translation of root to meaning. For example, knowing -*mort* refers to "death" may help with *mortal* or *immortal*, but probably does not help a person guess the meaning of *mortgage* or *mortify*. (p. 47)

Therefore, it is important for teachers to help students identify examples and nonexamples of words whose meaning can be determined using root words, prefixes, and suffixes.

After completing vocabulary activities, students should return to their vocabulary notebooks to update and augment their entries for various terms. Students might add information to their written description of the term or add to the picture they drew for a term. Alternatively, students might draw a new picture that helps them remember a nuance or abstract meaning for a term, record especially helpful metaphors or similes that they created, or record other terms they have discovered that are closely related to a target word.

Step 5: Periodically Ask Students to Discuss the Terms With One Another

Step 5 involves discussion of vocabulary terms. Stahl and Nagy (2006) explained the importance of discussion:

> Discussion adds an important dimension to vocabulary instruction. . . . Children benefit from the contributions of other children. . . . In open discussions, children are often able to construct a good idea of a word's meaning from the partial knowledge of the entire class. (p. 69)

Discussion can also surface and correct students' misconceptions about a word and help students look at a word from multiple perspectives. For example, during a discussion of the word *rhyme*, one student suggests that a rhyme occurs when two words are spelled the same except for the first letter, as in *cat* and *bat*. Another student offers a different set of rhyming words, such as *deep* and *leap*. The teacher displays the new set of words on the board and asks students to offer an updated description of *rhyme* based on the information that words can rhyme even if they aren't spelled the same. Another student explains that he calls his sister *Anna Banana* because those words rhyme, raising the issue of rhyming words with different numbers of syllables.

A teacher can facilitate effective vocabulary discussions in several ways. For instance, he or she can use response techniques that let all students know there is a possibility that they will be called on. Stahl and Charles Clark (1987) investigated the effects of discussion on vocabulary learning and found that students who anticipated being called on learned as much as students who were actually called on. Students who didn't expect to be called on learned less. In other words, students don't necessarily need to talk during a vocabulary discussion to learn. They just need to anticipate being asked to talk. Stahl and Clark (1987) offered two possible explanations for this effect. First, they suggested that students who expected to be called on "were rehearsing covert answers during discussion. . . . It may be that this rehearsal process produced more powerful effects on retention than passive listening" (p. 552). Alternatively, they hypothesized that students who expected to be called on "simply paid greater attention to the lesson. . . . If the students were generating responses and formulating cognitive links for the new material, they were paying attention to the discussion" (p. 552). One way to ensure that all students expect to be called on is to use a random names process to call on students. The teacher writes each student's name on a piece of paper or popsicle stick and then randomly draws a name after asking a question. That student's name should be returned to the pool before the next question is asked so that he or she continues to anticipate being called on.

The teacher can also create a structure for the discussion and give students prompts or "nudges" (Martinez & Roser, 2003) to help them talk together about what they know. As highlighted by Beck and her colleagues (2002), these prompts need not be overly complex:

They can be as simple as asking questions such as the following about newly introduced words:

When might you . . . ?

How might you . . . ?

Why might you . . . ? (pp. 45–46)

These questions can effectively stimulate whole-class or small-group discussions. Here, we describe three additional strategies that facilitate interaction about terms in pairs or small groups: role cards, paired thinking, and inside-outside circle (Kagan & Kagan, 2009).

Role Cards

To use role cards, the teacher identifies specific roles in a group that will help students in that group deepen and extend their knowledge of a vocabulary term. For example, a teacher creates the following four roles:

1. **Etymology expert**—This student looks for facts about where a term came from, such as its language of origin and how it came to have its current meaning.

2. **Root researcher**—This student identifies roots and affixes of a word and finds examples of other words with similar roots or affixes.

3. **Synonym/antonym explorer**—This student finds synonyms and antonyms for a word.

4. **Discussion leader**—This student makes sure that everyone has a turn to talk and summarizes the group's discussion for the class.

After explaining each role to students, the teacher groups the class into fours and passes out a different role card to each group member. Groups might have a list of terms to discuss or they might focus on one word. The teacher might also pass out the role cards in advance so that students have time individually to find information about their words before meeting with their group. Roles should be rotated so that students have the opportunity to perform each role.

Paired Thinking

This strategy involves students sharing their thinking about a term while in pairs. One especially popular variation of this strategy is called think-pair-share, where students think about what new information they have learned about a term, pair up with a partner, and share their thoughts. However, there are other variations that can also be useful. For example, after pairing up and sharing their thoughts, pairs identify their most important perception about a word and then join together with another pair, making a group of four. Both pairs in the group of four share their most important insight, and the group selects one insight to share with the class.

Paired thinking is also very useful in surfacing misconceptions or confusion about a word. Students can take their vocabulary notebooks with them when partnering or grouping with other students. Students then trade notebooks and each student looks in his or her partner's notebook for one piece of unfamiliar information and one error or misconception. After students have time to discuss their observations, each student retrieves his or her notebook, adds new details, and corrects misconceptions.

One form of paired thinking is referred to as give-one-get-one. This strategy takes very little time and provides a quick review of terms for students. Taking their vocabulary notebooks with them, students stand up and find a partner. The teacher instructs students to review their entries for a specific term or terms in order to give new information to their partner (give one) and get new information from their partner (get one). The teacher then answers any questions the pairs have in a whole-class discussion.

Inside-Outside Circle

This strategy allows students to have brief conversations with many different peers in a short amount of time. The teacher divides the class into two equal groups. One group stands in a circle, facing outward, and the other group forms an inward-facing circle around them. Each student should be facing one other student. The teacher asks students to have a quick conversation with their partner about a word or to discuss a specific question, such as, "What is your favorite vocabulary term from this unit and why?" After students converse briefly, the teacher gives a signal and students in the outside circle take one step to the left. With their new partner, students answer the same question from before or a different question provided by the teacher. This structure is an excellent way to quickly expose students to the vocabulary knowledge of a large number of other students in the class. After the activity, students should be given time to record new information or discoveries about words in their vocabulary notebooks.

While using these strategies or while leading whole-class discussions of terms, the teacher can facilitate and guide discussions in four ways: (1) acknowledging the contributions of each student to the discussion, (2) giving students positive feedback about correct parts of their responses, (3) helping students correct incorrect parts of their responses by giving hints or cues or restating a question, and (4) using techniques that allow students to rehearse their answers, such as asking students to share their answer with a partner before calling on someone to share his or her answer with the class. As in step 4, students should return to their vocabulary notebooks following a discussion to add to or revise previous entries for terms.

Step 6: Involve Students Periodically in Games That Allow Them to Play With Terms

In step 6, students play games with the terms they have learned. Academic games are an extremely effective (but typically underutilized) way to help students engage with academic content. Martin Covington (1992) pointed out that appropriate classroom games present students with challenges: "Outcomes and consequences cannot always be known in advance. . . . Players must cooperate to achieve common cause against obstacles not of their own making" (p. 217). Thomas Malone (1981a, 1981b) described three characteristics of effective games:

1. Games should present challenges that are appropriate and manageable for students.

2. Games should arouse students' curiosity.

3. Games should prompt students to imagine different circumstances and situations.

For all practical purposes, the number of potential vocabulary games is infinite. Some games, such as word walls—in which students are encouraged to look and listen for new words and add them to a classroom poster—are ongoing throughout the course of a year. Isabel Beck, Charles Perfetti, and Margaret

McKeown (1982) found that students who used a word wall learned more incidental vocabulary than students who were exposed only to direct vocabulary instruction.

Other games are confined to smaller periods of time. Here we briefly describe various games created by educators and researchers.

Alphabet Antonyms: Students write down a number of vocabulary words that all begin with the same letter. A student might choose *addition, area, angle, arc,* and *adjacent.* Then he or she writes an antonym for each word. For example:

- Addition—subtraction

- Area—perimeter

- Angle—side

- Arc—point

- Adjacent—opposite

The student then presents only the antonyms to the class (that is, *subtraction, perimeter, side, point,* and *opposite*). The class tries to guess the correct antonyms, all of which start with the same letter—*a* in this case (for middle and high school students; Blachowicz & Fisher, 2008).

Classroom Feud: Modeled after *Family Feud*, this game has students work in teams to answer questions about vocabulary terms (for all grade levels; Carleton & Marzano, 2010).

Create a Category: Students work together to categorize a list of terms in a limited amount of time (for upper elementary through high school students; Carleton & Marzano, 2010).

Definition, Shmefinition: Students try to identify the correct description of a vocabulary term out of a group of student-invented definitions (for upper elementary through high school students; Carleton & Marzano, 2010).

Digital Vocabulary Field Trip: Using an online program like TrackStar (trackstar.4teachers.org), teachers collect and annotate a series of websites that pertain to a vocabulary term or group of terms. Students then explore the websites to answer a series of teacher-designed questions (for upper elementary through high school students; Dalton & Grisham, 2011).

Draw Me: Modeled after *Pictionary*, this game involves one student drawing pictures of terms in a predetermined category while other students try to guess the terms (for all grade levels; Marzano & Pickering, 2005).

Magic Letter, Magic Word: Students try to identify the vocabulary term (beginning or ending with the "magic letter") that is the correct response to a teacher-provided clue (for elementary and middle school students; Carleton & Marzano, 2010).

Motor Imaging: Students create gestures for vocabulary terms. For example, for the word *consensus*, students might decide to stretch their arms wide and slowly bring them together until their fingers are interlaced to signify that consensus involves finding common ground from a wide range of views (for all grade levels; Casale, 1985).

Name It!: Students use vocabulary terms to express what they see in various photographs (for lower elementary students; Carleton & Marzano, 2010).

Name That Category: The teacher provides a secret list of categories, and a designated student tries to help his teammates guess each category by naming vocabulary terms that fit in it. As soon as his team guesses one category, the clue-giver starts naming terms in the next category. The first team to name all the categories correctly wins (for upper elementary through high school students; Marzano & Pickering, 2005).

Opposites Attract: Students work together to pair vocabulary terms with their antonyms (for elementary students; Carleton & Marzano, 2010).

Possible Sentences: The teacher selects six to eight words that students are not likely to know and four to six words that students are likely to know. Using that list, students create sentences, each of which must contain at least two of the words from the list. The teacher displays these sentences, and students discuss whether each one is correct, incorrect, or partially correct and modifies them as needed so that they are all correct (for middle and high school students; Stahl, 2005).

Puzzle Stories: Students construct a puzzle and then use vocabulary terms to describe the scene depicted in the puzzle (for upper elementary and middle school students; Carleton & Marzano, 2010).

Root Relay: From an array of prefixes, suffixes, and root words written on separate cards, students work in teams to construct words. One student from each team runs to the assortment of affixes and roots, selects one, and brings it back to her team. The next student does the same. The first team to form a complete word wins (for upper elementary and middle school students; Scott, Miller, & Flinspach, 2012).

Secret Language: Two students try to communicate the meaning of a vocabulary term to the class by using it in context over the course of a day or class period. At the end of the designated time period, the class tries to guess what the secret word was and explain its meaning (for upper elementary through high school students; Manzo & Manzo, 2008).

Semantic Feature Analysis: Students analyze a group of words to determine their unique and shared features. Table 2.9 shows how this might work with a set of ELA terms describing different literary genres.

Table 2.9: Semantic Feature Analysis

Literary Genres	Typical characteristics							
	Magic	**Facts**	**First Person**	**Third Person**	**Futuristic**	**Past**	**Informative**	**Suspenseful**
Fairy tale	X		X	X		X		X
Mystery			X	X				X
Myth	X			X		X	X	X
Essay		X	X	X			X	
Diary		X	X			X	X	
Science fiction			X	X	X		X	X
Fantasy	X		X	X	X	X		X

As shown in table 2.9, semantic feature analysis involves identifying typical characteristics for a group of words and then designating which words have which characteristics. These analyses can often lead to rich discussions. For example, a student who had just read Rick Riordan's *Percy Jackson and the Olympians* series might argue that myths can, in fact, be written in the first person (for middle and high school students; Graves, 2008).

Sentence Stems: The teacher creates a sentence stem that requires students to explain the vocabulary term in order to complete it. For example, "The *amplitude* of a trigonometric function can be determined from its graph because . . ." or "A *line segment* has two *endpoints* because . . ." (for middle and high school students; Beck et al., 2002).

Silly Questions: Students answer questions created by combining two vocabulary terms, such as "Can a *whole number* be an *integer*?," "Would an *integer* be *complex*?," and so on (for middle and high school students; McKeown et al., 1985).

Talk a Mile a Minute: The teacher prepares cards with lists of terms from different categories, as shown in figure 2.7.

Revise and Edit
topic
draft
peer review
audience
proofread
focus

Figure 2.7: Card for Talk a Mile a Minute.

The teacher passes a card out to one member of each team who is designated the "talker." The teacher starts a timer and, similar to the games *Taboo* and *Catch Phrase*, the talker tries to get his teammates to say each word in the list without saying any of the other words on the card or in the heading (for upper elementary through high school students; Marzano & Pickering, 2005).

Two of a Kind: Students match up homonyms in this *Memory*-style game (for elementary school students; Carleton & Marzano, 2010).

Vocabulary Charades: Students try to guess which vocabulary term their teammate is acting out (for all grade levels; Marzano & Pickering, 2005).

Vocab Vids: Students create sixty-second videos that exemplify the meaning of a vocabulary term (for middle and high school students; Dalton & Grisham, 2011).

What Is the Question?: In this *Jeopardy!*-like game, students have to come up with questions that describe teacher-provided vocabulary terms (for upper elementary through high school students; Carleton & Marzano, 2010).

Where Am I?: Students give clues to help a student guess his or her "secret location," a vocabulary term referring to a specific place, such as *western hemisphere* or *Bering Sea* (for all grade levels; Carleton & Marzano, 2010).

Which One Doesn't Belong?: Students try to identify the vocabulary term that doesn't belong with the other three words in a group of four (for all grade levels; Carleton & Marzano, 2010).

Who Am I?: Students give clues to help a selected student guess his or her "secret identity," a vocabulary term referring to a specific person, such as *Robert E. Lee* or *Sally Ride* (for upper elementary through high school students; Carleton & Marzano, 2010).

Word Associations: After explaining several new vocabulary terms, the teacher selects words and phrases and asks students to figure out which vocabulary term goes with which word or phrase. For example, if *infer, quote, explicit,* and *implicit* had been presented, the teacher might ask, "Which word goes with *assumptions*?" or "Which word goes with *quotation marks*?" Students should then explain the relationships behind their answers (for middle and high school students; Beck et al., 2002).

Word Harvest: Students "pick" words off of a construction paper tree or bush and sort them into baskets with different category labels (for lower elementary school students; Carleton & Marzano, 2010).

Wordle: Teachers use this electronic tool (www.wordle.net) to help students create visual representations of various vocabulary terms. When a block of text is pasted into the tool, Wordle produces a "word cloud" with high-frequency words from the passage appearing larger and low-frequency words appearing smaller. Students can manipulate the way the cloud looks and which words are included using different colors and configurations (for upper elementary through high school students; Dalton & Grisham, 2011).

Word Wizzle: Students make contrasting statements about words based on a rule. For example, for the rule *three-dimensional,* a student might say:

- "I like *spheres* but not *circles.*"

- "I like *prisms* but not *squares.*"

- "I like *pyramids* but not *triangles.*"

- "I like *cylinders* but not *rectangles.*"

The class tries to figure out the rule using the fewest clues possible (for middle and high school students; Scott et al., 2012).

These games and others like them are engaging and give students opportunities to extend their knowledge about specific vocabulary terms. Like steps 4 and 5, the games in step 6 should be followed by an opportunity for students to return to their vocabulary notebooks to record new knowledge and information about various terms.

In summary, the six-step process described here can be used to introduce terms to students, prompt students to represent terms linguistically and nonlinguistically, and help students work with, discuss, and play with the terms. In the next chapter, we narrow our focus and explain the process we used to identify, organize, and provide resources for specific vocabulary from the CCSS.

3 – domain specific
2 – gen. academic
Tier 1 – Basic

Vocabulary Terms From the Common Core State Standards

One of the most crucial components of direct vocabulary instruction involves selecting appropriate terms to teach. For example, most native English speakers do not need to be taught basic words like *clock*, *happy*, and *baby*. They learn these from the oral conversations described in chapter 1 and from day-to-day interactions with adults and other children. However, non-native English speakers often lack those experiences and require instruction in basic words. To facilitate conversations about different kinds of vocabulary terms, Beck and her colleagues (2002) designated three tiers of words: basic words like *clock*, *happy*, and *baby* are in Tier 1; more advanced general academic or literary words like *coincidence*, *absurd*, *imaginative*, *commercial*, *muscular*, *duplicate*, and *restrict* are in Tier 2; and domain-specific words such as *pronoun, algebra, isthmus*, and *quark* are in Tier 3.

As explained previously, most students will acquire Tier 1 words through conversation, reading, and daily experiences (with two notable exceptions: students from lower-SES families and English learners; for further information about providing direct instruction for Tier 1 words, see Marzano, 2010). Beck and her colleagues (2002) recommended focusing direct vocabulary instruction only on Tier 2 words (which they found resulted in a small but significant gain of 12 percentile points). They explained,

> Tier Two words are not only words that are important for students to know, they are also words that can be worked with in a variety of ways so that students have opportunities to build rich representations of them and of their connections to other words and concepts. (p. 20)

However, Stahl and Fairbanks (1986) found that teaching students Tier 3 words was associated with a gain of 33 percentile points, and Beck and her colleagues (2002), despite their belief that instruction about Tier 2 words was most efficacious, acknowledged that there is a place for instruction in Tier 3 words: "There may be . . . unfamiliar words that do not meet the criteria for Tier Two words but which nevertheless require some attention if students are to understand a selection" (p. 20).

In sum, students' academic success requires instruction in both general academic (Tier 2) and domain-specific (Tier 3) vocabulary. During our analysis of the CCSS, we documented both Tier 2 and Tier 3 words in the standards. Here, we describe how we identified and organized those words. The lists of terms themselves appear in parts II (general academic Tier 2 words) and III (domain-specific Tier 3 words). Additionally, the appendix contains an alphabetic master list of terms in both tiers so that teachers looking for a specific term can quickly locate it. For information about the sources of each term (for example, which Common Core standards it appears in), please see the online resources at **marzanoresearch.com/commoncore.**

Tier 2 Vocabulary From the Common Core State Standards

As we analyzed the CCSS, we identified 227 Tier 2 general academic terms, per the designations provided by Beck and her colleagues (Beck et al., 2002). We confined our identification of Tier 2 terms to verbs that describe cognitive processes such as *integrate, organize, comprehend, collaborate, distinguish, initiate, decide, recognize, elaborate, assess, employ, communicate, consider, infer, reflect, represent, solve, defend, diagnose, research,* and *apply.* Students need to know what these terms mean and how to use them to engage in learning in school, but they are not specific to any one subject area. This is not to say that all Tier 2 terms are verbs, only that we limited our identification of Tier 2 terms in the CCSS to verbs that describe cognitive processes.

Research indicates that teaching related words together can have a positive effect on students' learning of vocabulary terms. Antonio Marmolejo (1991) found that teaching related words helped students connect new vocabulary knowledge to their existing background knowledge. Candace Bos and her colleagues (Bos & Anders, 1990; Bos, Anders, Filip, & Jaffe, 1989) found that teaching related words and their features together led to increased vocabulary learning and reading comprehension. Stahl (1999) observed that "if words are stored [in the brain] in categories, then it makes sense to teach them that way" (p. 40). For these reasons, we sought an organizational structure for the identified terms that would allow us to group related words together. Unlike the domain-specific terms presented in part III, these terms are not specific to ELA or math, so we classified the verbs into twenty-four basic categories of cognitive processes. These twenty-four categories are based on previous research about critical thinking and reasoning skills and cognitive processes (see Marzano, 2007; Marzano et al., 1988 for more information).

1. Add To
2. Arrange
3. Collaborate
4. Compare/Contrast
5. Create
6. Decide
7. Define
8. Elaborate
9. Evaluate
10. Execute
11. Explain
12. Hypothesize
13. Infer
14. Measure
15. Problem Solve
16. Prove/Argue
17. Pull Apart
18. Redo
19. Reference
20. Seek Information
21. See the Big Picture
22. Symbolize
23. Think Metacognitively
24. Transform

To illustrate the idea of a basic cognitive process, consider the category Prove/Argue. There are fifteen verbs in this category (see page 74 in part II): *argue, assert, challenge, claim, confirm, defend, disagree, justify, persuade, promote, prove, qualify, specify, support*, and *verify*. Although each word means something different, they all describe actions associated with using logic to legitimize one's views or ideas. Thus, many of the instructional activities in chapter 2 regarding identifying similarities and differences could be used to teach words in this part II category.

Because many of these verbs are abstract and difficult to describe, we provide descriptions and examples for each term in part II. For example, consider the word *analyze*. Throughout the CCSS, students are asked to analyze many things: texts, ideas, documents, graphs, patterns, and so on. Most adults are comfortable with tasks that ask them to analyze information, but describing the word clearly and concretely can be more challenging. For *analyze* and all other words in part II, we provide (1) a description of the word using everyday language and (2) examples of when the word might be used. Teachers can use the description as a jumping-off point to further explain the features of each word. The examples are mainly drawn directly from the CCSS and are meant to give teachers ideas about further experiences, stories, images, and examples of the word for students. Essentially, the information provided in part II is designed to be used when introducing a term to students—step 1 in the six-step process. Consider our description of and examples for the term *analyze*:

> If you **analyze** something, you look closely at each of its parts and see if they fit together in a way that makes sense.
>
> ELA: When you analyze the development of a theme in a text, you find places where the author refers to the theme and examine how those parts work together to communicate the theme. To analyze a presentation, examine the words, visual aids, and information presented to see if they make sense and how they affect the overall presentation. To analyze the role of figures of speech in a text, find specific figures of speech and examine what they mean and how they affect the overall tone and feeling of the text.
>
> Math: When you analyze a problem or a situation, you look at each part of the problem or situation and decide what to do about each individual part. To analyze a shape, look carefully at its sides, angles, size, dimensions, color, and other characteristics. To analyze a graph, look closely at each data point and figure out what information is being given by each element of the graph. To analyze a relationship, look closely at each way that two or more things are related.

We provide examples for ELA and math because those are the areas covered by the CCSS. As mentioned previously, whenever possible, the examples were drawn directly from the CCSS. We searched for the term in the CCSS and tried to write examples that replicated how it was used in the standards. In some cases, the term was used so often that we had to select what we judged to be the most powerful and important examples. In other cases, a word was used only in one subject area in the CCSS, so we had to generate examples for the other subject area from experience and previous compilations of K–12 standards (Kendall & Marzano, 2000). The examples are also designed to give teachers clues about when might be the best time to focus on specific Tier 2 terms. For example, a teacher might notice that one of the examples of items students can *analyze* is a graph. Therefore, she might decide to focus on *analyze* as a vocabulary term while her students are studying specific kinds of graphs.

Besides the cognitive verbs we identified from the CCSS, part II also includes cognitive verbs that were previously identified by Marzano (2009). For example, verbs such as *discriminate, exemplify, judge, test, deduce, diagram, symbolize, overcome, argue*, and *diagnose* do not appear in the CCSS, but they work in tandem with the terms from the CCSS. A teacher who wants students to understand the nuances of *analyze* might ask students to compare it to another term that is closely related but slightly different, such as *judge* or *deduce*. Examining the cognitive verbs from the CCSS in concert with other verbs identified as important (Marzano, 2009) helps students create better representations and deeper understandings of the words from the CCSS. Therefore, we have also included these non-CCSS terms in part II, along with appropriate examples in ELA and math. As explained previously, for terms not appearing in the CCSS, we used experience and compilations of previous standards (Kendall & Marzano, 2000) to generate examples. For a list of how many verbs appear in each of the twenty-four categories, please see the online table at **marzanoresearch.com/commoncore**.

Tier 3 Vocabulary From the Common Core State Standards

Part III of this book contains domain-specific Tier 3 vocabulary terms from the CCSS, per the designations provided by Beck and her colleagues (Beck et al., 2002). To identify the important Tier 3 vocabulary terms in each subject area, we analyzed both the ELA and mathematics CCSS. We then compared that list of terms with the lists for ELA and mathematics presented in *Building Background Knowledge for Academic Achievement* (Marzano, 2004), which lists terms derived from an analysis of national standards documents in eleven subject areas.

As one might expect, many of the terms from the Marzano (2004) list and the CCSS overlapped. If terms overlapped, we included them. For terms that did not overlap, we included them if they were (a) in the CCSS or (b) in *Building Background Knowledge* and still relevant to the subject area. For example, the term *acronym* appears only in *Building Background Knowledge* but is an important term for ELA studies since acronyms are studied widely in ELA classrooms. Therefore, it is included in the lists in part III. In contrast, the term *card catalog* appears only in *Building Background Knowledge*, but most card catalogs have been replaced with electronic resources. Therefore, we decided not to include *card catalog* in the list of words in part III. Additionally, we limited our analysis of the mathematics CCSS to those standards without a + symbol (with one exception in the high school measurement topic Geometric Trigonometry). This is because the authors of the CCSS stated that "all standards without a (+) symbol should be in the common mathematics curriculum for all college and career ready students" (NGA & CCSSO, 2010b, p. 57).

Like the terms in part II, we sought to organize these terms in a way that allowed teachers to address related terms together. Unlike the terms in part II, the terms in part III are specific to ELA and mathematics; therefore, the categories from part II could not be used. Readers will also notice that instead of descriptions and examples, we provide suggested grade levels at which to teach each term. Since there are approximately ten times as many terms in part III as in part II, providing descriptions and examples for each term was outside the scope of this work.

For the domain-specific terms in part III, we settled on the organizational scheme known as *measurement topics* used by researchers at Marzano Research Laboratory to create scoring scales for the CCSS (Marzano et al., 2013). Measurement topics are categories of knowledge and skills found in the CCSS that extend across several grade levels. These categories are meant to help organize the Common Core standards in a way that makes the progression of learning from one grade level to the next more obvious and efficient. There are thirty-seven measurement topics in ELA and seventy-nine measurement topics in mathematics, as shown in table 3.1, and they are arranged into the CCSS strands for ELA (Reading, Reading Foundations, Writing, Speaking and Listening, and Language) and the CCSS domains in mathematics (Number and Quantity, Operations and Algebra, Functions, Geometry, and Measurement, Data, Statistics, and Probability). We used the same structure to organize the terms in part III of this book.

Table 3.1: Measurement Topics for ELA and Mathematics

English Language Arts	Mathematics
Reading: Questioning, Inference, and Interpretation; Themes and Central Ideas; Story Elements; Connections; Word Impact and Use; Academic Vocabulary; Text Structures and Features; Point of View / Purpose; Visual/Auditory Media and Information Sources; Argument and Reasoning; Literary Comparisons and Source Material; Rhetorical Criticism; Fluency	**Number and Quantity:** Number Names, Counting, Compare Numbers, Place Value, Foundations of Fractions, Fractions, Adding and Subtracting Fractions, Multiplying and Dividing Fractions, Decimal Concepts, Ratios and Unit Rates, Rational and Irrational Numbers, Exponents and Roots, Quantities, Operations With Complex Numbers, Polynomial Identities and Equations
Reading Foundations: Print Concepts, Phonological Awareness, Phonics and Word Analysis	**Operations and Algebra:** Addition and Subtraction, Multiplication and Division, Properties of Operations, Expressions and Equations, Factors and Multiples, Patterns, Equations and Inequalities, Dependent and Independent Variables, Slope, Systems of Equations, Structure of Expressions, Equivalent Expressions, Arithmetic Operations on Polynomials, Zeroes and Factors of Polynomials, Polynomial Identities, Rational Expressions, Creating Equations, Reasoning to Solve Equations, Solving Quadratic Equations, Graphs of Equations and Inequalities
Writing: Argumentative; Informative/Explanatory; Narrative; Task, Purpose, and Audience; Revise and Edit; Technology; Research; Access and Organize Information	**Functions:** Functions, Interpret Functions, Graph Functions, Properties of Functions, Model Relationships, Building New Functions, Linear and Exponential Models, Interpret Linear and Exponential Functions, Trigonometric Functions, Periodic Phenomena, Trigonometric Identities
Speaking and Listening: Collaborative Discussions, Evaluate Presented Information, Speech Writing, Presentation and Delivery	**Geometry:** Shapes, Compose and Decompose Shapes, Lines and Symmetry, Coordinate System, Area, Perimeter, Surface Area, Volume, Scale Drawings, Angles, Pythagorean Theorem, Congruence and Similarity, Transformations, Geometric Theorems, Geometric Constructions, Dilations, Theorems Involving Similarity, Trigonometric Ratios, Geometric Trigonometry, Circle Theorems, Arc Length and Sectors, Conic Sections, Geometric Modeling
Language: Grammar, Sentences, Capitalization and Punctuation, Spelling, Language Conventions, Context Clues, Word Origins and Roots, Reference Materials, Word Relationships	**Measurement, Data, Statistics, and Probability:** Measurement, Represent and Interpret Data, Time, Money, Data Distributions, Random Sampling, Probability, Multivariable Data Distributions, Linear Models, Rules of Probability

Source: Marzano et al., 2013, p. 52.

Our analysis of vocabulary terms in the CCSS and *Building Background Knowledge* produced 2,224 Tier 3 words: 1,100 in ELA and 1,124 in mathematics. In some cases, a word fit well into two or more measurement topics. For example, the word *angle* is appropriate for three measurement topics: (1) Angles, (2) Lines and Symmetry, and (3) Shapes. In such cases, we included the word in all applicable measurement topics. Additionally, we limited our use of the term to how it was used in the CCSS. For example, *angle* can also refer to "the precise viewpoint from which something is observed or considered" or "a special approach, point of attack, or technique for accomplishing an objective" ("Angle," 2005, p. 48) and these alternate definitions might fit within the scope of ELA. However, the word *angle* is not used that way in the ELA CCSS, so we do not include it in our ELA list.

In addition to organizing the terms by measurement topic, we also identified grade levels at which each term is especially appropriate for teaching. Unlike the terms in part II (which can apply to many different grade levels depending on the context in which they are taught), the terms in part III can be fitted into specific grade level ranges. We acknowledge that this is an inexact science; we used a combination of data from the CCSS and common sense to assign words to appropriate grade levels. As an example of how we made these determinations, consider the term *fraction*. This word appears in the CCSS starting at grade 3 and continues to be used all the way up to the high school level. However, by the time most students enter middle and high school, they need to fully understand this term and its uses. Therefore, we designated this term as important to learn in grades 3 through 5. In other cases, a word appeared in the CCSS at the high school level but not at lower grade levels, such as the term *play*. Since the term *drama* appears as early as grade 3, it made little sense to designate *play* as a high school word. Therefore, we designated a lower grade level for that term. For other terms, the CCSS used advanced terms such as *interrogative*, *preposition*, and *inflectional ending* at the kindergarten and first-grade levels. With many of these terms, the CCSS did not specifically state that students needed to know the terms; rather, the CCSS used those terms in lower grade-level standards to communicate to teachers what kinds of words students needed to know. For example, ELA standard L.1.1d says, "Use personal, possessive, and indefinite pronouns (e.g., *I, me, my; they, them, their; anyone, everything*)" (NGA & CCSSO, 2010a, p. 26). Here, we interpreted this to mean that students need to be able to *use* personal, possessive, and indefinite pronouns, but not necessarily know what they were called. However, the CCSS's use of the terms *personal pronoun*, *possessive pronoun*, and *indefinite pronoun* here indicates that they are important terms. Therefore, we included them but suggest that the terms themselves should be taught in grades 3–5.

It is important to keep in mind that most Tier 3 terms are designated for a range of grade levels; for example, the term *inference* is designated for grades 2, 3, and 4. As seen in table 3.2, the eleven terms for Questioning, Inference, and Interpretation at the kindergarten level are the same ones that appear at grade 1, and eight of the same terms also appear at grade 2. A kindergarten teacher might introduce the eleven terms (or a selection of those eleven terms), a first-grade teacher might help students master the terms (focusing especially on the three that do not overlap into second grade), and a second-grade teacher might review the eight terms that students have already learned in kindergarten and first grade and introduce the remaining three terms that do not overlap with lower grade levels. As shown by this example, coordinating direct vocabulary instruction across grade levels is an important part of building an effective schoolwide vocabulary program, a topic we discuss in more depth in chapter 4.

Table 3.3 shows how many words are unique at each grade level, meaning the same word included in several measurement topics is only counted once for each grade level. Visit **marzanoresearch.com /commoncore** for more detailed charts listing the unique terms for each grade level in ELA and mathematics.

Teachers should feel free to adjust the grade levels and measurement topics of terms according to their students' needs and the details of their curricula. For example, a fourth-grade ELA teacher might decide to include the term *couplet* as part of his unit on poetry, even though we have designated it as a high school term. A middle school math teacher might determine that her students need more practice with the term *whole number*, even though we have designated it as an upper elementary school term. During a unit on Themes and Central Ideas, a fifth-grade teacher might include the term *plot development*, even though we placed it in the measurement topic Story Elements. Or an eighth-grade math teacher might decide to include the term *addition property of equality* in his unit on Addition and Subtraction in spite of the fact that it appears in Properties of Operations in part III. We consider adjustments like these to be completely appropriate.

Table 3.2: Repetition of Terms Across the Measurement Topic Questioning, Inference, and Interpretation

K	1	2	3	4	5	6	7	8	9–10	11–12
answer	answer	detail	inference	inference	evidence	analysis	analysis	analysis		
ask	ask	how	reason	reason	support	cite	cite	cite		
question	question	what	example	example	quote	explicit	explicit	explicit		
detail	detail	when	evidence	evidence		implicit	implicit	implicit		
how	how	where	support	support		textual evidence	textual evidence	textual evidence		
what	what	who	quote	quote						
when	when	why								
where	where	text								
who	who	inference								
why	why	reason								
text	text	example								
Total Unique Terms: 22										

Table 3.3: Number of Unique ELA and Mathematics Terms

	K	1	2	3	4	5	6	7	8	9–10	11–12
Unique ELA Terms	109	149	216	370	379	324	344	289	279	272	263
Unique Mathematics Terms	93	137	209	290	314	291	360	309	314	384	

As we explain in chapter 4, it is important for teachers to consider the needs of their students and the opportunities and constraints of their individual situations when designing a program to build vocabulary for the CCSS. Our lists in parts II and III are a starting point for that process. As mentioned previously, we do not recommend that teachers try to teach all of the terms in parts II and III. Rather, teachers and teams of teachers should select those words that they deem most necessary to the content they will be teaching. We describe strategies for this selection process in chapter 4.

Building a Vocabulary Program

In chapters 1 and 2, we examined research and theory highlighting the importance of vocabulary knowledge and described a research-based six-step process for vocabulary instruction. Chapter 3 explained how we identified and organized the CCSS vocabulary terms in parts II and III. In this chapter, we address two issues that are important when implementing vocabulary programs in classrooms and schools: educators must (1) select which terms they will teach from parts II and III and (2) create systems to assess and track the knowledge that students gain as a result of direct vocabulary instruction.

Selecting Terms to Teach

As explained in chapter 3, parts II and III are designed to be a menu from which educators select the terms they consider most critical to the content being taught. It is not our expectation that teachers address all of the terms in parts II and III. In fact, attempting to teach them all would not allow teachers or students time enough with each term to facilitate learning. Instead, our collection of terms represents a starting point from which teachers should exercise their professional judgment and select appropriate terms for instruction.

In general, teachers are fairly skilled at identifying essential and supplemental vocabulary terms (Beck et al., 2002; Breland, Jones, & Jenkins, 1994; Calderón, Hertz-Lazarowitz, & Slavin, 1998; Carlo et al., 2004; Marzano, 2002; Shapiro, 1969). Thus, this selection process can be completed by individual teachers, but it is more effective when done with larger groups, such as grade-, school-, or district-level teams. Here we review how individuals and groups of teachers would go about selecting terms for direct instruction.

Selection of Terms by Individual Teachers

An individual teacher working in a self-contained classroom would begin by estimating how many terms he or she thinks can be taught during the school year. For example, a third-grade teacher in a self-contained classroom might estimate that he can teach ten words per week across all of his subject areas or 320 words during the year (assuming that a year involves thirty-two weeks of instruction). (For a more extensive discussion of how many terms can be taught during a year, see Marzano, 2004). Next, the teacher would determine how many different subjects he was responsible for teaching. This teacher teaches four subjects: science, social studies, mathematics, and ELA. Since mathematics and ELA each comprise a quarter of the subjects, the teacher estimates that he will be able to teach eighty math words and eighty ELA words during the school year. Although social studies and science are outside the scope of this book, the teacher would also create vocabulary lists for those subject areas (most likely with eighty words on each list).

A high school mathematics teacher, on the other hand, estimates that she will be able to teach five terms per week over the course of a year for a total of 160 mathematics terms.

Once a teacher has estimated how many terms he or she can teach in a year, the next step is to examine the lists in parts II and III, asking whether or not each term is critical to the content that he or she will be teaching that year. The measurement topics into which part III terms are categorized are a useful tool to this end. For example, a seventh-grade mathematics teacher might decide that the measurement topic of Angles (among many others) is important to a unit he will be teaching. At grade 7, that topic includes the following terms:

- Adjacent angle
- Alternate interior angle
- Angle bisector
- Complementary angle
- Exterior angle
- Inscribed angle

- Interior angle
- Intersection
- Similarity
- Supplementary angle
- Vertical angle

Of these, he selects the following:

- Interior angle
- Exterior angle
- Supplementary angle

- Complementary angle
- Vertical angle
- Adjacent angle

He does so because these terms can easily be taught as a set of related words. He might also include related Tier 2 words (such as *measure*, *model*, or *construct*). Because the terms are related, many of the instructional activities in chapter 2 regarding similarities and differences could be used. In addition, the terms *supplementary angle*, *complementary angle*, *vertical angle*, and *adjacent angle* are central to one of the goals of his unit:

> Use facts about supplementary, complementary, vertical, and adjacent angles in a multi-step problem to write and solve simple equations for an unknown angle in a figure. (7.G.B.5; NGA & CCSSO, 2010b, p. 50)

When considering each measurement topic, a teacher could put a check mark next to the terms he or she considers critical to that year's content. Teachers might also scan terms at other grade levels or create a list of terms not included in parts II and III but which they feel are important to the content.

If a teacher identifies more terms as critical than he or she originally planned to teach each year, the teacher will need to adjust his or her plan. For example, if the third-grade teacher described previously (who planned to teach eighty mathematics terms and eighty ELA terms) discovered that there were seventy mathematics terms and ninety ELA terms that he considered critical, he would simply teach seventy mathematics terms and ninety ELA terms instead of eighty math and eighty ELA terms. If the same teacher discovered that there were ninety math terms and ninety ELA terms that he considered critical, he would need to teach one extra term each week for twenty weeks to accommodate the additional terms. Alternatively, the teacher could re-examine his list of critical terms, asking himself once again which terms are most critical to the content being taught.

Selection of Terms by School or District Teams

Although individual teachers can use the process just described to select a set of vocabulary terms for their classrooms, school- or districtwide vocabulary programs can be even more powerful. Marzano and Pickering (2005) recommended a five-phase process that schools or districts can use. The process includes the following phases:

1. Decide the target number of words to be taught at each grade level and across each grade-level interval (K–2, 3–5, 6–8, or 9–12) or multigrade span (such as K–6 or K–12).

2. For each subject area, create a rank-ordered list of critical words by selecting words from parts II and III and adding words that reflect local standards and curriculum materials.

3. Based on the number of critical words identified, determine how many terms should be taught in each subject area.

4. Generate a final list of terms for each subject area by adding terms, deleting terms, or otherwise altering the lists.

5. Assign terms in each subject area list to specific grades.

A group working to select vocabulary terms for a school or district should include teachers from all grade levels in both mathematics and ELA. During the first phase, this group estimates how many terms can be addressed each year in each subject at each grade level. This step is similar to the first step for individual teachers described previously. During the second phase, the group selects words from parts II and III for instruction at each grade level. The group might decide to use a more detailed system for identifying words than that described for individual teachers. For example, rather than simply asking if the term is critical to the content being taught that year, the group could use a scale like the one in table 4.1 to rate each term's importance.

Table 4.1: Rating Scale for Potential Vocabulary Terms

4	This word should definitely be included.
3	This word should probably be included.
2	This word should probably not be included.
1	This word should definitely not be included.

Teachers in each group individually rate the words and then compare their ratings. This method allows teachers to make determinations about which words should definitely be included or excluded, and which words may require more discussion. In all cases, a group working to select words should remain aware that their initial selections are not set in stone. Revisions, additions, and deletions will almost certainly be necessary as schools and districts implement vocabulary programs and receive feedback from teachers and students.

During phase 3, the group counts the number of terms identified and compares that number to the original estimate of how many words it is feasible to teach at each grade level. During phase 4, the group makes additions, deletions, or revisions so that the number of terms in each list matches the total identified during phase 1. Finally, in phase 5, the group assigns terms to specific grade levels.

Whether teachers work individually or in school- or districtwide groups to select terms for instruction, it is also important to allow students to identify terms that they consider important to learn. To that end, many teachers designate a section of each student's vocabulary notebook as a place where students can record terms they learn independently. Recall from chapter 2 the benefits gained when a teacher prompted students to post their "found" words on a word wall. It stands to reason that some of the same benefits can be gained by allowing students to collect terms in their vocabulary notebooks. Students can find terms through their reading or select terms from teacher-provided lists. For example, a teacher might show students a list of terms not considered critical to the content being taught and allow them to select one or two words that they would like to investigate independently and record in their vocabulary notebooks.

Creating Systems to Assess and Track Students' Vocabulary Knowledge

Teachers can assess students' vocabulary knowledge formally and informally. The six-step process described in chapter 2 is designed to allow many opportunities for teachers and students to identify and clarify any errors or misconceptions in students' understanding of a term. Teachers might also periodically look through students' vocabulary notebooks to identify areas of confusion or uncertainty about the meaning of a term. By moving around the room and listening to students' conversations during activities, discussions, and games, teachers can also informally and unobtrusively assess students' vocabulary knowledge.

If a teacher wants to assess students' vocabulary knowledge more formally, he or she might design a quiz or test for the purpose. However, Marzano and Pickering (2005) warned teachers to use caution when designing these tests:

> The six-step teaching process we have described allows for great variation in the ways students describe and represent terms. Consequently, a multiple-choice or matching test might not be a valid assessment, especially if words within the test items are unfamiliar to the student. We recommend constructing tests with open-ended questions that allow the students to show what they understand about the terms. (pp. 33–34)

For example, a teacher might ask students to explain a term in their own words, draw a picture or other graphic representation of a term, or write a short dialogue between two characters that uses the term and makes its meaning clear. If a teacher does want to use multiple-choice items, Beck et al. (2002) recommended creating items that require students to apply their knowledge of a term to different situations. They offered the examples of weak and strong multiple-choice items shown in table 4.2.

Table 4.2: Weak and Strong Multiple-Choice Vocabulary Items

Weak	Strong

Diligent means:
  a. fast
  b. hardworking
  c. lost
  d. punished
	Diligent means:
	  a. making a lot of money
	  b. working at an interesting job
	  c. always trying one's best
	  d. remembering everything

Source: Beck et al., 2002, p. 96.

The column on the left side of table 4.2 simply asks students to select the closest synonym for *diligent*. The item on the right side, however, requires that students understand the characteristics and defining features of someone who is *diligent*.

As explained in chapter 2, asking students to assess their own knowledge of a vocabulary term is an excellent way to help them become more aware of how well they understand a term. Students' self-evaluation scores on the four-point scale in their vocabulary notebooks (presented on page 22) should be revised as their knowledge of a term improves. For example, during step 2 of the six-step process (restate the description, explanation, or example in your own words), a student might decide that she has a general idea of what a term means but is still uncertain. She would circle the number 2 (*I'm a little uncertain about what the term means, but I have a general idea.*) on the self-assessment scale in her vocabulary notebook for that term. However, during step 4, she might complete an activity that clarifies and extends her knowledge of the term. After adding information to her entry for the term, the student might change her self-assessment rating to a 3 (*I understand the term, and I'm not confused about any part of what it means.*) in her notebook. If the same student later encounters that term while reading in a way that further extends her knowledge of it, she could return to that entry, add information, and change her self-assessment rating to a 4 (*I understand even more about the term than I was taught.*). This scale also allows teachers to get an idea of a student's comfort level with different words by looking at the student's vocabulary notebook. Terms that the student has self-assessed as a level 1 (*I'm very uncertain about the term. I don't understand what it means.*) are those the teacher may want to provide further lessons about or focus on during games and activities.

Another way to utilize the self-assessment scales in students' vocabulary notebooks is by asking students to look at all of their entries and tally how many words they have rated at each level. A tracking chart like the one in table 4.3 could be used to summarize their results. The bar graph created by the *x*'s provides a visual representation of the vocabulary learning recorded in students' vocabulary notebooks.

Table 4.3: Tracking Chart for Vocabulary Knowledge

Number of Terms	Level 1	Level 2	Level 3	Level 4
10			X	
9			X	
8		X	X	
7		X	X	
6		X	X	
5		X	X	X
4		X	X	X
3	X	X	X	X
2	X	X	X	X
1	X	X	X	X

Teachers might ask students to fill out a chart like the one in table 4.3 (page 53) weekly, monthly, or once per grading period. If such a chart is completed in pencil or electronically, students can easily move the x's around to reflect changes in their vocabulary knowledge.

In summary, building a strong program of vocabulary instruction requires teachers to select terms to teach, assess students' knowledge of vocabulary terms, and help them evaluate their understanding and track their progress with different terms. Combined with the six-step process for teaching vocabulary from chapter 2, these elements support students as they learn new words.

Part II

Tier 2 Vocabulary Terms From the Common Core State Standards

Part II contains Tier 2 general academic terms from the CCSS. In our analysis of the CCSS, we limited our identification of Tier 2 terms to verbs that describe cognitive processes. We also included a number of verbs from *Designing & Teaching Learning Goals & Objectives* (Marzano, 2009) that work in tandem with the verbs from the CCSS. The words in Part II are organized into the categories introduced on page 42. Abbreviations for each category align with the appendix. For a complete alphabetical listing of the terms in this section and the source of each term, please consult the online resource at **marzanoresearch.com /commoncore**. An alphabetical master list of all the words in parts II and III and their category (for part II words) or measurement topic (for part III words) is included in the appendix (page 215). Teachers can use the appendix to locate specific words in parts II and III.

Each word is accompanied by a description of the word and examples of how that word might be used in ELA and mathematics. The examples are largely drawn directly from the CCSS. For example, to write the examples for the term *build*, we searched both the ELA CCSS and the mathematics CCSS for the term and wrote examples based on how it was used in each document. If a term was used extensively throughout the CCSS, we focused our examples on what we judged to be the most useful occurrences. If a word was used in only one subject area, we generated examples for the other subject area from experience and by consulting previous compilations of K–12 standards (Kendall & Marzano, 2000). Teachers can use the examples as clues about the best contexts in which to teach the terms in part II. The examples for the word *deepen*, for instance, indicate that it is probably best taught in the context of research or information-gathering.

The terms in this section are not designated to be taught at a specific grade level, because these terms are appropriate for a wide range of grade levels. Teachers should use the descriptions and examples offered here as starting points for their classes' exploration of each term. If a teacher feels that the examples given are too advanced or too simple for her class, she can revise them to apply more directly to the content being taught. Teachers can also personalize and extend the examples presented here by sharing experiences, stories, and images of how they use the word in their own lives.

Add To (ADD)

combine   If you **combine** things, you put them together.

ELA: When you have lots of short, choppy sentences in your writing, combine some of them to improve the rhythm of your piece. When you want to tell a story that also proves a point, combine elements of narrative and argumentative writing. When learning to read, combine knowledge about letter sounds with context clues to figure out words.

Math: Combine addition and multiplication to figure out a math problem. Combine smaller shapes, like triangles, to form a larger shape, like a square. Addition and multiplication both involve combining groups or quantities.

deepen   If you **deepen** your knowledge of something, you learn more about it or strengthen what you already know.

ELA: Ask questions or make observations to deepen your understanding of a topic or issue. To deepen your research, investigate specific topics or issues related to your research question.

Math: When you already know about two-dimensional shapes and you learn about three-dimensional shapes, your knowledge of shapes will deepen.

improve   If you **improve** something, you make it better.

ELA: When you think your writing is too choppy, improve it by combining some of your sentences and using more transition words. When you think your speaking style is too timid, improve it by speaking louder or making eye contact with audience members more often.

Math: Improve the solution to a problem by providing more explanation for it. Improve the quality of your conclusions by making sure your data are accurate.

incorporate   If you **incorporate** something, you add it or include it.

ELA: In a discussion, incorporate quieter members of a group by asking them questions.

Math: Incorporate pictures or drawings in your explanation of a problem to make it clearer.

integrate   If you **integrate** something, you combine it with other things to form a complete whole.

ELA: When you integrate information from oral, visual, quantitative, and media sources, you put all the different kinds of information together to form one idea. When writing a research report, it is important to integrate information from several sources.

Math: When you integrate several strategies to solve a math problem, you put together several processes like adding tens, dividing, and subtracting to help you solve it.

introduce   If you **introduce** something, you present it for the first time.

ELA: When you are writing an argumentative or informative piece, introduce your topic or issue at the beginning of your piece. In a narrative piece, authors normally introduce the main characters at the beginning, although sometimes new characters can be introduced later in the story.

Math: When you figure out a new strategy for solving a problem, introduce your classmates to it by telling them about it.

Arrange (ARR)

arrange   If you **arrange** items, you place each one in a particular place or location.

ELA: When you are writing a narrative, arrange the events chronologically or according to each character's perspective.

Math: Arrange items in a straight line to count them more easily. You might also arrange items into equal groups or an array and use multiplication to figure out how many there are all together. Arrange several shapes in a specific way to figure out their angle measures, or arrange the elements of a graph to best represent the data.

list   If you **list** things, you write them down or say them one after the other.

ELA: In an opinion piece, list all the reasons for your opinion before describing each one in detail. You should list all the sources you used in your report or paper in a bibliography or reference list at the end. When you brainstorm, you list everything you can think of without judging any of the ideas.

Math: To determine the probability of a specific outcome, start by listing all the possible outcomes. The domain of a function lists all its possible inputs, and the range lists all the possible outputs.

organize   If you **organize** things, you arrange them in a certain order or plan them in a certain way.

ELA: When writing, organize information so that it is easy to read and understand. In an argumentative piece, organize claims and reasons logically. In an informative piece, organize main ideas and details. In a narrative, the author might organize events according to time order. A speaker might organize his points so that they build on each other.

Math: It is important to organize data before trying to draw conclusions from them.

sort   If you **sort** items, you put them into different groups based on what they are like.

ELA: When you have a lot of information, you might sort it according to what information supported your argument and what did not. Sort words according to their part of speech, number, person, tense, or other attributes.

Math: Sort numbers according to whether they are even or odd, composite or prime, or positive or negative. Sort shapes according to their sides or angles.

Collaborate (COLL)

collaborate   If you **collaborate**, you work together with other people.

ELA: Collaborate with other students by sharing ideas with each other. You could also collaborate by splitting up work among members of a group. Websites or technology tools that allow multiple users to contribute ideas or add to projects can help people collaborate.

Math: Collaborate with a partner to solve a math problem by each using a different strategy to solve it and then comparing your answers. Collaborate with someone to do research by assigning each person different tasks and then putting your work together to produce a final project.

contribute   If you **contribute**, you give or add something to a situation.

ELA: In a discussion, each person can contribute by saying his or her ideas. In a story, different characters and events contribute to the development of the plot. When you are giving a presentation or speech, contribute to your credibility by speaking clearly and audibly, looking audience members in the eye, and presenting material in an organized way.

Math: When your group is building a model, contribute to the work by getting the appropriate supplies or by building a specific part of the model.

engage   If you **engage** in something, you participate in it. If you **engage** someone in something, you keep him or her interested in it.

ELA: When you engage in a discussion, you talk and listen to others in a group. Keep a reader engaged in a story by presenting a series of problems that the protagonist has to solve. Keep a reader engaged in an informative or argumentative piece by using interesting evidence or facts that he or she hasn't heard before.

Math: When you are explaining your solution to a math problem, engage your listeners by using pictures in addition to numbers.

interact	If you **interact** with someone, your actions affect each other.
	ELA:　Characters in a story might interact by talking, fighting, becoming friends, or going somewhere together. Events in a story interact when they overlap or have a cause/effect relationship. You can interact with others by talking face to face, writing, or using technology tools such as email, web conferences, social media, blogs, or other Internet sites.
	Math:　When you are having trouble solving a problem, interact with someone else so he or she can tell you his or her ideas and hear yours.
participate	If you **participate** in something, you take part in it.
	ELA:　When you participate in a research project, you work with others on it. When you participate in a discussion, you talk and share your ideas.
	Math:　Participate in class by offering to write out the steps of a problem and explain your work to others.
share	If you **share** information, you let someone else know about it.
	ELA:　When you do research, you normally share your findings by writing a report. During a discussion, people should share what they are thinking.
	Math:　Share your solution to a problem by drawing pictures, showing it with numbers, or using words to explain it.

Compare/Contrast (C/C)

associate	If something is **associated** with something else, the two are connected or related in some way.
	ELA:　When learning to read, you associate sounds and words with the printed letters on the page.
	Math:　A number line associates numbers with points on a line. A coordinate plane associates ordered pairs with points in space. A function describes two values that are associated with each other. Data are often associated with specific categories.
categorize	If you **categorize** items, you put them in groups.
	ELA:　Categorize information according to what source it is from (book, magazine, journal, Internet).
	Math:　When you categorize data according to when they were collected, you group them by date. If you want to categorize a group of numbers, sort them into rational numbers, irrational numbers, and complex numbers.
classify	If you **classify** things, you organize them into groups based on their attributes.
	ELA:　Classify evidence for an argument into groups such as common knowledge, expert opinion, experimental evidence, and factual information. Classify words into groups such as those with prefixes, those with suffixes, and those with Greek or Latin roots. Sometimes you classify things by putting them into groups that already exist, and other times you classify them by creating groups that things will fit into.
	Math:　Classify shapes according to their number of sides or angles. You could also classify shapes as two-dimensional (square, circle, triangle) or three-dimensional (sphere, pyramid, prism).
compare	If you **compare** things, you identify ways that they are the same.
	ELA:　Compare two texts by looking for things the authors did the same. Compare two characters by pointing out similarities in their personalities, experiences, or appearances. Compare different uses of English by pointing out how you talk in formal and informal contexts.
	Math:　Compare your predictions with the actual results of an experiment by looking to see how they were similar. When you compare numbers, equations, or expressions, consider which ones represent larger or smaller amounts. Compare several items according to attributes that can be measured, such as length, height, weight, volume, size, or orientation.

connect   If you **connect** things, you make a link between them.

ELA: When you express opinions or arguments, connect them to reasons that explain why you think they are true. When writing, use linking words, phrases, and clauses to connect ideas. In discussions, questions that connect ideas from several different people are often helpful.

Math: When you connect counting to cardinality, you understand that each number corresponds to one thing in a group. When you connect area to multiplication, you understand that multiplying involves counting groups of items in the same way that area often involves counting columns and rows.

contrast   If you **contrast** things, you find the differences between them.

ELA: To contrast two characters, settings, or events, find ways that they differ. Contrast the point of view in several texts showing how different narrators saw or described things differently. To contrast two narrative structures, show how one is chronological and the other is cause/effect.

Math: To contrast fractions and decimals, show that they are different because fractions use many kinds of fractional parts (halves, thirds, fourths, fifths, and so on) and decimals are expressed in terms of tenths, hundredths, thousandths, and so on.

differentiate   If you **differentiate** between two things, you show how they are different.

ELA: Differentiate between how you use English to speak to your friends and how you use English in a formal presentation. When doing research, it is important to differentiate between primary and secondary sources.

Math: The negative number sign differentiates positive from negative numbers. Differentiate between prime and composite numbers or between odd and even numbers.

discriminate   If you **discriminate** between things, you see or perceive a difference between them and treat them differently based on the difference.

ELA: Discriminate between fiction and nonfiction by finding out if a book is true or made up. When doing research, discriminate between reliable and unreliable sources.

Math: Discriminate different shapes by counting their number of sides, corners, and angles. Discriminate logical arguments from illogical arguments by examining the reasons and evidence behind each one.

distinguish   If you **distinguish** something, you recognize it for a specific reason.

ELA: When you write an argument, distinguish your claim from opposing or alternate claims by explaining how it is different. When you are considering several words to describe something, distinguish between those that have positive and negative connotations. When you listen to an argument or debate, distinguish between facts, opinions, and reasoned judgment.

Math: When you are listening to an argument, try to distinguish if the logic and reasoning are correct or incorrect. Distinguish defining and nondefining attributes of shapes. Distinguish linear growth from exponential growth by examining whether things are growing at a constant or expanding rate.

link   If you **link** things together, you connect them.

ELA: It is important to link opinions to reasons and evidence that support them. Use words like *because* and *also* to link ideas. To link one web page to another, use a hyperlink. In discussions, link your ideas to what has already been said by paraphrasing previous comments before giving your own.

Math: Use a model to link mathematical expressions or equations to their real-world uses.

match   If you **match** things, you pair up two things that are alike in some way.

ELA: To match claims to reasons, explain why you think the things you do. To match your writing style to your favorite author's, try to write like him or her.

Math: When you are trying to figure out which of two groups contains more items, match items from each group up to see which group had items left over. When you fold a shape in half and both sides match each other, it is symmetrical.

relate

If you **relate** things, you find connections between them.

ELA: Relate the first scene of a play to the last scene by describing how characters are portrayed in each one. Examine how the author relates different elements of a story, such as the characters, settings, and events. During a discussion, it is important to ask questions that relate to the topic at hand.

Math: Relate addition to multiplication by saying that they both result in larger numbers. To relate addition and subtraction to a number line, show that addition involves moving to the right and subtraction involves moving to the left. Relate the domain of a function to its graph by showing how each value on the horizontal axis corresponds to a value in the domain.

Create (CRE)

accomplish

If you **accomplish** something, you do it successfully.

ELA: Write an argumentative piece to accomplish the task of convincing someone that renewable energy is a worthwhile cause.

Math: Use math to accomplish a goal, such as keeping a ledger of costs and revenues from an art sale fundraiser.

achieve

If you **achieve** something, you succeed at it.

ELA: You can use language to achieve particular effects, such as using conditional verb forms (*might, could,* and *would*) to express uncertainty.

Math: Use math to achieve a goal, such as calculating the angle at which you need to cut wood when building a set of shelves.

build

If you **build** something, you join separate items or concepts together to create something new.

ELA: Build on someone else's ideas during a discussion by connecting your ideas to his or hers to form new ideas. To build knowledge, join new information with what you already know to form new conclusions. Texts often build on themselves, with later paragraphs or chapters adding to previously presented material.

Math: To build a shape, use smaller shapes to create the new shape. When you build your understanding of something, you learn more about it. Build a fraction such as $5/8$ by adding $3/8$ and $1/4$ or by adding $1/8$ five times. To build a model of something, put materials together to create a representation of the thing. To build a function, combine numbers and variables to create an equation that describes a relationship.

compose

If you **compose** something, you put it together using several separate parts.

ELA: To compose a written piece, put words, phrases, and sentences together to create an essay, report, article, book, or other written work. Compose an argument by putting ideas and evidence together to defend a particular viewpoint on an issue.

Math: When you want to compose the number 143, combine 1 hundred, 4 tens, and 3 ones. When you add 8 ones and 4 ones, you can compose a ten, with 2 ones left over. Smaller shapes can be used to compose larger shapes.

construct

If you **construct** something, you build it by putting separate parts together.

ELA: When you construct an argument, you put several reasons together to form a conclusion.

Math: Use simple shapes to construct more complex shapes. To display a lot of numbers, construct a table, a graph, or a chart.

create   If you **create** something, you make it for the first time.

ELA: Once you have collected information to write about, you have to create an organization scheme for it. Use transition words and phrases to create smooth movement from one section of a written or oral piece to the next. Create cohesion in a written piece or presentation by pointing out connections between information and ideas.

Math: When you want to describe a relationship, create an equation to describe it. Many shapes can be created by combining other shapes.

develop   If you **develop** something, you work on it over a period of time, during which it grows or changes.

ELA: When you are writing a narrative, use details and description to develop a setting and characters. Ask a friend to read your writing and give you advice on how to develop better organization or sentence fluency. When you are making an argument, present a simple claim at the beginning and then develop it with evidence and facts.

Math: To develop understanding, learn more and more about something over time. To develop a strategy or method for doing something, figure out better and better ways of doing it over time. Develop fluency with something by becoming faster and more accurate at it. To develop a model for something, design and build it over time.

draft   If you **draft** something, you write it down for the first time, with the intention of revising it.

ELA: When you write or type a written piece for the first time, you are drafting it.

Math: To build a model, draft an initial plan for it.

form   If you **form** something, you create it.

ELA: Form most regular plural nouns by adding -s or -es to the end of the word. Form most regular past-tense verbs by adding -ed to the end of the word. Apostrophes can be used to form possessives or contractions.

Math: Use simple shapes like triangles, squares, pentagons, and hexagons to form more complex shapes. Form ordered pairs using an x-coordinate and a y-coordinate.

generate   If you **generate** something, you bring it into being or existence.

ELA: During a research project, you might discover new information that causes you to generate new research questions.

Math: When you measure something, you generate measurements. To generate equivalent fractions, create new fractions that refer to the same amount as a given fraction. Use rules to generate patterns and commutative and distributive properties to generate equivalent expressions. When you collect data from a population, you generate a data set. Use a computer to generate graphs, tables, plots, or statistical measurements from a set of data.

initiate   If you **initiate** something, you make it begin.

ELA: Initiate a discussion by asking everyone to share their initial thoughts on an issue.

Math: Initiate a research project by asking everyone who will be involved to meet together to talk about the project.

produce   If you **produce** something, you make it.

ELA: To produce a written piece, type it in a word processor or write it out on paper. If asked to produce rhyming words for candle, you might say *handle*, *sandal*, *scandal*, or *vandal*.

Math: Produce an equivalent fraction by multiplying the numerator and denominator of a fraction by the same, non-zero number. One way to produce equivalent expressions is to use properties of operations.

publish   If you **publish** something, you prepare and distribute it.

ELA: When you publish a book, you print copies of it to sell or give away. When you publish something on the Internet, you post it where the public can access it. When you publish an article, it is printed in a journal, magazine, or newspaper.

Math: When you publish your findings after completing a research project, you write about what you found out and give it to people to read.

record

If you **record** something, you create a written, audio, or video version of it that can be looked at or listened to in the future.

ELA: Record information found during a web search in your notes. Video record yourself giving an oral presentation and watch the recording to figure out ways to improve your speaking style.

Math: Record the decomposition of 10 by writing $10 = 4 + 3 + 2 + 1$. When you compare two numbers, record the result using the symbols $>$, $<$, or $=$. Record measurements by writing them in a column or table.

stimulate

If you **stimulate** something, you encourage it to be more active.

ELA: Stimulate a discussion by asking questions, paraphrasing others' ideas, or introducing a controversial idea.

Math: Stimulate your brain by solving riddles or brain teasers.

Decide (DEC)

choose

If you **choose** something, you pick that thing instead of something else.

ELA: When you need to modify a noun, you should choose an adjective instead of an adverb. When writing, choose words, phrases, and sentences that express your ideas precisely or create the effects you want. When you want a sentence to communicate excitement, choose to use an exclamation mark at the end instead of a period.

Math: Choose a specific strategy to add three-digit numbers. You might choose to use meters instead of centimeters to measure the length of a table. For a repeating decimal, you could choose to round it to the thousandths place.

decide

When you **decide** something, you think about several choices and then choose one of them.

ELA: When your teacher gives you several choices of novels to read for class, decide which one you want to read. When you decide to write a narrative piece, you might choose to write a fictional story.

Math: When you listen to someone's reasoning, you have to decide if it makes sense. To solve problems, you normally have to decide on a correct answer.

select

If you **select** something, you choose it.

ELA: Select a bar graph to display data during a presentation. To search a wide range of information, select a search engine online.

Math: Select the best unit to measure something, depending on how large or small it is. To measure an angle, you would probably select a protractor tool.

Define (DEF)

define

If you **define** something, you explain what it means very clearly and specifically.

ELA: In a discussion, define everyone's role so they know what they are expected to contribute. Define a word by telling what category it belongs in and how it is different from other things in that category.

Math: Define a shape by describing its sides, corners, and angles. Functions are defined by different equations and expressions (like the quadratic equation or a polynomial) because those equations describe exactly how the function relates inputs and outputs.

delineate

If you **delineate** something, you show where it is or what it is.

ELA: To delineate the claims and evidence in a text, circle or mark each claim and piece of evidence in the actual text or make a list of the claims and evidence to present to others.

Math: In place value, use a decimal point to delineate where the ones column is. In geometry, use two lines, like this | |, to delineate that two lines are parallel.

determine   If you **determine** something, you discover it or decide on it.

ELA: To determine the main idea of a book, you have to read the book and decide which message or theme in it is most important. To determine the meaning of an unknown word, it can be helpful to look at the words around it and the sentence it appears in or to look it up in a dictionary.

Math: When comparing two shapes, determine whether one is a reflection of the other. Determine if an equation or inequality is true or false, or find the number or numbers that will make it true. Determine if a number is odd or even or if it is a multiple or factor of another number. Often, you measure something to determine how large or small it is. Formulas and theorems can be used to determine measurements such as area, volume, surface area, and side length. Calculate probabilities to determine the likelihood of an event. In a function, the input determines the output.

discern   If you **discern** something, you see or perceive how it is different.

ELA: To discern the main points of a speaker's argument, listen carefully and take notes.

Math: Use a mirror to discern if a shape is symmetrical. Discern whether a shape has been transformed by rotation, reflection, or translation.

establish   If you **establish** something, you create it or show that it is true.

ELA: Establish a debate club in your school by finding people who are interested and planning a time to meet. Establish that your claim is accurate by providing evidence and reasons for it. In narrative pieces, it is important to establish a setting, characters, and a narrator in the introduction. In argumentative and informative pieces, it is important to establish a formal style and objective tone. In a discussion, it is sometimes helpful to establish roles for each participant.

Math: Cut apart triangles and arrange the angles of each one to form a straight line to establish that the angle sum of a triangle is always 180 degrees. Use the properties of similarity transformations to establish the angle-angle criterion.

exemplify   If you **exemplify** something, you give examples of it.

ELA: When you are writing about an abstract concept such as *patriotism*, exemplify it by telling stories of people who were especially patriotic. When you are arguing in favor of a change, exemplify a situation where the same change had positive results.

Math: Exemplify the identity property of one with the example $8 \times 1 = 8$. Exemplify the quantity of one-fourth by drawing a circle and dividing it into four equal parts.

identify   If you **identify** something, you say what it is.

ELA: When you are asked to identify the characters in a story, list their names. When you are asked to identify the main events in a story, describe what happened in each event or circle the passages that describe them. Often you can identify things by pointing to them. When you are reading or listening to an argument, identify which reasons and evidence support which points.

Math: When you identify a shape, you say what its name is. Identify shapes that are larger or smaller than other shapes. Identify patterns by recognizing them and describing them. Identify data on a graph by labeling them. Gathering data can help you identify relationships.

interpret   If you **interpret** something, you figure out what you think it means.

ELA: Words and phrases in a text can be interpreted literally (the words mean exactly what they say) or figuratively (the words have an implied or nonliteral meaning). When you use visual aids during a presentation, you may need to help the audience interpret the information they present.

Math: You can interpret data in many different ways. When you use division to solve a problem, you need to interpret the remainder to decide whether to express it as a fraction, a decimal, or in some other way.

label   If you **label** something, you assign a name, number, or symbol to it.

ELA: When you are writing an argumentative or informative piece, label each section with a heading. When you use a pie chart in a presentation, label each part of the pie with what it represents and its exact percentage.

Math: It is important to label the axes of a graph so that people know what types of data they represent and what values are associated with each data point. Label sides, angles, or whole shapes using a combination of letters and symbols.

locate

If you **locate** something, you find it or figure out where it is.

ELA: In books, use the table of contents or index to quickly locate specific information. Circle, underline, or copy key information into your notes to help you easily locate it later. Use keywords, hyperlinks, and sidebar menus to help you locate information on the Internet.

Math: To locate a number on a number line, point to where it is or draw a dot there. To locate a point in the coordinate plane, first find the x-coordinate on the horizontal axis and then move up or down depending on what the y-coordinate is.

name

If you **name** something, you say what it is.

ELA: When you are asked to name the author and illustrator of a book, say their names. When you are asked to name the letters of the alphabet, recite the *abc*'s. When you are writing about a book, name it by including the title in your piece. When you are asked to name the steps in a process, describe each step.

Math: When you are asked to name all the ways to make 50, you might say $25 + 25$, 5×10, $45 + 5$, and so on. When you are asked to name the properties used to simplify an expression, you might say *the associative property* and *the distributive property*.

recall

If you **recall** something, you remember it.

ELA: Before writing about an experience, you have to recall what happened. When you are trying to solve a problem, recall a solution that worked in the past.

Math: When you have memorized certain addition, subtraction, multiplication, or division facts, you can recall the answers to them quickly.

recognize

If you **recognize** something, you know what it is because you have seen it before.

ELA: When you have read an epic poem like the *Odyssey* or the *Aeneid*, you may recognize the structure of other epic poems, such as Dante's *Inferno* or *Paradise Lost*. Learn to read irregularly spelled words by recognizing what they look like. When you edit a composition, it is important to recognize errors and correct them.

Math: Try to recognize a shape in the real world or recognize an equivalent form of a fraction. Recognize concepts you already know that are attributes of shapes, such as area, perimeter, or angle.

Elaborate (ELAB)

broaden

If you **broaden** something, you make it bigger.

ELA: When you broaden an Internet search, you look at more resources. If you broaden the topic of a piece of writing, you write about more than you originally planned.

Math: When you broaden a research project, you look at more data or ask more questions. If the sample size you chose was too small to get reliable results from the data, broaden your research project to collect more data.

derive

If you **derive** something, you take information from a specific source and use it logically to create something new.

ELA: Derive a narrative from a poem that you like by thinking about what events led up to the situation described in the poem.

Math: Derive the equation of a line by using the coordinates of a point on the line and the slope of the line. Derive the quadratic formula from a quadratic equation by completing the square.

elaborate

If you **elaborate** on something, you tell more about it.

ELA: In a discussion or after an oral presentation, you might ask someone to elaborate on something he or she said. When an event in a narrative is not very clear, someone editing your work might ask you to elaborate on it by adding more detail.

Math: When you present only your solution to a math problem, you might be asked to elaborate on it by showing how you got that answer.

enhance   If you **enhance** something, you make it better.

ELA: Visual aids like charts, tables, graphs, or diagrams enhance written pieces. Digital media such as slides, audio or video clips, or interactive elements enhance oral presentations. To enhance the development of an idea, add more details that relate to it or more evidence to support it.

Math: Enhance a model by adding more detail to it. Enhance your solution to a problem by making it more exact.

expand   If you **expand** something, you make it larger.

ELA: Expand a sentence by adding descriptive words (like adjectives and adverbs) to it. Expand your vocabulary by studying specific words or by reading in your spare time.

Math: Expand numbers and expressions by writing them using more terms. To expand a number, you separate the ones, tens, hundreds, and so on. 783 expanded is $700 + 80 + 3$. To expand an expression, you distribute the terms. $2(x + y)$ expanded is $2x + 2y$.

Evaluate (EVAL)

assess   If you **assess** something, you estimate its value or quantity.

ELA: When you assess the credibility of a source, you decide how trustworthy the source is. When you assess the accuracy of a source, you decide how truthful the source is. To assess how an author's point of view affects a text, count how many passages contain evidence of the author's particular viewpoint and decide if those passages affect the text a lot or a little.

Math: When you assess the reasonableness of your answer to a division problem, you decide if it is reasonable or unreasonable, perhaps by estimating an answer and seeing how closely the estimate matches your actual answer. When you collect data, assess how closely it matches what you predicted by graphing the data and predictions and looking at how closely the graphs match.

check   If you **check** something, you make sure that it is accurate.

ELA: During a discussion, it is a good idea to check your understanding of the information being presented by asking questions. Check the spelling or meaning of a word by looking it up in a dictionary.

Math: To check your answer to a problem, solve it a different way and see if the answers match.

critique   If you **critique** something, you look at it carefully to find things that could be improved.

ELA: You might critique someone's argument by saying that he or she is using inaccurate evidence. When you critique someone's presentation or draft, tell him or her specific things he or she can do to make it better.

Math: You might critique someone's strategy for solving a mathematical problem by saying how to make it faster or more accurate. When you critique someone's reasoning, point out evidence or reasons he or she gave that don't make sense.

evaluate   If you **evaluate** something, you decide if it is good or bad or right or wrong.

ELA: You can evaluate information, ideas, texts, evidence, points of view, and arguments. Evaluate yourself, your progress, or your own work, and try something different if you don't like your results.

Math: To evaluate a mathematical expression, replace the variables with numbers and perform the operations and see if the expression is true. Sometimes there are guidelines to help you evaluate something. When you evaluate expressions, you have to pay attention to the order of operations. When you evaluate your friend's work, your teacher might ask you to say one good thing he or she did and suggest one change he or she could make.

judge

If you **judge** something, you form an opinion about it.

ELA: When giving an objective summary, tell what a text or speaker said without judging whether it was right or wrong, accurate or inaccurate. When you are writing an argumentative piece, judge the facts and evidence you collect to decide which are most credible and what conclusions to form.

Math: Look at data to judge whether or not they have a linear association.

Execute (EXEC)

advance

If you **advance** something, you move it forward.

ELA: When you advance the plot in a narrative piece, you move it forward, perhaps by causing something to happen to one of the characters. When you advance a point of view or purpose, you try to convince more people to agree with it.

Math: Advance a group's thinking by explaining a new way to solve a problem they are working on.

calculate

If you **calculate** something, you think very carefully about all of its details and create a plan to make it happen. If you **calculate** something in math, you figure out a solution using numbers and mathematical operations.

ELA: In a narrative, one of the characters might calculate how to kidnap the princess. When you want to convince your audience of something during an oral presentation, calculate which evidence and arguments are most likely to persuade them.

Math: You can calculate in your head, on paper, or using a calculator or computer. When you calculate whether or not you have enough money to buy everything you want, you add up all the prices to find the total cost of all the items. When you calculate how much time you will need to complete a set of tasks, you add up how long each task will take.

compute

When you **compute** something, you figure out an answer or solution using math.

ELA: When you have a word limit on a piece of writing, use a word-processing program to compute how many words are in your piece.

Math: When you solve a math problem using addition, subtraction, multiplication, or division, you are computing an answer to it. You can compute in your head, using a calculator, or using a computer.

conduct

If you **conduct** something, you plan and do it.

ELA: When you conduct a research project, you create a research question, collect data, and write a final report.

Math: To practice graphing, conduct surveys of your classmates and represent the data in different ways.

employ

If you **employ** something, you use it to accomplish a task.

ELA: When you want to publish a blog, you have to employ technology. Tasks like word processing, data analysis, and Internet publishing are easier if you employ certain software programs.

Math: Employ the distributive property to solve an equation or the commutative property to simplify an expression.

execute

If you **execute** something, you do it.

ELA: When you execute a piece of writing, you write it. When you execute a plan, you put it into action.

Math: When you execute a strategy, you use it to solve a problem. When you execute a process, you use it.

navigate

If you **navigate** something, you find your way through it.

ELA: Navigate through the Internet by clicking on hyperlinks, searching, or typing in web addresses. Navigate a computer program by using the menus, icons, and keyboard commands. Navigate a database by using keyword searches and opening folders.

Math: Navigate through a particularly difficult math problem by writing out your thinking for each step of your solution.

Explain (EXP)

answer   If you **answer** someone or something, you respond with information you think is correct or true.

ELA: When you answer questions about a text, go back and look at the text to explain your answer. Write an informative or argumentative piece to answer a specific question. After giving an oral presentation, answer questions from listeners to clarify what you said. Research projects are also designed to answer questions.

Math: When someone asks you how many there are of something, count the items before answering. To answer a question, use words, numbers, or pictures. To answer a statistical question, you might need to collect data.

articulate   If you **articulate** something, you express it clearly.

ELA: When you articulate your ideas, you explain them in detail.

Math: When you articulate the strategy you used to solve a math problem, you explain it in detail.

clarify   If you **clarify** something, you explain it in a way that makes it easier to understand.

ELA: When someone doesn't understand what you wrote, revise your piece to clarify your main points. When you don't understand a word, ask a question or use context clues to try to clarify its meaning. Informative pieces often contain diagrams or drawings to clarify information.

Math: You could clarify the strategy you used to solve a problem by writing it out or drawing a picture. You could clarify data on a graph by adding labels to each axis.

communicate   When you **communicate**, you share information with others, usually by speaking or writing.

ELA: When you want to communicate with a small group of people, tell them or write them a note, an email, or a letter. When you want to communicate with a larger group, give a speech or presentation, create an advertisement, send a mass email, or write a book or article about your topic.

Math: When you want to share your solution to a problem, communicate it by telling, writing, or drawing a picture. When you communicate precisely, you are careful to make sure that others understand exactly what you are trying to convey.

convey   If you **convey** something, you communicate it.

ELA: Use descriptive words and phrases to convey an image. The goal of informative/explanatory writing is to convey information to the reader. Often, in narrative writing, authors use details to convey a theme or central idea. A speaker conveys emotion through his tone of voice or through gestures.

Math: Use a drawing to convey your solution to a math problem or your idea for a model.

describe   If you **describe** something, you explain what it is like.

ELA: Describe the structure of a work of fiction by using words such as *introduction*, *rising action*, *climax*, *falling action*, and *conclusion*. Describe the structure of a nonfiction work by using terms such as *thesis*, *support*, *evidence*, and *conclusion*. Describe connections and relationships by explaining how things are related. In a narrative piece, it is important to describe the characters, main events, and setting. Describe an oral presentation by explaining what the speaker's purpose was, what he or she said, and what visual aids he or she used.

Math: You can use the equation $10 - 5 = 5$ to describe a situation in which you had 10 marbles, lost 5 of them, and had 5 left. Functions can describe how one quantity depends on another quantity. When you want to describe a shape, tell about its sides, corners, angles, orientation, faces, color, or dimensions. Describe an object by measuring it and reporting its length, width, height, weight, volume, area, perimeter, or surface area. Fractions can describe parts of a whole.

explain   If you **explain** something, you give information about it or reasons for it that make it easier to understand.

ELA: Use details and examples to explain what a text is about. The purpose of informative/explanatory texts is to explain information or concepts. In a discussion, you should explain your ideas so that others can understand them.

Math: An important part of solving mathematics problems is explaining how you got your answer. When you say that two items or concepts are connected, you should also explain how they are connected. When you notice a pattern, figure out how to explain why it occurs.

express   When you **express** something, you show or tell about it.

ELA: When you express your opinion about something, you tell what you think. When you express information or ideas clearly, you present them in an organized and logical way. Using descriptive words and details can help you express your feelings clearly.

Math: When you express your reasoning in a logical way, you tell about your thinking in an ordered way. When you express an answer precisely, you make sure to write it as clearly and accurately as possible.

inform   If you **inform** someone of something, you tell him or her facts or information about it.

ELA: The purpose of informative/explanatory texts is to inform about a topic. It is important to use precise language and appropriate vocabulary when you inform someone about something.

Math: Inform your peers about the data you collected by displaying the data in a graph or histogram.

narrate   If you **narrate** something, you describe a sequence of events.

ELA: When you narrate a story, you tell what happened in the story. When you narrate a play, you tell what is happening while others act it out. When you narrate a musical piece, you tell a story that goes along with the music.

Math: To show your solution to a problem in front of your class, narrate by explaining what you were thinking at each step of the problem while you write using numbers.

present   If you **present** something, you show or give it to someone.

ELA.   Present information, findings, and evidence in a written piece, in an oral presentation, in a video or audio clip, or on a website. Use a diagram or graphic organizer to present relationships.

Math: Present data using charts, tables, graphs, or pictures.

recount   If you **recount** a story or event, you describe what happened.

FI A: After reading a story, recount it to a friend. When you recount a real or imagined event in writing, it is usually called a narrative.

Math: Recount your experiences collecting data to explain why there are outliers or why the data look a certain way.

report   If you **report** something, you tell about it.

ELA: Report about research you conducted by writing an informative piece. Report on a book you read by summarizing the main events and characters.

Math: When you use a survey to do research, it is important to report how many people completed the survey, what the response choices were, and other details. When you report the answer to a measurement problem, it is important to report what type of units were used. When you report your conclusions, you tell people what you decided based on the information you collected.

respond   If you **respond** to something, you react to it.

ELA: When members of your audience look confused, respond by speaking more slowly or restating your point. When you respond to something you read, you tell what you thought about it. When someone asks you a question, respond by answering him or her. When you respond to someone's argument, explain why you agree or disagree with him or her. When writing a narrative, you have to decide how the characters will respond to different situations and challenges.

Math: When you respond to someone's argument, explain why you agree or disagree with him or her.

retell

If you **retell** something, you tell it again.

ELA: When you retell a story that you read or heard, you tell it to someone else. When you retell an experience, you usually tell the events that happened and give the important details of each event. When you retell an informative or argumentative text, tell the main points and supporting details.

Math: To make sure you understand, your teacher might ask you to retell how to perform long division.

state

If you **state** something, you say it clearly and definitely.

ELA: When you state your opinion, you say what you think about an idea, issue, or text.

Math: When you use a symbol, you should state what it means.

summarize

If you **summarize** something, you tell the most important information from it.

ELA: To summarize a narrative text, tell the main characters, setting, main events, and important details. To summarize an informative or argumentative text, tell the main ideas or claims and supporting details. Summarize a discussion by listing what the group agreed about and what they disagreed about.

Math: Summarize a data set by describing its median, mean, interquartile range, standard deviation, and outliers. Summarize the shape of a data distribution using words such as *symmetric*, *skewed*, *flat*, or *bell shaped*. Summarize data for two categories using a two-way frequency table.

synthesize

If you **synthesize** information, you combine it in a logical way.

ELA: When you read information in several different sources, synthesize it by generating a conclusion based on what you read. To synthesize the comments of a group during a discussion, say what points the group agrees and disagrees on. If you don't know how to perform a task, look at several explanations on the Internet and synthesize them into one method for accomplishing the task.

Math: Collect data using several different techniques, such as interviews, surveys, and observations, and then synthesize the data to form conclusions.

Hypothesize (HYP)

anticipate

If you **anticipate** something, you predict that something will happen and prepare for it.

ELA: When you are writing an argumentative piece, anticipate questions that readers will have and answer them. When you are preparing for a debate, anticipate the opposing arguments to your viewpoint and prepare to rebut them.

Math: When you are collecting data on how old students in your middle school are, anticipate students' answers by creating a data collection sheet that has places to mark *10 years*, *11 years*, *12 years*, *13 years*, and *14 years*.

approximate

If you **approximate** something, you make a guess about its size or value.

ELA: Approximate the length of a book by looking at the size of the print and number of chapters. Approximate the length of an oral presentation by counting the number of slides you plan to use and multiplying that number by how much time you plan to spend on each slide.

Math: When you round the prices of several items up to the next dollar and add them together to figure out how much your purchase will cost, you are approximating your total cost. When you guess about how likely it is that something will happen, you are approximating the probability of that event. When you round a repeating decimal to the nearest hundredth, you are approximating its quantity or size.

conjecture

If you **conjecture**, you say something that you think is true but aren't completely sure about.

ELA: When you make a claim but don't have any evidence to support it, you are conjecturing.

Math: When you guess about the solution to a problem before solving it, you are conjecturing.

consider

If you **consider** something, you think carefully about it.

ELA: When you consider a word's meaning, think carefully about it and look it up in a dictionary. When you consider the meaning of a passage or line of text, reread it several times or have a conversation with someone else about it.

Math: When you are trying to solve a problem and you think about other problems that are like the one you're working on, you are considering those other problems. When you think about tools (like graphs, rulers, or a calculator) that might help you solve a problem, you are considering those tools.

estimate

If you **estimate** something, you guess about its amount or size without trying to be exact.

ELA: Estimate how long it will take you to read a book by looking at how many pages it has. Estimate the length of a presentation by timing yourself while you make your first point and multiplying that time by how many points you have.

Math: People often use the word *about* when estimating, as in "I think that she is about five feet tall." Estimate measurements such as length, height, weight, or volume. One way to estimate is to round numbers to the nearest multiple of ten before solving a problem. When you estimate how much something is going to cost, it is important to overestimate so that you know you will have enough money. Estimate the solution to a problem to get an idea of how large or small the exact answer should be. Random sampling is a way of estimating the frequency or value of something in a larger population or sample.

experiment

When you **experiment**, you do a scientific test to find out something specific.

ELA: When you make a claim and need evidence for it, experiment to collect evidence.

Math: Experiment with algebraic expressions or transformations of geometric shapes. Computer software programs are often useful for experimenting with algebraic expressions or transformations of geometric shapes.

explore

If you **explore** something, you try to find out more about what it is like.

ELA: In discussions, keeping an open mind is a good way to explore different ideas. Some people learn to use new software programs or new digital tools by exploring them.

Math: Explore fractions by using pattern blocks to create wholes and parts. Explore algebraic expressions or geometric sequences using a computer.

hypothesize

If you **hypothesize** about something, you say what you think will happen or be proven true.

ELA: After you hypothesize that global warming is just a myth, do research to support or discredit that hypothesis.

Math: Before doing research, it is good to hypothesize about what you think you will find based on the information you have at that time.

pose

If you **pose** something, you present it.

ELA: When you pose a question, you ask it.

Math: When you pose a problem, you describe it.

predict

If you **predict** something, you say that you think it will happen.

ELA: Predict the meaning of a word based on what you know about prefixes, suffixes, and root words. While reading a story or watching a play, predict what you think will happen by explaining how you think the story is going to end.

Math: Use data to predict events. You can also predict the frequency of an event. Use your knowledge of reflections, rotations, and translations to predict the effects of a rigid motion on a figure.

test

If you **test** something, you try it out to see how well it works.

ELA: When you write an ending for a story, test its quality by writing a different ending and asking your friends to read both and say which one they like best.

Math: You might think that you can use a calculator to simplify fractions until you test that strategy and find out it converts them to decimals. If you think that most of the students in your school would like school to start later, test that idea by asking a random sample of students what they prefer.

Infer (INF)

conclude

If you **conclude** something, you decide whether it is true or correct after considering related information. **Conclude** also means to end something.

ELA: When you conclude an argument, you say what you think is true based on all the information you've just presented. When you conclude a narrative, you explain what happened as a result of the story you just told. When you conclude that a source is not trustworthy, it means that you found information that showed the source was biased or inaccurate.

Math: When you notice that a decimal number is repeating the same digits over and over again, you could conclude that it is a repeating decimal. When you use three different strategies for a problem and get the same answer each time, you could conclude that the answer is correct.

deduce

If you **deduce** something, you figure out that it is true because you know other things are true.

ELA: When you are investigating a research question, deduce the answer from the data you collect. When you are presenting an argument, your audience should be able to deduce your conclusions from the evidence you present.

Math: When you figure out that 5×25 is 125 because you already know that $4 \times 25 = 100$ and $100 + 25 = 125$, you are deducing the answer to 5×25.

generalize

If you **generalize**, you take what you know about one situation or thing and apply it to other situations or things.

ELA: When you know how to spell *light*, you can generalize that knowledge to spell *fight*, *might*, *right*, *sight*, *slight*, *tonight*, and *delight*.

Math: When you know that in place value, the number in the tens place is ten times the number in the ones place, you can generalize that the number in the hundreds place is ten times the number in the tens place, the number in the thousands place is ten times the number in the hundreds place, and so on.

infer

If you **infer** something, you decide that it is true after gathering and considering information about it.

ELA: When a character in a story runs away from a battle, you might infer that he or she is not very brave. When you infer something from a text, you should also provide quotes or other information from the text to support what you are saying. When you encounter an unknown word while reading, infer its meaning from the words around it.

Math: You can infer things about populations by collecting data from a random sample of the population.

reason

If you **reason**, you think about something in an orderly, logical way.

ELA: When you defend an argument or opinion, reason about your facts and evidence to come to a logical conclusion. When you reason about someone else's argument, you think about whether his or her evidence is closely related to and supports his or her conclusions.

Math: Reason about a problem by creating a picture or diagram of the problem, thinking about how to solve each part of the problem, solving each part of the problem, and then checking to make sure each part is correct and makes sense with the other parts. When you reason about data, you think about how and where the data were collected, look at the data with those factors in mind, and think about interpretations of the data that make sense in light of those factors.

Measure (MEAS)

gauge

If you **gauge** something, you measure it.

ELA: When you gauge an audience's reaction to your message, you try to figure out what they are feeling.

Math: When you gauge the variation between different estimates, you figure out how far apart they are. When you gauge the accuracy of a prediction, you measure how close it is to what actually happened.

measure	If you **measure** something, you describe its size using units.
	ELA: To measure the length of a discussion, you could time it in minutes and seconds or say that it took an entire class period.
	Math: To measure length or distance, you could use inches, feet, yards, miles, centimeters, meters, or kilometers. To measure weight, you could use ounces, pounds, grams, or kilograms. To measure volume, you could use cups, pints, quarts, gallons, or liters.
quantify	If you **quantify** something, you say how much of it there is using numbers.
	ELA: In argumentative pieces, using evidence that quantifies the effect of something is better than just saying "often" or "a lot."
	Math: When you say that the probability of getting heads when tossing a coin is 1 : 2, you have quantified the likelihood of that event.

Problem Solve (PS)

figure out	If you **figure out** how to do or solve something, you find a way to do it.
	ELA: To figure out how to create a web page, try different things until you find one that works. Figure out which gestures to use during an oral presentation by trying different gestures out for your friend and asking him which ones are best.
	Math: When you figure out the solution to a mathematical problem, you succeed in solving it. To figure out the best way to build a model, you might draw several pictures of how you want it to look.
overcome	If you **overcome** something, you stop it from being an obstacle to your goal.
	ELA: Overcome a lack of information by doing research.
	Math: Overcome a lack of data by collecting more. Overcome a wrong answer by reworking the problem. Overcome time restraints by working quickly.
problem solve	If you **problem solve**, you figure out how to overcome obstacles and find a solution.
	ELA: In a collaborative discussion, problem solve a disagreement by encouraging the people who disagree to explain why and to figure out what they do agree about. When you don't like the organization of your writing, problem solve by moving things around to see if there is a structure you like better.
	Math: Problem solve a mathematical problem by performing a calculation or rearranging an expression. Problem solve a geometric problem by applying theorems, postulates, or criteria.
resolve	If you **resolve** a problem, contradiction, or issue, you find a solution for it.
	ELA: When you resolve something in a narrative, you show how it ended. When a contradiction arises in a discussion, try to resolve it by asking questions.
	Math: When you get stuck while solving a math problem, resolve the situation by starting over again or asking for help.
solve	If you **solve** something, you find an answer or a solution for it.
	ELA: To solve a problem, you need to gather information about it. To solve a disagreement, you need to help each person discuss and resolve their differences.
	Math: Solve mathematical problems by using addition, subtraction, multiplication, and division. Solve an equation by figuring out what numbers the variables represent.
surmount	If you **surmount** something, you overcome it.
	ELA: When you surmount the difficult vocabulary in a text, you figure out what the text is saying even though the words are difficult to understand. When you surmount an obstacle while solving a problem, you stop the obstacle from getting in your way.
	Math: To surmount difficulty with division, practice doing it, ask for help, or learn more about different division strategies.

Prove/Argue (P/A)

argue   If you **argue** for or against something, you try to convince someone who disagrees with you that something is right or wrong using reasons and evidence.

ELA: When you write a piece or give a speech arguing that global warming is a serious concern, present evidence and reasons that support what you are saying. When you argue for a specific perspective, you try to convince people with other perspectives to agree with you, usually by explaining why you think your perspective is best.

Math: When you and a friend disagree about the solution to a math problem, show your friend how you solved the problem to argue for your answer. If your friend stated that her solution was correct, she might show you a graph of her solution to argue for her answer.

assert   If you **assert** something, you say it confidently.

ELA: When you are participating in a debate, begin by asserting the position you intend to defend. When speaking, people usually use confident body language (like eye contact and slightly elevated volume) when they assert things.

Math: The difference between an expression and an equation is that the equation asserts that something is true (using =, >, or <) but an expression does not.

challenge   If you **challenge** something, you question it or dispute it.

ELA: When you challenge an idea or a conclusion during a discussion, you might ask the speaker to provide evidence to show why he thinks it is true.

Math: When you think someone's solution to a problem is wrong, you might challenge it by showing how you got a different answer.

claim   If you **claim** something, you say it is true.

ELA: In a discussion, you might claim that your idea is better than someone else's idea. In a debate, each side claims that their position is the best view of the issue and defends that position. An informative text might claim to have the most recent and accurate information about a topic.

Math: When you claim that your solution to an equation is correct, you may need to show how you solved it, especially if others have different solutions.

confirm   If you **confirm** something, you make sure that it is true.

ELA: To confirm that you understand someone or that someone understands you, each of you should ask questions. To confirm that a fact is true, look it up using several different sources and see if they all say the same thing. Confirm your understanding of a text by talking to someone else who has read it or by reading what others have written about it.

Math: To confirm that your solution to a math problem is correct, solve it several different ways.

defend   If you **defend** something, you say why you think it is true.

ELA: When you defend a claim, you present facts and evidence that show why you think that claim is true.

Math: Defend your answer to a problem by explaining the strategy you used to come up with it or by showing that a different strategy produces the same answer.

disagree   If you **disagree**, you have a different opinion than someone or something.

ELA: Read two texts on the same topic and notice whether the authors disagree on various points.

Math: When you disagree with someone about how to prove a geometric theorem, show what you did and explain your reasoning.

justify   If you **justify** something, you explain why it is reasonable or appropriate.

ELA: When writing an argument or giving a presentation, present information to justify your opinions and conclusions. When someone shows you new evidence related to your opinion about something, you might need to justify your opinion in light of the new evidence.

Math: Use an array to justify using multiplication to find area. Your teacher might ask you to justify your solution to a problem by explaining your thinking and describing why your method for solving the problem was best.

persuade   If you **persuade** someone to do something, you convince him or her to do it.

ELA: The purpose of an argumentative piece or presentation is to persuade listeners to agree with the writer's or speaker's point of view.

Math: If you and a friend got different answers to a math problem, try to persuade your friend that your answer was correct by explaining how you got it.

promote   If you **promote** something, you help it succeed.

ELA: When you promote civil behavior during discussions, you are polite and you help others be polite. To promote a specific perspective, provide reasons and evidence for it.

Math: To promote using surveys to collect data, tell about other successful projects that used surveys to collect data.

prove   If you **prove** something, you give evidence to show that it is true.

ELA: In an argumentative piece, you present evidence that proves your claims are true. When you cite a source, give details about the author you cite to prove that he or she is trustworthy.

Math: Prove a linear function grows in equal intervals by graphing it. Use the criteria for triangle similarity to prove theorems about triangles, quadrilaterals, and other geometric shapes. In geometry, you might be asked to prove that two angles are congruent, that the sum of the angles in a triangle is 180 degrees, or that the opposite sides of a parallelogram are congruent.

qualify   If you **qualify** something, you tell about an exception to it or add some information to it to make it less general.

ELA: Qualify a claim by telling about a situation in which it wouldn't be true. Qualify an argument by saying that it only makes sense in certain situations.

Math: When you say that a number is irrational, you might qualify your answer by saying that it did not repeat within the first ten decimal places.

specify   If you **specify** something, you describe or explain it clearly and in detail.

ELA: In an argument, it is important to specify the claims you are making and the evidence you are using to support them.

Math: In an equation, put parentheses around an expression to specify that it should be evaluated first. If you specify a sequence of transformations, you explain what transformations to use and what order to use them in.

support   If you **support** something, you help it succeed.

ELA: When you support an argument, you help others agree with it by providing reasons and evidence. In informative pieces, the details should support the main idea.

Math: When doing research, if the data you collect support your hypothesis, then your hypothesis is probably true.

verify   If you **verify** something, you make sure that it is true.

ELA: When a speaker or a text makes a claim, verify it by examining its evidence and sources.

Math: Verify that something is true by experimenting or investigating it. Verify an answer or measurement by reworking the problem or remeasuring. Verify that a shape is symmetrical by putting a mirror along the line of symmetry and looking to see if the reflection matches the original shape.

Pull Apart (PULL)

analyze

If you **analyze** something, you look closely at each of its parts and see if they fit together in a way that makes sense.

ELA: When you analyze the development of a theme in a text, you find places where the author refers to the theme and examine how those parts work together to communicate the theme. To analyze a presentation, examine the words, visual aids, and information presented to see if they make sense and how they affect the overall presentation. To analyze the role of figures of speech in a text, find specific figures of speech and examine what they mean and how they affect the overall tone and feeling of the text.

Math: When you analyze a problem or a situation, you look at each part of the problem or situation and decide what to do about each individual part. To analyze a shape, look carefully at its sides, angles, size, dimensions, color, and other characteristics. To analyze a graph, look closely at each data point and figure out what information is being given by each element of the graph. To analyze a relationship, look closely at each way that two or more things are related.

decompose

To **decompose** something means to take it apart.

ELA: Decompose someone's argument by finding each claim that was made and the evidence that supports or contradicts it.

Math: To decompose the number 10 into pairs of numbers, say 1 + 9, 2 + 8, 3 + 7, 4 + 6, or 5 + 5. To decompose the number 526 into hundreds, tens, and ones, break it into 5 hundreds, 2 tens, and 6 ones. Fractions can be decomposed into equal parts ($\frac{2}{5} = \frac{1}{5} + \frac{1}{5}$), and shapes can be decomposed into equal or unequal portions.

decontextualize

If you **decontextualize** something, you think about it apart from its normal surroundings.

ELA: When you read a book without first learning about its author or the situation in which it was written, your experience reading the book is decontextualized from its original writing.

Math: When you decontextualize a problem, you focus only on the numbers and not what they represent.

diagnose

If you **diagnose** something, you figure out what is wrong with it.

ELA: Your friend or peer might read your writing or listen to your oral presentation to diagnose its weaknesses.

Math: If your teacher told you that your answer to a mathematical problem was wrong, you might diagnose the problem by figuring out that you added numbers when you should have multiplied them.

examine

If you **examine** something, you look at it closely.

ELA: When you want to examine a topic but don't have an opinion about it, write an informative/explanatory piece about it.

Math: When someone gives an answer to a problem, you normally have to examine the process he or she used to solve it to decide if his or her answer is correct. After you collect data, you have to examine them to see if there are patterns or deviations.

grapple

If you **grapple** with something, you struggle to figure it out.

ELA: When you don't understand a text when you first read it, you may have to grapple with it by rereading it, comparing it to other texts, and finding out what others have said about it.

Math: When a math problem is particularly hard, grapple with it by trying again, trying different strategies to solve it, or asking for help.

investigate   If you **investigate** something, you study or examine it closely.

ELA: To investigate the circumstances surrounding the stock market crash of 1929, read several accounts of it and identify similarities and differences between them. To investigate the relationship between vegetation and insects, collect data in several locations and compare them.

Math: To investigate the probability of a certain outcome or event, count how many times it happens during a number of trials. Investigate data by looking for patterns, outliers, or positive or negative associations.

partition   If you **partition** something, you divide it into parts.

ELA: Partition a book into segments based on major events, casts of characters, or themes. Partition an oral presentation or a piece of writing into introductory, explanatory, and concluding sections.

Math: To partition a shape, use a fraction to describe each part. When you partition a rectangle into equal rows and columns, count the resulting squares to find its area. When you use division, you are partitioning a quantity into an equal number of parts. The denominator of a fraction describes how many parts the whole has been partitioned into.

probe   If you **probe** something, you explore or examine it closely.

ELA: You could ask questions to probe someone's reasoning and evidence during a discussion.

Math: When you probe the meaning of the symbols in a math problem, you try to figure out what they represent in the real world.

Redo (REDO)

redo   If you **redo** something, you do it over again.

ELA: When you redo a piece of writing, you write it over again. When you redo an oral presentation, you give it again.

Math: When you initially get an unreasonable answer to a math problem, redo it using a different strategy.

repeat   If you **repeat** something, you do it again.

ELA: Repeat your main point throughout an oral presentation to remind the audience of it. Repeat the same theme in each stanza of a poem to emphasize its importance. Authors sometimes repeat words or sequences of events to emphasize themes or important ideas.

Math: One strategy for multiplication is to repeat the addition process. If you find yourself repeating the same calculation for a decimal number, it may be a repeating decimal. Repeat measurements before cutting a piece of wood or fabric to make sure that you measured correctly.

reread   If you **reread** something, you read it again.

ELA: When you read a sentence or paragraph but don't understand what it says, go back and reread it.

Math: When you don't understand the directions for a problem, reread them to try to understand.

revisit   If you **revisit** a topic, you think about or talk about it again.

ELA: If you didn't finish discussing something in a previous conversation with someone, revisit it when you talk to him or her again. When you revisit a piece of writing, you reread it and think about ways to improve it.

Math: If you learned about functions once but didn't understand them very well, revisit them to learn more.

Reference (REF)

acknowledge   If you **acknowledge** something, you show that you agree that it exists.

ELA: Acknowledge different characters' points of view in a story by using different voices for them when reading aloud. When making an argument, acknowledge conflicting evidence or opposing viewpoints.

Math: In geometry, it is acknowledged that parallel lines do not intersect.

cite   If you **cite** something, you quote, paraphrase, or refer to it.

ELA: If you said that the theme of a text was "greed as downfall," cite a passage in the text where a greedy person was ruined as evidence. When you quote another author in your writing, cite that source by giving the page number of the quote and including the source in your reference list. When you make a claim, cite examples that prove that claim.

Math: When you talk or write about research by someone else that relates to your research, cite that person by telling who he or she is and where he or she said or wrote the ideas that you're referring to.

consult   If you **consult** something or someone, you ask for advice or information.

ELA: When you don't know how to spell, pronounce, or define a word, consult a dictionary or glossary. When you need to know synonyms for a word, consult a thesaurus. When you need advice about your writing, consult a friend.

Math: When you're not sure how to use a strategy, consult your peers or teacher to find out how. You can also consult the Internet or print sources for information.

plagiarize   If you **plagiarize** something, you copy it without giving credit to the original author.

ELA: When you copy someone's words and don't use quotation marks or a citation to give credit to the author, you are plagiarizing his or her words. If you copy someone's ideas or the organization of someone's work, and don't give him or her any credit, you could still be plagiarizing. Anytime you claim that words or ideas are your own when they aren't, you are plagiarizing.

Math: When you copy a friend's answers to math problems, you are plagiarizing her work.

refer   If you **refer** to something, you direct attention to it by specifically mentioning it.

ELA: When you refer to details and examples in a text while summarizing it, you mention them to support what you are saying. Refer to the structural elements of poems by using terms like *verse*, *rhythm*, and *meter*.

Math: Numbers (1, 2, 3, and so on) each refer to specific quantities. A fraction refers to a part of a whole. In place value, each place refers to ten times the value of the place to its right.

reference   If you **reference** something, you mention it in a formal way.

ELA: In a piece of writing, it is important to reference each source you took ideas or quotes from. In an oral presentation, reference an expert's opinion or scientific evidence to support your claims.

Math: Reference postulates or theorems when completing a proof in geometry.

trace   If you **trace** something, you follow it closely.

ELA: When you trace the reasoning in an argument, you look carefully at each piece of evidence one by one. When you trace the claims in a text, you find each point the author makes over the course of a text.

Math: When you trace the reasoning in an argument, you look carefully at each piece of evidence one by one. When you trace a shape or figure, you put a piece of paper over it and draw over each line.

Seek Information (SI)

acquire   If you **acquire** something, you obtain it or gain it.

ELA: When you acquire a large vocabulary, you know and use lots of words. To acquire information, search online. Many people try to acquire good habits.

Math: When you acquire data, you collect them from people or situations. When you acquire skill, you learn how to do something well.

ask   If you **ask** a question, you are trying to find an answer or get some information.

ELA: You can ask questions of others or yourself. When you don't understand a text, ask questions about specific parts or details that are confusing. When you don't know a word, ask what it means. When you are listening to someone else speak and you don't understand something he or she says, ask him or her to clarify. Ask questions if you want to learn more about or deepen your understanding of a topic.

Math: You can ask questions of others or yourself. When you are solving a math problem, ask yourself if your answer makes sense. When you are listening to someone else's explanation of something, ask a question about something that you don't understand. When you collect data about something, ask questions about that data.

capture   If you **capture** something, you describe it vividly and accurately.

ELA: To capture the action in a scene, use descriptive details. To capture a character's thoughts and feelings, use sensory language.

Math: Use video or computer imaging to capture what happens to a model under certain strains and stresses.

compile   If you **compile** something, you collect information and put it together.

ELA: Before finishing a report, compile a list of all the sources you used. After doing research about a topic, compile all your notes to start writing a report.

Math: Compile a list of the names of different-sided polygons.

detect   If you **detect** something, you notice or find it.

ELA: In a novel, you might detect certain details that indicate a character is not trustworthy.

Math: Detect errors in mathematical solutions by estimating or using a different strategy to check your initial answer.

elicit   If you **elicit** a response or feeling from someone, you draw it out of him or her.

ELA: Asking a question during a discussion can elicit comments from group members. Dramas and speeches are often designed to elicit an emotional response from the audience. Written words can also elicit responses from readers.

Math: You might elicit your friend's strategy for solving a math problem by asking her questions about how she solved it.

encounter   If you **encounter** something, you experience it.

ELA: When you encounter a word you don't know, look it up in a dictionary or glossary or try to figure out its meaning from context.

Math: Doing math problems with fractions or functions may be difficult when you encounter them for the first time.

evoke

If something **evokes** something else, it brings it to mind.

ELA: When a story is set in Ireland, use the phrase "bonnie lass" to evoke a sense of that particular place. When a story is set in the future, include robots, spaceships, or other technological elements to evoke a sense of that particular time. When you want to evoke an informal tone, use slang. When you want to evoke a formal tone, use only third-person pronouns.

Math: The relationship between multiplication and division or between squares and square roots might evoke the relationship between addition and subtraction.

find out

If you **find out** about something, you learn about it.

ELA: Find out about a topic by reading about it; listening to a live, audio, or video presentation about it; investigating it on the Internet; or by doing an experiment.

Math: When you find out that circles have 360 degrees, you'll better understand why right angles are 90 degrees. When you want to find out more about patterns that occur in nature, read an article about the Fibonacci sequence.

gather

If you **gather** things, you collect them together in a group.

ELA: To gather information for a research project, read journal articles, books, or information on the Internet. You can gather information by taking notes, collecting quotes from different sources, making stacks or electronic files of information, or by audio recording interviews or oral notes.

Math: Gather useful mathematical formulas together on one page of your notes.

listen

If you **listen** to someone, you hear and try to understand what he or she is saying.

ELA: When you listen to a speaker, you might agree or disagree with what he or she is saying, but you don't interrupt; you keep listening. During a discussion, show that you are listening by nodding your head or paraphrasing what was just said. Read a book yourself or listen to someone else read it.

Math: When you listen to someone, you hear and think about what the person is saying. After he or she is done speaking, use the information you heard while listening to ask questions if there is anything you don't understand.

note

If you **note** something, you notice it or write it down.

ELA: When you note examples of the word *colorful*, you look for colorful things. To note that the spelling test will be on Monday, write it in your planner.

Math: You could note a number of things about a number: whether it is positive or negative, composite or prime, and rational or irrational.

notice

If you **notice** something, you become aware of it.

ELA: While reading a book, you might notice that the author includes many details that have to do with time. While listening to a speaker, you might notice that he breaks eye contact with the audience when he is unsure of what he is saying. In a collaborative discussion, you might notice that everyone participates more if you sit in a circle.

Math: If you notice a pattern of repeating numbers after a decimal, you know that it is a rational number.

observe

If you **observe** something, you see it happen or you look carefully to find out what will happen.

ELA: When you compare how people talk to the rules of writing, you might observe that people do not always speak in complete sentences. If you are writing a narrative, perhaps write about a situation you observed at school.

Math: When you observe a graph or table with data in it, you can draw conclusions about the data. When you observe a probability model and actual events, you can describe differences between what the model predicts and what actually happens.

question

If you **question** something, you express doubt or skepticism about it.

ELA: When you don't believe what a speaker is saying, question him or her about his or her evidence.

Math: Question your answer to a math problem if it is significantly different from your estimated answer.

request
If you **request** something, you ask for it.

ELA: When you don't understand what a speaker is saying, request clarification by asking a question. When you don't know how to complete a task, request help from a friend or teacher.

Math: When you don't understand how to perform a strategy, request help with certain steps of that strategy.

research
If you **research** something, you look for information about it.

ELA: To research the Mars exploration program, look at NASA's website. Research the views of students in your school by asking them questions on a survey or in interviews. It is a good idea to research the topic of a discussion beforehand.

Math: When you want to know what most students' favorite subject is, research by asking a random sample of students what their favorite subjects are.

search
If you **search** for something, you look for it.

ELA: You could search for information on the Internet using a search engine. When you search a database, use several different keywords to find as much information as possible related to your topic.

Math: When you are looking at data, search for regularity or trends.

seek
If you **seek** something, you try to find it or obtain it.

ELA: To seek help with something, ask someone to lend a hand or look for information related to your difficulty. To seek specific information, ask people who are likely to know it or look in places (like books, articles, or on the Internet) where it is likely to be.

Math: To calculate how much wind resistance a vehicle would have to withstand at a certain speed, seek a formula to help you calculate it.

study
If you **study** something, you work to learn about it.

ELA: Study a text by reading it, thinking about it, and reading and listening to others' opinions and thoughts about it. Study a topic by reading information about it or talking to experts.

Math: To study the relationship between two variables (like height and weight), collect data to learn more about it.

See the Big Picture (SBP)

comprehend
If you **comprehend** something, you understand it completely.

ELA: When you comprehend what you are reading, you understand what the text means. When you don't comprehend what the speaker is saying, ask a question to help you understand his or her message.

Math: You might not comprehend fractions the first time you hear about them, but you will comprehend them after studying them and learning how they are related to whole numbers and decimals.

contextualize
If you **contextualize** something, you think about its normal surroundings.

ELA: When you are writing a narrative, contextualize your characters by explaining where they live, what they wear, who their family members are, and what they think about things.

Math: When you are solving a word problem, contextualize it by remembering what the numbers in the problem refer to.

orient
If you **orient** people to something, you show them where they are relative to what they know.

ELA: In a narrative, it is important to orient the reader by introducing the main characters and describing their setting and situation.

Math: When you are explaining your solution to a problem, orient your listeners by giving some background, such as where the problem came from and other ways that have been tried to solve it.

understand   If you **understand** something, you know what it means, how it occurs, why it happens, or why it is important.

ELA: You could understand a personal narrative because someone explained it to you, you read it, or you experienced it yourself.

Math: You could understand an equation or concept because someone explained it to you, you studied it, or you used digital models to visualize it.

Symbolize (SYM)

act out   When you **act out** something, you move your body to show what it looks and sounds like.

ELA: To act out the meaning of a verb, do what that verb says (such as *run*). To act out the meaning of a noun, pretend to be that thing (such as a *cow*).

Math: Act out addition by moving toward someone else and subtraction by moving apart from someone else.

chart   When you **chart** something, you measure it over time and keep track of those measurements on a graph or in a table.

ELA: When you want to make a claim but aren't sure it is true, collect information to use as evidence and chart whether that evidence supports or contradicts your claim.

Math: Chart something's growth or decay. Chart a series of temperature measurements over the course of a week or month.

conceptualize   When you **conceptualize** something, you form an idea of it in your brain.

ELA: When you are writing a narrative and you know what story you want to tell, conceptualize it by picturing the characters and setting and thinking about what perspective to tell the story from.

Math: Conceptualize addition by thinking of two groups of items coming together, and conceptualize subtraction by thinking of part of a group being taken away. Conceptualize the number ten by holding up all of your fingers or looking at ten objects on a table. When you conceptualize a problem, it means you understand all of its parts.

demonstrate   If you **demonstrate** something, you show how to do it.

ELA: Demonstrate your knowledge of language conventions by using them correctly in your writing. Demonstrate that you understand someone else's perspective by paraphrasing it.

Math: Demonstrate how to use the multiplication algorithm by explaining what you are doing as you complete the strategy. Demonstrate how to graph a linear equation by graphing it and explaining each step as you do it.

depict   If you **depict** something, you create a picture of it.

ELA: The illustrations of a story usually depict what is happening in the text. Use descriptive words to help readers depict a process or event in their minds.

Math: To depict the situation described in a word problem, draw a picture of it. A graph is often used to depict equations or sets of data.

diagram   If you **diagram** something, you draw a picture of it using mostly lines and simple pictures, words, or numbers.

ELA: Diagram connections between concepts or things by writing words and drawing lines between them. Diagram the reasons for an argument and how they logically fit together. When planning a written piece or oral presentation, it can be helpful to diagram your main points or ideas and show how you will move from one to the next.

Math: Use a number line to diagram the location of a number. Diagram the angle and side measurements for a shape. To diagram networks or multiple relationships, use a tree diagram.

graph	If you **graph** something, you create a picture that represents it using a grid or horizontal and vertical lines.

ELA: Graph your level of skill with different elements of writing such as ideas, organization, voice, sentence fluency, and word choice to see what you are good at and what you still need to work on.

Math: Graph data on picture, bar, or line graphs. Graph ordered pairs, equations, inequalities, relationships, and functions on a coordinate plane. Often, graphing a problem can help you solve it.

illustrate If you **illustrate** something, you use images to explain it.

ELA: When you write a narrative, illustrate it by drawing pictures that help tell the story. When you write an informative piece, illustrate it with diagrams or photographs. Illustrate with descriptive words that help readers or listeners create a mental picture of something. Illustrate an idea or point by providing an example of it.

Math: Illustrate a multiplication problem by drawing an array. Using computer software, illustrate the way that changing an equation changes its graph. Use a tape diagram to illustrate number relationships.

imagine If you **imagine** something, you form a mental image or idea of it.

ELA: When you write a narrative, you could write about something that actually happened to you or something you imagined.

Math: When doing mental math, it is often helpful to imagine groups of ones, tens, hundreds, and so on.

map If you **map** something, you create a diagram or picture that shows what it looks like.

ELA: Map relationships by drawing lines between items or concepts.

Math: Map numbers on a number line, or map out a plan of action to solve a problem.

model If you **model** something, you create a structure or system that illustrates it.

ELA: When you are writing an informative piece about a process, model the process using a diagram or picture. In a presentation, model a process by giving a demonstration or acting out a scenario.

Math: Use addition and subtraction equations to model what happens when things are joined together or separated in the real world. Model three-dimensional objects using shapes and lines. Model a relationship using a graph, an equation, or a function.

represent If you **represent** something, you create a sign or symbol that reminds people of the original idea or object.

ELA: Two accounts of the same event might be different because they represent two different people's perspectives of the event. When you sort a group of objects into categories, the name of each category represents what is the same about all the objects in the category (such as *round* or *pink*).

Math: Numerals (0, 1, 2, 3, and so on) are symbols that represent quantities. You can represent mathematical operations or mathematical concepts with objects, your fingers, mental images, drawings, sounds, gestures, spoken words, expressions, or equations.

symbolize If you **symbolize** something, you create an image, gesture, or word to represent it.

ELA: Symbolize a paragraph break with the symbol ¶ when revising or editing a written piece. In a narrative piece, symbolize concepts like *bravery* or *courage* with certain animals, like an eagle or lion.

Math: In mathematics, the letters x and y usually symbolize the horizontal and vertical axes of a coordinate plane. Other letters symbolize other quantities or measurements.

visualize If you **visualize** something, you create a picture of it in your head.

ELA: Visualize what happens in a narrative before you write it, or visualize yourself in front of an audience giving a speech before delivering the speech.

Math: Visualize groups of ones, tens, and hundreds to help you do mental math. Visualize parts of a whole to help you understand fractions. When a three-dimensional shape is drawn on paper, you have to visualize what it would look like in real life.

Think Metacognitively (TM)

appreciate   If you **appreciate** something, you understand why it is important.

ELA: Good speakers and writers appreciate the small differences that need to be made for different audiences and purposes. When you appreciate people's differences, you pay attention to and respect different perspectives. When you learn to appreciate nuances in words, you learn how their meanings can change depending on the context and how they are used.

Math: You might not appreciate the need to measure precisely until you try to make or build something and discover that different pieces don't fit correctly.

attend   If you **attend** to something, you pay attention to it.

ELA: When writing, it is important to attend to conventions such as capitalization and punctuation. When you attend to the norms of a group, you make sure that you follow them.

Math: When you keep in mind what the numbers refer to when solving a word problem, you are attending to the meaning of the numbers. When you attend to precision, you pay attention to making sure your solutions are clear and exact. When you attend to details, you pay attention to them and make sure they are resolved appropriately.

design   If you **design** something, you create a plan for it.

ELA: Design a presentation by making an outline of the main points and drawing sketches of the visual aids you will use.

Math: Use geometry to design art, machines, or structures. It is a good idea to design a research project or an experiment before you conduct it. Design simulations to study what might happen in certain situations. Designing before you create or do something can help you save time and money and solve problems quickly.

monitor   If you **monitor** something, you check its progress over a period of time.

ELA: When you monitor your own progress, you take time every once in a while to see if you've moved closer to or further away from your goal.

Math: Use charts or graphs to monitor the progress or growth of something.

persevere   If you **persevere** with something, you keep doing it even though it is difficult.

ELA: After you write something or draft a speech, it is important to persevere through the editing and revision process.

Math: When you get the wrong answer the first three times you try to solve a problem, you should persevere and try again.

plan   If you **plan** to do something, you decide in advance what you are going to do.

ELA: Use an outline to plan an argumentative or informative piece. Use a story web or storyboard to plan a narrative piece. When you plan an oral presentation, think about how you will gesture or where you will stand during each part of the presentation.

Math: Before trying to solve a problem, plan what strategy you are going to use to solve it.

prepare   If you **prepare** for something, you get ready for it.

ELA: To prepare for a discussion, read about the topic or think about your position on the issue that will be discussed.

Math: Prepare for a quiz by reviewing and memorizing the formulas you will need to know and use.

reflect   If you **reflect** on something, you think about it.

ELA: Reflect on what has been said before sharing your own ideas during a discussion. Read material about a topic and reflect on it before participating in a discussion about that topic.

Math: Stop after solving a problem to reflect on how you solved it and whether your answer is correct. After you collect and analyze data, reflect on how to do it better next time.

self-correct   If you **self-correct**, you fix a mistake you made.

ELA: When you read a sentence and realize it doesn't make sense, you might self-correct a word you read incorrectly earlier in the sentence.

Math: Self-correct your answers to problems by solving each problem several different ways and making sure the answers match.

Transform (TRANS)

accentuate   When you **accentuate** something, you make it stand out so it's easier to see or notice.

ELA: When you want to accentuate a point in a presentation, use a gesture or a visual aid, or raise the volume of your voice.

Math: Accentuate data by graphing it or presenting it in a table. Accentuate your answer to a math problem by circling it.

adapt   If you **adapt** something, you change it so that you can use it differently.

ELA: You can adapt writing and speech to different audiences and purposes. When you give the same speech to a group of students and a group of adults, adapt the examples in your speech to help each group understand as clearly as possible.

Math: When you know that the formula for area is length multiplied by width, and you already know the area and width of a shape, you can adapt that formula to help you find the length of the shape.

adjust   If you **adjust** something, you change it a little.

ELA: When you are writing an argument and realize that your evidence is weak, adjust your argument to better fit the evidence. When you are giving a speech and see that the audience doesn't understand, adjust your pacing or vocabulary to provide more clarity.

Math: When your answer to a math problem is correct but you didn't include enough decimal places, adjust your answer.

alter   If you **alter** something, you change it.

ELA: Sometimes authors alter real-life events and include them in fiction books. When an author is writing nonfiction, he or she should not alter the facts.

Math: It is important not to alter the numbers or variables in a math problem while solving it. When you collect data, you should also be careful not to alter them.

apply   If you **apply** something, you use it for a specific purpose.

ELA: When you are learning to read, apply what you know about letter sounds to sound out words. Apply a new word you learn by using it in your writing. When you understand how language works, apply that knowledge to make decisions about how to phrase things when you are writing or speaking. When you use what you know about language to better understand something you read or hear, you have applied your knowledge.

Math: Apply your knowledge of addition to add up the prices of several items you intend to buy at the store. When you know that $5 \times 3 = 15$, and you know that you can reverse the order of multiplication problems (the commutative property), you can apply that knowledge to solve 3×5. When you know the formula for area ($l \times w$), you can apply that formula to a rectangle to calculate its area.

conform   If you **conform**, you make your actions match what something or someone says.

ELA: To make your writing conform to the guidelines in a style manual, make sure that you follow the rules in the style manual.

Math: When you use an algorithm to solve a math problem, what you do needs to conform to the guidelines of the algorithm.

convert   If you **convert** something, you change it from one form to another.

ELA: When you convert a story into a poem, you change it from prose to poetry. When you convert a speech into a written piece, you write down what you would say, paying attention to the conventions of writing (rather than speaking).

Math: When you measure something in inches but want to know how many yards long it is, you will need to convert inches to yards. You can convert a fraction to a decimal by dividing the numerator by the denominator.

edit   If you **edit** something, you look for and correct mistakes in it.

ELA: Edit a text to correct errors or to make sure that it conforms to a style manual.

Math: If your solution to a problem is wrong, edit the strategy you used to solve it.

emphasize   If you **emphasize** something, you draw attention to it because it is important.

ELA: In written pieces, emphasize words using bold print or italics. In oral presentations, emphasize a point by speaking louder, using gestures, or using a visual aid. You can also emphasize information by addressing it first or last or by providing more evidence for it.

Math: Different data displays emphasize different aspects of data sets.

manipulate   If you **manipulate** something, you control it or move it around for a specific purpose.

ELA: Manipulate time in a narrative by making it speed up or slow down or by using flashbacks.

Math: When you want to add three measurements and one is in inches, one is in feet, and one is in centimeters, you will need to manipulate the units. Use tools like matrices to manipulate data to show it in a certain way. When you rewrite an expression so that it is in an easier form to work with, you manipulate the symbols in the expression.

modify   If you **modify** something, you change it a little, usually to make it better.

ELA: Finding out new information about a topic might cause you to modify your views about it.

Math: When your answer to a problem is incorrect, modify the strategy you used to solve it.

paraphrase   If you **paraphrase** something, you say it using different words.

ELA: When you want to write about what another author said, quote him or her using his or her exact words or paraphrase what he or she said using your own words. When you paraphrase someone else's ideas, it is important to give him or her credit for the ideas. Paraphrase what someone else said during a discussion to let him or her know that you heard correctly.

Math: When you explain your solution to an equation and others don't understand it, paraphrase what you said to help them understand.

rearrange   If you **rearrange** items, you change where they are placed or located.

ELA: When a sentence's meaning isn't clear, rearrange the words to make more sense. When your writing isn't well-organized, rearrange the sections or ideas in it to help it flow better.

Math: When you want to solve for a specific variable, rearrange a formula to isolate that variable on one side of the equal sign.

refine   If you **refine** something, you make it clearer, better, or more precise.

ELA: When you refine your knowledge of a topic, you learn more about it or correct wrong ideas you may have had about it.

Math: When you refine a model, you make it reflect reality more closely.

replace

If you **replace** something, you take it away and put something else in its place.

ELA: Strengthen a piece of writing by replacing the passive voice with active voice. When you realize that your argument is using biased evidence, replace it with evidence from a better source.

Math: To add or subtract fractions, replace each fraction with an equivalent fraction so that all the denominators match. In a system of two equations in two variables, replace one of the equations with the sum of that equation and a multiple of the other.

revise

If you **revise** something, you change it to make it better or more accurate.

ELA: When you revise a piece of writing, look for and correct awkward sentence constructions, imprecise vocabulary, or illogical organization.

Math: When you realize that your original answer to a math problem was wrong, revise it to be correct.

rewrite

If you **rewrite** something, you write it differently.

ELA: Rewrite a narrative from the third-person perspective rather than first-person. Rewrite an oral presentation for a more formal audience.

Math: When you rewrite an expression, use the properties of operations or exponents to change its form.

shape

If you **shape** something, you make it look a particular way.

ELA: Shape a narrative by controlling the setting, characters, and events. Shape the meaning or tone of a written piece by choosing certain words.

Math: Shape a model to more accurately represent a certain situation by adding or deleting parts of it.

shift

If you **shift** something, you move it.

ELA: When you change the way you think about something, you shift your perspective.

Math: To simplify an equation, shift variables from one side of the equal sign to the other.

simplify

If you **simplify** something, you make it smaller or easier to understand.

ELA: When you simplify an argument, you get rid of complex details and leave just the claim and main pieces of evidence.

Math: When you need to simplify a situation, focus on the most obvious issues. To simplify an algebraic expression, eliminate the parentheses, combine like terms, and combine constants.

strengthen

If you **strengthen** something, you make it stronger.

ELA: The purpose of revision is to strengthen writing. Strengthen an oral presentation by using visual aids.

Math: Strengthen your answer to a problem by showing how you arrived at it.

substitute

If you **substitute** something, you use it in place of something else.

ELA: When you substitute the /o/ sound for the /e/ sound in *let*, it becomes *lot*.

Math: Substitute the variable *l* for length or *w* for width.

tailor

If you **tailor** something, you make it appropriate for a specific purpose.

ELA: Tailor an online search using Boolean operators like AND, OR, and BUT. Tailor your research to only include information published in books and journal articles.

Math: Tailor a model to show a specific problem or situation by making changes to it.

transform

If you **transform** something, you change it.

ELA: When an author alludes to a previous work like the Bible or an ancient work, he or she usually transforms material from the original source rather than quoting it directly.

Math: Transform shapes by rotating them, reflecting them, or translating them. When you transform a shape by resizing it, it is called dilation.

translate   If you **translate** something, you express it in a different way.

ELA: When you translate information in text into a visual display, you show it with a chart, graph, or diagram. When you translate data into text, you describe it with words.

Math: When you want to write an equation for a conic section, translate its geometric description into equation form.

update   If you **update** something, you add information to it or make it more current.

ELA: When you publish work on the Internet, you can update it more easily than if you publish it in print.

Math: When you solve a problem in your homework but then learn something in class that shows you your answer is wrong, update your answer before handing it in.

Part III

Tier 3 Vocabulary Terms From the Common Core State Standards

Part III contains Tier 3 domain-specific terms from the CCSS. In our analysis of the CCSS, we sought to include every important word that appeared in the grade-level standards. Additionally, we included terms that appeared in an earlier compilation of vocabulary from standards documents (Marzano, 2004). Please visit **marzanoresearch.com/commoncore** for a complete alphabetical listing of the terms in this section and the sources of each term. Teachers can use the appendix (page 215) to locate specific words in parts II and III.

Because the words in part III are all subject-specific (math or ELA), they are organized into measurement topics rather than categories (as in part II). A measurement topic is simply a category of related words. Also, because there are approximately ten times as many terms in part III as in part II, providing descriptions and examples (as in part II) for each Tier 3 term was beyond the scope of this work. In lieu of descriptions and examples for the part III terms, each term in part III is accompanied by a suggested grade-level range. This allows teachers to quickly locate appropriate words for their current topic of study at their assigned grade level.

English Language Arts

Reading

1. Questioning, Inference, and Interpretation

	K	1	2	3	4	5	6	7	8	9–10	11–12
answer	X	X									
ask	X	X									
question	X	X									
detail	X	X	X								
how	X	X	X								
what	X	X	X								
when	X	X	X								
where	X	X	X								
who	X	X	X								
why	X	X	X								
text	X	X	X								
inference			X	X	X						
example			X	X	X						
reason			X	X	X						
evidence				X	X	X					
quote				X	X	X					
support				X	X	X					
analysis							X	X	X		
cite							X	X	X		
explicit							X	X	X		
implicit							X	X	X		
textual evidence							X	X	X		

2. Themes and Central Ideas

	K	1	2	3	4	5	6	7	8	9–10	11–12
retell	X	X									
central idea	X	X	X								
detail	X	X	X								
main idea	X	X	X								
story	X	X	X								
text	X	X	X								
central message		X	X	X							
lesson		X	X	X							
moral		X	X	X							
convey				X	X	X					
drama				X	X	X					
summarize				X	X	X					
summary				X	X	X					
supporting idea/detail				X	X	X					
theme				X	X	X					
emerge							X	X	X		
judgment							X	X	X		
objective summary							X	X	X		
personal opinion							X	X	X		
cultural theme										X	X
historical theme										X	X
pastoral theme										X	X
recurring theme										X	X
universal theme										X	X

3. Story Elements

	K	1	2	3	4	5	6	7	8	9–10	11–12
character	X	X	X								
detail	X	X	X								

	K	1	2	3	4	5	6	7	8	9–10	11–12
story	X	X	X								
main character		X	X	X							
setting		X	X	X							
conclusion (ending)			X	X	X						
event			X	X	X						
introduction			X	X	X						
order of events			X	X	X						
action				X	X	X					
challenge				X	X	X					
character development				X	X	X					
character trait				X	X	X					
decision				X	X	X					
development				X	X	X					
dialogue				X	X	X					
drama				X	X	X					
line (in a script)				X	X	X					
minor character				X	X	X					
plot				X	X	X					
plot development				X	X	X					
role				X	X	X					
sequence / sequential order				X	X	X					
villain				X	X	X					
climax							X	X	X		
conflict							X	X	X		
episode							X	X	X		
incident							X	X	X		
physical description							X	X	X		
provoke							X	X	X		
resolution							X	X	X		

continued →

	K	1	2	3	4	5	6	7	8	9–10	11–12
story element							X	X	X		
subordinate character							X	X	X		
suspense							X	X	X		
archetype										X	X
characterization										X	X
clincher sentence										X	X
dramatic element										X	X
external/internal conflict										X	X
motivation										X	X
red herring										X	X

4. Connections

	K	1	2	3	4	5	6	7	8	9–10	11–12
category		X	X	X							
connection		X	X	X							
event			X	X	X						
example			X	X	X						
information			X	X	X						
procedure			X	X	X						
relationship			X	X	X						
cause/effect				X	X	X					
comparison				X	X	X					
historical event				X	X	X					
scientific concept/idea				X	X	X					
series				X	X	X					
sequence / sequential order				X	X	X					
technical procedure				X	X	X					
analogy							X	X	X		

	K	1	2	3	4	5	6	7	8	9–10	11–12
influence							X	X	X		
interaction							X	X	X		
allegory										X	X
anecdote										X	X
distinction										X	X

5. Word Impact and Use

	K	1	2	3	4	5	6	7	8	9–10	11–12
word	X										
feeling	X	X	X								
poem	X	X	X								
rhyme	X	X	X								
song	X	X	X								
story	X	X	X								
text	X	X	X								
language		X	X	X							
descriptive language			X	X	X						
meaning			X	X	X						
mental image			X	X	X						
rhythm			X	X	X						
word choice			X	X	X						
adage				X	X	X					
definition				X	X	X					
effect				X	X	X					
idiom				X	X	X					
imagery				X	X	X					
irony				X	X	X					
metaphor				X	X	X					
mood				X	X	X					

continued →

	K	1	2	3	4	5	6	7	8	9–10	11–12
phrase				X	X	X					
proverb				X	X	X					
sensory language				X	X	X					
simile				X	X	X					
alliteration					X	X	X				
allusion					X	X	X				
figurative language					X	X	X				
figure of speech					X	X	X				
foreshadowing					X	X	X				
hyperbole					X	X	X				
onomatopoeia					X	X	X				
personification					X	X	X				
pun					X	X	X				
symbolism					X	X	X				
analogy							X	X	X		
association							X	X	X		
biblical allusion							X	X	X		
connotation							X	X	X		
connotative meaning							X	X	X		
context							X	X	X		
degree of certainty							X	X	X		
denotation							X	X	X		
denotative meaning							X	X	X		
emphasis							X	X	X		
figurative meaning							X	X	X		
formal							X	X	X		
humor							X	X	X		
impact							X	X	X		
informal							X	X	X		

	K	1	2	3	4	5	6	7	8	9–10	11–12
literal language							X	X	X		
literal meaning							X	X	X		
literary allusion							X	X	X		
mythological allusion							X	X	X		
nonliteral language							X	X	X		
nonliteral meaning							X	X	X		
shade(s) of meaning							X	X	X		
slang							X	X	X		
state of mind							X	X	X		
style							X	X	X		
tone							X	X	X		
aesthetic impact										X	X
ambience										X	X
ambiguity										X	X
contrasting expressions										X	X
cultural expression										X	X
cultural influence										X	X
cultural nuance										X	X
cumulative impact										X	X
emotional appeal										X	X
euphemism										X	X
evoke										X	X
literary device										X	X
nuance										X	X
oxymoron										X	X
parable										X	X
paradox										X	X
sense of place										X	X
sense of time										X	X

continued →

	K	1	2	3	4	5	6	7	8	9–10	11–12
truth in advertising										X	X
verbal irony										X	X

6. Academic Vocabulary

	K	1	2	3	4	5	6	7	8	9–10	11–12
word	X										
dictionary	X	X	X								
vocabulary	X	X	X								
category		X	X	X							
topic		X	X	X							
meaning			X	X	X						
academic vocabulary				X	X	X					
action				X	X	X					
content-area vocabulary				X	X	X					
definition				X	X	X					
description				X	X	X					
phrase				X	X	X					
signal word/phrase/ clause/sentence				X	X	X					
spatial relationship				X	X	X					
temporal relationship				X	X	X					
emotion					X	X	X				
state of being					X	X	X				
addition relationship						X	X	X			
compare/contrast						X	X	X			
logical relationship						X	X	X			
context							X	X	X		
inferred meaning							X	X	X		
specialized language							X	X	X		
technical meaning							X	X	X		

7. Text Structures and Features

	K	1	2	3	4	5	6	7	8	9–10	11–12
back cover	X										
book	X										
front cover	X										
picture book	X										
storybook	X										
title page	X										
beginning	X	X	X								
detail	X	X	X								
ending	X	X	X								
rhyme	X	X	X								
sentence	X	X	X								
text	X	X	X								
chapter		X	X	X							
margin		X	X	X							
setting		X	X	X							
body (of a text)			X	X	X						
caption			X	X	X						
conclusion (ending)			X	X	X						
event			X	X	X						
introduction			X	X	X						
paragraph			X	X	X						
rhythm			X	X	X						
appendix				X	X	X					
cast of characters				X	X	X					
cause/effect				X	X	X					
chapter title				X	X	X					
chronological order				X	X	X					
comparison				X	X	X					
contrast				X	X	X					

continued →

	K	1	2	3	4	5	6	7	8	9–10	11–12
dialogue				X	X	X					
direct quote				X	X	X					
headline				X	X	X					
passage				X	X	X					
plot				X	X	X					
preface				X	X	X					
problem/solution				X	X	X					
scene				X	X	X					
section				X	X	X					
sequence / sequential order				X	X	X					
series				X	X	X					
stanza				X	X	X					
structure				X	X	X					
summary sentence				X	X	X					
verse				X	X	X					
chronology					X	X	X				
meter (of a poem)					X	X	X				
stage direction					X	X	X				
symbolism					X	X	X				
footnote							X	X	X		
juxtaposition							X	X	X		
page format							X	X	X		
resolution							X	X	X		
soliloquy							X	X	X		
sonnet							X	X	X		
subliminal message							X	X	X		
subplot							X	X	X		
tempo							X	X	X		
written exchange							X	X	X		

	K	1	2	3	4	5	6	7	8	9–10	11–12
ballad										X	X
blurring of genres										X	X
comedy										X	X
couplet										X	X
digressive time										X	X
direct address										X	X
divided quotation										X	X
dramatic dialogue										X	X
exposition										X	X
extended quotation										X	X
flashback										X	X
hierarchic structure										X	X
interior monologue										X	X
lyric poem										X	X
memorandum										X	X
ode										X	X
opening monologue										X	X
overview										X	X
parallel plots										X	X
stream of consciousness										X	X
surprise										X	X
temporal change										X	X
tension										X	X
tragedy										X	X

8. Point of View / Purpose

	K	1	2	3	4	5	6	7	8	9–10	11–12
author	X	X	X								
character	X	X	X								

continued →

	K	1	2	3	4	5	6	7	8	9–10	11–12
illustration	X	X	X								
illustrator	X	X	X								
text	X	X	X								
narrator		X	X	X							
purpose		X	X	X							
reader		X	X	X							
topic		X	X	X							
event			X	X	X						
information			X	X	X						
speaker			X	X	X						
voice			X	X	X						
convey				X	X	X					
custom				X	X	X					
dialogue				X	X	X					
effect				X	X	X					
firsthand				X	X	X					
first person				X	X	X					
irony				X	X	X					
narration				X	X	X					
point of view				X	X	X					
role				X	X	X					
role playing				X	X	X					
secondhand				X	X	X					
second person				X	X	X					
third person				X	X	X					
account (version of a story)					X	X	X				
similarity						X	X	X			
author's purpose							X	X	X		
dramatic irony							X	X	X		
humor							X	X	X		

	K	1	2	3	4	5	6	7	8	9–10	11–12
influence							X	X	X		
native culture							X	X	X		
objective view							X	X	X		
perspective							X	X	X		
position							X	X	X		
stereotype							X	X	X		
subjective view							X	X	X		
suspense							X	X	X		
understatement							X	X	X		
viewpoint							X	X	X		
conflicting evidence									X	X	X
conflicting viewpoints									X	X	X
author's bias										X	X
belief system										X	X
clarity of purpose										X	X
cultural experience										X	X
drastic mood change										X	X
limited point of view										X	X
omniscient point of view										X	X
parody										X	X
persona										X	X
rhetoric										X	X
sarcasm										X	X
satire										X	X

9. Visual/Auditory Media and Information Sources

	K	1	2	3	4	5	6	7	8	9–10	11–12
actor	X	X	X								
cartoon	X	X	X								
directions	X	X	X								

continued →

	K	1	2	3	4	5	6	7	8	9–10	11–12
guest speaker	X	X	X								
illustration	X	X	X								
illustrator	X	X	X								
map	X	X	X								
movie	X	X	X								
music	X	X	X								
photograph	X	X	X								
photographer	X	X	X								
play	X	X	X								
sign	X	X	X								
television program	X	X	X								
text	X	X	X								
video recording	X	X	X								
audio recording			X	X	X						
diagram			X	X	X						
fiction			X	X	X						
folktale			X	X	X						
graphics			X	X	X						
information			X	X	X						
nonfiction			X	X	X						
presentation			X	X	X						
advertisement				X	X	X					
animation				X	X	X					
atlas				X	X	X					
chart				X	X	X					
checklist				X	X	X					
commercial				X	X	X					
digital text				X	X	X					
drama				X	X	X					

	K	1	2	3	4	5	6	7	8	9–10	11–12
graph				X	X	X					
graphic artist				X	X	X					
graphic novel				X	X	X					
host				X	X	X					
hostess				X	X	X					
image				X	X	X					
interview				X	X	X					
news				X	X	X					
oral presentation				X	X	X					
pamphlet				X	X	X					
radio program				X	X	X					
rating				X	X	X					
script				X	X	X					
skit				X	X	X					
sound effect				X	X	X					
source				X	X	X					
special effect				X	X	X					
spoken text				X	X	X					
theme music				X	X	X					
time line				X	X	X					
web page				X	X	X					
audio version					X	X	X				
faithful representation					X	X	X				
media/medium					X	X	X				
multimedia					X	X	X				
musical					X	X	X				
quiz show					X	X	X				
scriptwriter					X	X	X				
speech					X	X	X				

continued →

	K	1	2	3	4	5	6	7	8	9–10	11–12
video version					X	X	X				
almanac							X	X	X		
broadcast							X	X	X		
broadcast advertising							X	X	X		
camera angle							X	X	X		
camera focus							X	X	X		
camera shot							X	X	X		
catalog							X	X	X		
children's program							X	X	X		
current affairs							X	X	X		
documentary							X	X	X		
electronic media							X	X	X		
film							X	X	X		
film director							X	X	X		
film producer							X	X	X		
filmed production							X	X	X		
format							X	X	X		
lecture							X	X	X		
lighting							X	X	X		
live production							X	X	X		
logo							X	X	X		
mass media							X	X	X		
multimedia presentation							X	X	X		
news broadcast							X	X	X		
news bulletin							X	X	X		
oral tradition							X	X	X		
political cartoonist							X	X	X		
political speech							X	X	X		
portrayal							X	X	X		

	K	1	2	3	4	5	6	7	8	9–10	11–12
production							X	X	X		
quantitative format							X	X	X		
sitcom							X	X	X		
staged version							X	X	X		
talk show							X	X	X		
time lapse							X	X	X		
visual format							X	X	X		
advertising code										X	X
advertising copy										X	X
celebrity endorsement										X	X
cinematographer										X	X
computer-generated imagery (CGI)										X	X
consumer document										X	X
court opinion										X	X
dictation										X	X
drama-documentary										X	X
FCC regulation										X	X
film review										X	X
filter (in photography)										X	X
media-generated image										X	X
packaging										X	X
production cost										X	X
reaction shot										X	X
set design										X	X
soap opera										X	X
somber lighting										X	X
theater										X	X
visual text										X	X

10. Argument and Reasoning

	K	1	2	3	4	5	6	7	8	9–10	11–12
claim			X	X	X						
reason			X	X	X						
argument				X	X	X					
evidence				X	X	X					
point (in an argument)				X	X	X					
source				X	X	X					
support				X	X	X					
appeal to authority							X	X	X		
appeal to emotion							X	X	X		
appeal to logic							X	X	X		
conclusions (in an argument)							X	X	X		
counter argument							X	X	X		
glittering generality							X	X	X		
irrelevant							X	X	X		
logic/logical							X	X	X		
logical argument							X	X	X		
reasoning							X	X	X		
relevant							X	X	X		
valid							X	X	X		
advocacy										X	X
attack ad hominem										X	X
bandwagon										X	X
circumlocution										X	X
exaggerated claim										X	X
fallacious reasoning										X	X
false causality										X	X
false statement										X	X

	K	1	2	3	4	5	6	7	8	9–10	11–12
faulty mode of persuasion										X	X
legal reasoning										X	X
logical fallacy										X	X
overgeneralization										X	X
overstatement										X	X
philosophical assumption										X	X
premise										X	X
principle										X	X

11. Literary Comparisons and Source Material

	K	1	2	3	4	5	6	7	8	9–10	11–12
adventure	X	X	X								
fairy tale	X	X	X								
magazine	X	X	X								
newspaper	X	X	X								
play	X	X	X								
poem	X	X	X								
story	X	X	X								
textbook	X	X	X								
fable			X	X	X						
fiction			X	X	X						
folktale			X	X	X						
nonfiction			X	X	X						
autobiography				X	X	X					
biography				X	X	X					
children's literature				X	X	X					
contract				X	X	X					
culture				X	X	X					

continued →

	K	1	2	3	4	5	6	7	8	9–10	11–12
diary				x	x	x					
fantasy				x	x	x					
genre				x	x	x					
journal				x	x	x					
legend				x	x	x					
memoir				x	x	x					
mystery				x	x	x					
myth				x	x	x					
mythology				x	x	x					
novel				x	x	x					
prose				x	x	x					
quest				x	x	x					
science fiction				x	x	x					
series				x	x	x					
short story				x	x	x					
source				x	x	x					
tall tale				x	x	x					
version				x	x	x					
account (version of a story)							X	X	X		
almanac							X	X	X		
Bible							X	X	X		
biographical sketch							X	X	X		
citation							X	X	X		
cross-reference							X	X	X		
editorial							X	X	X		
essay							X	X	X		
feature story							X	X	X		
historical fiction							X	X	X		
historical novel							X	X	X		

	K	1	2	3	4	5	6	7	8	9–10	11–12
life story							X	X	X		
periodical							X	X	X		
publication date							X	X	X		
supernatural tale							X	X	X		
tabloid newspaper							X	X	X		
trickster tale							X	X	X		
allegory										X	X
American literature										X	X
ancient literature										X	X
British literature										X	X
copyright law										X	X
credit										X	X
epic										X	X
excerpt										X	X
feature article										X	X
historical significance										X	X
Homeric Greek literature										X	X
medieval literature										X	X
modern literature										X	X
neoclassic literature										X	X
primary source										X	X
religious literature										X	X
romantic period literature										X	X
secondary source										X	X
Shakespeare										X	X
traditional literature										X	X
warranty										X	X
world literature										X	X

12. Rhetorical Criticism

	K	1	2	3	4	5	6	7	8	9–10	11–12
topic		X	X	X							
claim			X	X	X						
information			X	X	X						
presentation			X	X	X						
argument				X	X	X					
evidence				X	X	X					
point (in an argument)				X	X	X					
subject				X	X	X					
similarity						X	X	X			
concept							X	X	X		
conflicting information							X	X	X		
criticism							X	X	X		
document							X	X	X		
emphasis							X	X	X		
interpretation							X	X	X		
logical argument							X	X	X		
logic/logical							X	X	X		
censorship										X	X
commercialization										X	X
controlling idea										X	X
critical standard										X	X
deconstruct										X	X
faulty mode of persuasion										X	X
literary criticism										X	X
literary significance										X	X
rhetorical device										X	X
rhetorical feature										X	X
rhetorical question										X	X
structural analysis										X	X

13. Fluency

	K	1	2	3	4	5	6	7	8	9–10	11–12
poetry	X	X	X								
story	X	X	X								
text	X	X	X								
informational text		X	X	X							
literature		X	X	X							
purpose		X	X	X							
expression			X	X	X						
drama				X	X	X					
prose				X	X	X					
rate (speed)				X	X	X					
reading strategy				X	X	X					
literary nonfiction							X	X	X		
speed reading							X	X	X		
speed writing										X	X

Reading Foundations

14. Print Concepts

	K	1	2	3	4	5	6	7	8	9–10	11–12
alphabet	X										
left to right	X										
page	X										
space	X										
top to bottom	X										
word	X										
end punctuation	X	X									
letter (of the alphabet)	X	X									
lowercase	X	X									
uppercase	X	X									

continued →

	K	1	2	3	4	5	6	7	8	9–10	11–12
capitalization	X	X	X								
print	X	X	X								
sentence	X	X	X								
symbol		X	X	X							

15. Phonological Awareness

	K	1	2	3	4	5	6	7	8	9–10	11–12
sound	X										
word	X										
beginning sound	X	X									
ending sound	X	X									
consonant	X	X	X								
long vowel sound	X	X	X								
pronounce	X	X	X								
rhyme	X	X	X								
segment	X	X	X								
short vowel sound	X	X	X								
vowel	X	X	X								
beginning consonant		X	X								
consonant blend		X	X								
ending consonant		X	X								
middle vowel sound		X	X								
syllable		X	X	X							

16. Phonics and Word Analysis

	K	1	2	3	4	5	6	7	8	9–10	11–12
sound	X										
word	X										
letter (of the alphabet)	X	X									
blend (sounds together)	X	X	X								

	K	1	2	3	4	5	6	7	8	9–10	11–12
consonant	X	X	X								
long vowel sound	X	X	X								
short vowel sound	X	X	X								
sight word	X	X	X								
vowel	X	X	X								
vowel sound	X	X	X								
consonant blend		X	X								
final -*e*		X	X								
vowel team/ combination		X	X								
irregular spelling		X	X	X							
pattern		X	X	X							
syllable		X	X	X							
affix				X	X	X					
correspondence				X	X	X					
miscue				X	X	X					
multisyllable				X	X	X					
root				X	X	X					

Writing

17. Argumentative

	K	1	2	3	4	5	6	7	8	9–10	11–12
detail	X	X	X								
opinion	X	X	X								
closing sentence		X	X	X							
fact		X	X	X							
topic		X	X	X							
claim			X	X	X						
conclusion (ending)			X	X	X						

continued →

	K	1	2	3	4	5	6	7	8	9–10	11–12
information			X	X	X						
introduction			X	X	X						
reason			X	X	X						
statement			X	X	X						
argument				X	X	X					
evidence				X	X	X					
organization				X	X	X					
point of view				X	X	X					
source				X	X	X					
support				X	X	X					
clarification						X	X	X			
accuracy							X	X	X		
alternate claim							X	X	X		
appeal to authority							X	X	X		
appeal to emotion							X	X	X		
appeal to logic							X	X	X		
counter argument							X	X	X		
counterclaim							X	X	X		
credible/credibility							X	X	X		
fair							X	X	X		
logical argument							X	X	X		
logic/logical							X	X	X		
objective tone							X	X	X		
opposing claim							X	X	X		
reasoning							X	X	X		
thesis							X	X	X		
thesis statement							X	X	X		
valid							X	X	X		
attack ad hominem										X	X

	K	1	2	3	4	5	6	7	8	9–10	11–12
attend (pay attention to)										X	X
bias										X	X
circumlocution										X	X
discipline										X	X
limitation										X	X
logical fallacy										X	X
norm										X	X
significant/significance										X	X
substantive										X	X

18. Informative/Explanatory

	K	1	2	3	4	5	6	7	8	9–10	11–12
detail	X	X	X								
directions	X	X	X								
illustration	X	X	X								
closing sentence		X	X	X							
fact		X	X	X							
topic		X	X	X							
conclusion (ending)			X	X	X						
example			X	X	X						
explanation			X	X	X						
heading			X	X	X						
information			X	X	X						
informative/explanatory			X	X	X						
introduction			X	X	X						
paragraph			X	X	X						
topic sentence			X	X	X						
cause/effect				X	X	X					
chart				X	X	X					
definition				X	X	X					

continued →

	K	1	2	3	4	5	6	7	8	9–10	11–12
graphic				X	X	X					
organization				X	X	X					
quotation				X	X	X					
section				X	X	X					
table				X	X	X					
domain-specific vocabulary					X	X	X				
multimedia					X	X	X				
clarification						X	X	X			
observation						X	X	X			
accuracy							X	X	X		
analysis							X	X	X		
classification							X	X	X		
comparison/contrast							X	X	X		
concept							X	X	X		
format							X	X	X		
logic/logical							X	X	X		
objective tone							X	X	X		
preview							X	X	X		
technical directions							X	X	X		
technical language							X	X	X		
discipline										X	X
figure										X	X
implication										X	X
norm										X	X
significant/significance										X	X

19. Narrative

	K	1	2	3	4	5	6	7	8	9–10	11–12
character	X	X	X								

	K	1	2	3	4	5	6	7	8	9–10	11–12
detail	x	x	x								
experience	x	x	x								
feeling	x	x	x								
closing sentence		x	x	x							
narrator		x	x	x							
reader		x	x	x							
setting		x	x	x							
conclusion (ending)			x	x	x						
event			x	x	x						
introduction			x	x	x						
order of events			x	x	x						
problem			x	x	x						
action				x	x	x					
chronological order				x	x	x					
description				x	x	x					
descriptive detail				x	x	x					
dialogue				x	x	x					
narrative				x	x	x					
organization				x	x	x					
plot				x	x	x					
point of view				x	x	x					
response				x	x	x					
sensory detail/image				x	x	x					
sensory language				x	x	x					
sequence / sequential order				x	x	x					
story map				x	x	x					
observation						x	x	x			
pacing						x	x	x			
reflection						x	x	x			

continued →

	K	1	2	3	4	5	6	7	8	9–10	11–12
context							X	X	X		
personal narrative							X	X	X		
resolution							X	X	X		
suspense							X	X	X		
time frame							X	X	X		
autobiographical narrative										X	X
biographical narrative										X	X
outcome										X	X
vivid										X	X

20. Task, Purpose, and Audience

	K	1	2	3	4	5	6	7	8	9–10	11–12
message	X	X	X								
plan	X	X	X								
audience		X	X	X							
prewriting		X	X	X							
purpose		X	X	X							
apology				X	X	X					
friendly letter				X	X	X					
goal				X	X	X					
invitation				X	X	X					
pen pal				X	X	X					
personal letter				X	X	X					
prior knowledge				X	X	X					
stay on topic				X	X	X					
task				X	X	X					
thank-you letter				X	X	X					
deadline							X	X	X		
private audience							X	X	X		

	K	1	2	3	4	5	6	7	8	9–10	11–12
public audience							X	X	X		
sales technique							X	X	X		
special interests							X	X	X		
style							X	X	X		
target audience							X	X	X		
tone							X	X	X		
viewer perception							X	X	X		
cohesion										X	X
ethics										X	X
expressive writing										X	X
friendly audience										X	X
hostile audience										X	X
job application										X	X
job interview										X	X
marketing										X	X
negotiate										X	X
performance review										X	X
policy statement										X	X
résumé										X	X

21. Revise and Edit

	K	1	2	3	4	5	6	7	8	9–10	11–12
question	X	X									
detail	X	X	X								
suggestion	X	X	X								
audience		X	X	X							
draft		X	X	X							
edit		X	X	X							
purpose		X	X	X							
topic		X	X	X							

continued →

	K	1	2	3	4	5	6	7	8	9–10	11–12
peer			X	X	X						
revise			X	X	X						
composition				X	X	X					
multiple drafts				X	X	X					
peer review				X	X	X					
proofread				X	X	X					
transition				X	X	X					
try a new approach				X	X	X					
composition structure							X	X	X		
focus							X	X	X		
peer-response group							X	X	X		
redundancy							X	X	X		
rewrite							X	X	X		
strengthen							X	X	X		
wordiness							X	X	X		
clarity of purpose										X	X
criteria										X	X
redraft										X	X

22. Technology

	K	1	2	3	4	5	6	7	8	9–10	11–12
publish	X	X	X								
technology	X	X	X								
typing	X	X	X								
Internet		X	X	X							
CD/DVD			X	X	X						
digital tool			X	X	X						
information			X	X	X						
password			X	X	X						

	K	1	2	3	4	5	6	7	8	9–10	11–12
username			X	X	X						
website			X	X	X						
blog				X	X	X					
collaboration				X	X	X					
cursor				X	X	X					
email				X	X	X					
hyperlink				X	X	X					
keyboarding				X	X	X					
pull-down menu				X	X	X					
source				X	X	X					
word processing				X	X	X					
citation							X	X	X		
desktop							X	X	X		
efficient							X	X	X		
hardware							X	X	X		
programming							X	X	X		
software							X	X	X		
status indicator							X	X	X		
cloud										X	X
display										X	X
dynamic										X	X
feedback										X	X
secure site										X	X
software update										X	X
writing product										X	X
text boundary										X	X
URL (uniform resource locator)										X	X

23. Research

	K	1	2	3	4	5	6	7	8	9–10	11–12
question	X	X									
topic		X	X	X							
library catalog			X	X	X						
problem			X	X	X						
report			X	X	X						
search			X	X	X						
investigation				X	X	X					
learning log				X	X	X					
multiple sources				X	X	X					
research				X	X	X					
source				X	X	X					
citation							X	X	X		
conclusions (in an argument)							X	X	X		
exploration							X	X	X		
focus							X	X	X		
inquiry							X	X	X		
knowledge base							X	X	X		
log							X	X	X		
plagiarism							X	X	X		
public opinion trend							X	X	X		
refocus							X	X	X		
research paper							X	X	X		
research project							X	X	X		
research question							X	X	X		
resource material							X	X	X		
self-generated question							X	X	X		
thesis							X	X	X		
thesis statement							X	X	X		

	K	1	2	3	4	5	6	7	8	9–10	11–12
artifact										X	X
field study										X	X
literature review										X	X
methodology										X	X
microfiche										X	X
primary source										X	X
questionnaire										X	X
secondary source										X	X

24. Access and Organize Information

	K	1	2	3	4	5	6	7	8	9–10	11–12
experience	X	X	X								
text	X	X	X								
category		X	X	X							
electronic menu		X	X	X							
fact		X	X	X							
glossary		X	X	X							
icon		X	X	X							
table of contents		X	X	X							
bold print			X	X	X						
caption			X	X	X						
heading			X	X	X						
index			X	X	X						
information			X	X	X						
subheading			X	X	X						
digital source				X	X	X					
evidence				X	X	X					
graphic organizer				X	X	X					
hyperlink				X	X	X					
keyword				X	X	X					

continued →

	K	1	2	3	4	5	6	7	8	9–10	11–12
notes				X	X	X					
outline				X	X	X					
paraphrase				X	X	X					
print source				X	X	X					
quote				X	X	X					
scan				X	X	X					
search term				X	X	X					
search tool				X	X	X					
sidebar				X	X	X					
skim				X	X	X					
source				X	X	X					
source list				X	X	X					
accuracy							X	X	X		
bibliography							X	X	X		
conclusions (in an argument)							X	X	X		
credible/credibility							X	X	X		
data							X	X	X		
efficient							X	X	X		
plagiarism							X	X	X		
relevant							X	X	X		
standard citation format							X	X	X		
advanced search										X	X
anecdotal scripting										X	X
annotated bibliography										X	X
authoritative										X	X
conceptual map										X	X
flow of ideas										X	X
limitation										X	X
overreliance										X	X

Speaking and Listening

25. Collaborative Discussions

	K	1	2	3	4	5	6	7	8	9–10	11–12
ask	X	X									
question	X	X									
conversation	X	X	X								
listen	X	X	X								
take turns	X	X	X								
talk	X	X	X								
vote	X	X	X								
comment		X	X	X							
confused		X	X	X							
connection		X	X	X							
participate		X	X	X							
topic		X	X	X							
discussion			X	X	X						
explanation			X	X	X						
information			X	X	X						
peer			X	X	X						
presentation			X	X	X						
speaker			X	X	X						
brainstorm				X	X	X					
check understanding				X	X	X					
collaboration				X	X	X					
discussion leader				X	X	X					
evidence				X	X	X					
one-on-one discussion				X	X	X					
paraphrase				X	X	X					
point of view				X	X	X					
remark				X	X	X					

continued →

	K	1	2	3	4	5	6	7	8	9–10	11–12
response				x	x	x					
review				x	x	x					
role				x	x	x					
rules of conversation				x	x	x					
small-group discussion				x	x	x					
clarification						x	x	x			
elaboration						x	x	x			
observation						x	x	x			
reflection						x	x	x			
active listening							x	x	x		
conclusions (in an argument)							x	x	x		
discourse							x	x	x		
diverse							x	x	x		
etiquette							x	x	x		
explicit							x	x	x		
facilitator							x	x	x		
formal							x	x	x		
gain the floor							x	x	x		
implicit							x	x	x		
informal							x	x	x		
issue							x	x	x		
perspective							x	x	x		
position							x	x	x		
preparation							x	x	x		
small talk							x	x	x		
verbal cue							x	x	x		
collegial discussion										x	x
consensus										x	x
contradiction										x	x

	K	1	2	3	4	5	6	7	8	9–10	11–12
creative										X	X
democratic										X	X
divergent										X	X
personal space										X	X
persuasion/persuasive										X	X
point of agreement										X	X
point of disagreement										X	X
synthesis										X	X
well-reasoned										X	X

26. Evaluate Presented Information

	K	1	2	3	4	5	6	7	8	9–10	11–12
ask	X	X									
question	X	X									
main idea	X	X	X								
claim			X	X	X						
information			X	X	X						
reason			X	X	X						
speaker			X	X	X						
argument				X	X	X					
evidence				X	X	X					
paraphrase				X	X	X					
point (in an argument)				X	X	X					
source				X	X	X					
study				X	X	X					
support				X	X	X					
media/medium					X	X	X				
clarification						X	X	X			
accuracy							X	X	X		

continued →

	K	1	2	3	4	5	6	7	8	9–10	11–12
appeal to authority							X	X	X		
appeal to emotion							X	X	X		
appeal to logic							X	X	X		
credible/credibility							X	X	X		
data							X	X	X		
extraneous information							X	X	X		
glittering generality							X	X	X		
inconsistency							X	X	X		
irrelevant							X	X	X		
issue							X	X	X		
jargon							X	X	X		
logic/logical							X	X	X		
logical argument							X	X	X		
reasoning							X	X	X		
commercial motive									X	X	X
motive									X	X	X
political motive									X	X	X
social motive									X	X	X
debate										X	X
discrepancy										X	X
distort										X	X
exaggerate										X	X
fallacious reasoning										X	X
false causality										X	X
faulty mode of persuasion										X	X
incongruity										X	X
logical fallacy										X	X
overgeneralization										X	X
overstatement										X	X

	K	1	2	3	4	5	6	7	8	9–10	11–12
philosophical assumption										X	X
point of emphasis										X	X
premise										X	X
rhetoric										X	X
slanted material										X	X
stance										X	X

27. Speech Writing

	K	1	2	3	4	5	6	7	8	9–10	11–12
detail	X	X	X								
experience	X	X	X								
main idea	X	X	X								
story	X	X	X								
audience		X	X	X							
fact		X	X	X							
topic		X	X	X							
claim			X	X	X						
event			X	X	X						
example			X	X	X						
listener			X	X	X						
report			X	X	X						
description				X	X	X					
descriptive detail				X	X	X					
evidence				X	X	X					
organization				X	X	X					
support				X	X	X					
theme				X	X	X					
speech					X	X	X				
concise							X	X	X		

continued →

	K	1	2	3	4	5	6	7	8	9–10	11–12
discourse							X	X	X		
emphasis							X	X	X		
formal							X	X	X		
jargon							X	X	X		
logic/logical							X	X	X		
perspective							X	X	X		
relevant							X	X	X		
style							X	X	X		
tone							X	X	X		
reasoning							X	X	X		
valid							X	X	X		
circumlocution										X	X
exchange of ideas										X	X
line of reasoning										X	X
proposition of fact speech										X	X
proposition of policy speech										X	X
proposition of problem speech										X	X
proposition of value speech										X	X
supporting evidence										X	X

28. Presentation and Delivery

	K	1	2	3	4	5	6	7	8	9–10	11–12
talk	X	X	X								
complete sentence		X	X	X							
audio recording			X	X	X						
digital media			X	X	X						
expression			X	X	X						

	K	1	2	3	4	5	6	7	8	9–10	11–12
graphics			x	x	x						
presentation			x	x	x						
volume			x	x	x						
body language				x	x	x					
cue				x	x	x					
eye contact				x	x	x					
facial expression				x	x	x					
gesture				x	x	x					
image				x	x	x					
memory aid				x	x	x					
oral presentation				x	x	x					
oral report				x	x	x					
pace				x	x	x					
posture				x	x	x					
pronunciation				x	x	x					
prop				x	x	x					
situation				x	x	x					
typeface				x	x	x					
voice level				x	x	x					
formal English					x	x	x				
multimedia					x	x	x				
speech					x	x	x				
clarification						x	x	x			
audible							x	x	x		
delivery							x	x	x		
enunciation							x	x	x		
formal language							x	x	x		
informal language							x	x	x		
intonation							x	x	x		

continued →

	K	1	2	3	4	5	6	7	8	9–10	11–12
layout							X	X	X		
manner of speech							X	X	X		
native speaker							X	X	X		
nonverbal cue							X	X	X		
physical gesture							X	X	X		
projection							X	X	X		
recitation							X	X	X		
sound system							X	X	X		
speech pattern							X	X	X		
visual aid							X	X	X		
visual display							X	X	X		
voice inflection							X	X	X		
articulation										X	X
audio element										X	X
diction										X	X
directionality										X	X
interactive element										X	X
modulation										X	X
poise										X	X
speech action										X	X
subvocalize										X	X
textual element/feature										X	X
visual element										X	X

Language

29. Grammar

	K	1	2	3	4	5	6	7	8	9–10	11–12
action word	X	X	X								
noun	X	X	X								

	K	1	2	3	4	5	6	7	8	9–10	11–12
verb	X	X	X								
article (part of speech)		X	X	X							
future tense		X	X	X							
past tense		X	X	X							
plural		X	X	X							
present tense		X	X	X							
singular		X	X	X							
adjective			X	X	X						
contraction			X	X	X						
common noun			X	X	X						
linking word			X	X	X						
pronoun			X	X	X						
proper noun			X	X	X						
verb tense			X	X	X						
adverb				X	X	X					
antecedent				X	X	X					
conjunction				X	X	X					
gender				X	X	X					
grammar				X	X	X					
irregular noun				X	X	X					
irregular verb				X	X	X					
numerical adjective				X	X	X					
personal pronoun				X	X	X					
preposition				X	X	X					
subject-verb agreement				X	X	X					
abstract					X	X	X				
action verb					X	X	X				
comparative					X	X	X				
concrete					X	X	X				

continued →

	K	1	2	3	4	5	6	7	8	9–10	11–12
coordinating conjunction					X	X	X				
determiner					X	X	X				
helping verb					X	X	X				
interjection					X	X	X				
linking verb					X	X	X				
number					X	X	X				
person					X	X	X				
prepositional phrase					X	X	X				
pronoun-antecedent agreement					X	X	X				
superlative					X	X	X				
collective noun						X	X	X			
coordinate adjective						X	X	X			
correlative conjunction						X	X	X			
modifier						X	X	X			
predicate						X	X	X			
proper adjective						X	X	X			
relative pronoun						X	X	X			
subordinating conjunction						X	X	X			
active voice							X	X	X		
dangling modifier							X	X	X		
demonstrative pronoun							X	X	X		
indefinite pronoun							X	X	X		
intensive pronoun							X	X	X		
object pronoun							X	X	X		
objective case							X	X	X		
passive voice							X	X	X		
perfect tense							X	X	X		
progressive tense							X	X	X		

	K	1	2	3	4	5	6	7	8	9–10	11–12
possessive case							X	X	X		
reflexive pronoun							X	X	X		
relative adverb							X	X	X		
subject pronoun							X	X	X		
subjective case							X	X	X		
usage							X	X	X		
conditional mood									X	X	
gerund									X	X	
imperative mood									X	X	
indicative mood									X	X	
interrogative mood									X	X	
noun clause/phrase									X	X	
parallel structure									X	X	
participle									X	X	
subjunctive mood									X	X	
conjunctive adverb										X	X
infinitive										X	X
modal auxiliary										X	X
pronominal										X	X

30. Sentences

	K	1	2	3	4	5	6	7	8	9–10	11–12
question	X	X									
sentence	X	X	X								
complete sentence		X	X	X							
command			X	X	X						
compound sentence			X	X	X						
simple sentence			X	X	X						
statement			X	X	X						

continued →

	K	1	2	3	4	5	6	7	8	9–10	11–12
complex sentence				x	x	x					
exclamatory sentence				x	x	x					
linking phrase				x	x	x					
object				x	x	x					
phrase				x	x	x					
sentence structure				x	x	x					
subject				x	x	x					
clause					x	x	x				
run-on sentence					x	x	x				
sentence combining					x	x	x				
sentence fragment					x	x	x				
declarative sentence						x	x	x			
imperative sentence						x	x	x			
interrogative sentence						x	x	x			
adjectival clause							x	x	x		
adjectival phrase							x	x	x		
adverbial clause							x	x	x		
adverbial phrase							x	x	x		
compound-complex sentence							x	x	x		
phrase grouping							x	x	x		
absolute phrase										x	x
dependent clause										x	x
independent clause										x	x
nonrestrictive clause										x	x
participial phrase										x	x
relative clause										x	x
restrictive clause										x	x
syntax										x	x
verb phrase										x	x

31. Capitalization and Punctuation

	K	1	2	3	4	5	6	7	8	9–10	11–12
capitalization	X	X	X								
exclamation mark	X	X	X								
first name	X	X	X								
last name	X	X	X								
letter (sent to someone)	X	X	X								
period (punctuation mark)	X	X	X								
question mark	X	X	X								
sentence	X	X	X								
title	X	X	X								
underline	X	X	X								
apostrophe		X	X	X							
comma		X	X	X							
date		X	X	X							
punctuation		X	X	X							
closing			X	X	X						
colon			X	X	X						
geographic name			X	X	X						
greeting			X	X	X						
holiday			X	X	X						
product name			X	X	X						
signature			X	X	X						
address (street address)				X	X	X					
italics				X	X	X					
quotation marks				X	X	X					
salutation				X	X	X					
acronym					X	X	X				
parentheses					X	X	X				

continued →

	K	1	2	3	4	5	6	7	8	9–10	11–12
semicolon					x	x	x				
dash						x	x	x			
hyphen						x	x	x			
ellipsis							x	x	x		
tag question							x	x	x		

32. Spelling

	K	1	2	3	4	5	6	7	8	9–10	11–12
sound	x										
word	x										
letter (of the alphabet)	x	x									
spell/spelling	x	x									
consonant	x	x	x								
dictionary	x	x	x								
long vowel sound	x	x	x								
short vowel sound	x	x	x								
irregular spelling		x	x	x							
spelling pattern		x	x	x							
word family		x	x	x							
generalization			x	x	x						
prefix			x	x	x						
r-controlled			x	x	x						
suffix			x	x	x						
word part			x	x	x						
root				x	x	x					
syllabication				x	x	x					
syllable pattern				x	x	x					
syllabic system							x	x	x		

33. Language Conventions

	K	1	2	3	4	5	6	7	8	9–10	11–12
English	X	X	X								
everyday language	X	X	X								
audience		X	X	X							
language		X	X	X							
abbreviation			X	X	X						
cursive				X	X	X					
double negative				X	X	X					
indentation				X	X	X					
precise				X	X	X					
standard English				X	X	X					
convention					X	X	X				
formal English					X	X	X				
informal English					X	X	X				
sentence patterns					X	X	X				
business letter						X	X	X			
dialect						X	X	X			
context							X	X	X		
mechanics (language)							X	X	X		
polite form							X	X	X		
stress							X	X	X		
style							X	X	X		
tone							X	X	X		
vernacular							X	X	X		
American Psychological Association										X	X
assonance										X	X
bylaw										X	X
consonance										X	X

continued →

	K	1	2	3	4	5	6	7	8	9–10	11–12
discipline										X	X
Modern Language Association										X	X
register										X	X
style manual										X	X
style sheet format										X	X
syntax										X	X

34. Context Clues

	K	1	2	3	4	5	6	7	8	9–10	11–12
word	X										
clue	X	X	X								
prediction	X	X	X								
text	X	X	X								
self-correct		X	X	X							
example			X	X	X						
meaning			X	X	X						
meaning clue			X	X	X						
comparison				X	X	X					
confirm				X	X	X					
definition				X	X	X					
restatement				X	X	X					
context							X	X	X		
context clue							X	X	X		
textual clue							X	X	X		
word function							X	X	X		
word position							X	X	X		
sociocultural context										X	X

35. Word Origins and Roots

	K	1	2	3	4	5	6	7	8	9–10	11–12
word	X										
compound word			X	X	X						
meaning			X	X	X						
prefix			X	X	X						
suffix			X	X	X						
affix				X	X	X					
part of speech				X	X	X					
root				X	X	X					
foreign word					X	X	X				
Greek affix					X	X	X				
Greek root					X	X	X				
Latin affix					X	X	X				
Latin root					X	X	X				
Anglo-Saxon affix							X	X	X		
Anglo-Saxon root							X	X	X		
derivation							X	X	X		
derivational suffix							X	X	X		
word borrowing							X	X	X		
word origin							X	X	X		
cognate										X	X
infinitive										X	X
inflection										X	X
word change pattern										X	X

36. Reference Materials

	K	1	2	3	4	5	6	7	8	9–10	11–12
dictionary	X	X	X								
picture dictionary	X	X	X								
glossary		X	X	X							

continued →

	K	1	2	3	4	5	6	7	8	9–10	11–12
index			X	X	X						
encyclopedia				X	X	X					
guide words				X	X	X					
part of speech				X	X	X					
pronunciation				X	X	X					
references / reference materials				X	X	X					
rhyming dictionary				X	X	X					
thesaurus				X	X	X					
etymology										X	X
Readers' Guide to Periodical Literature										X	X
standard usage										X	X

37. Word Relationships

	K	1	2	3	4	5	6	7	8	9–10	11–12
opposite	X										
word	X										
number word	X	X	X								
category		X	X	X							
meaning			X	X	X						
relationship			X	X	X						
antonym				X	X	X					
cause/effect				X	X	X					
compare/contrast				X	X	X					
homophone				X	X	X					
multimeaning word				X	X	X					
synonym				X	X	X					
homograph					X	X	X				
analogy							X	X	X		

	K	1	2	3	4	5	6	7	8	9–10	11–12
homonym							x	x	x		
item/category relationship							x	x	x		
part/whole relationship							x	x	x		
logographic system										x	x

Mathematics

Number and Quantity

38. Number Names

	K	1	2	3	4	5	6	7	8	HS
count	x	x	x							
eight	x	x	x							
eighteen	x	x	x							
eighth (ordinal number)	x	x	x							
eighty	x	x	x							
eleven	x	x	x							
fifteen	x	x	x							
fifth (ordinal number)	x	x	x							
fifty	x	x	x							
first	x	x	x							
five	x	x	x							
forty	x	x	x							
four	x	x	x							
fourteen	x	x	x							
fourth (ordinal number)	x	x	x							
hundred	x	x	x							
nine	x	x	x							
nineteen	x	x	x							
ninety	x	x	x							

continued →

	K	1	2	3	4	5	6	7	8	HS
ninth (ordinal number)	X	X	X							
number	X	X	X							
number name	X	X	X							
one	X	X	X							
ones	X	X	X							
second (ordinal number)	X	X	X							
seven	X	X	X							
seventeen	X	X	X							
seventh (ordinal number)	X	X	X							
seventy	X	X	X							
six	X	X	X							
sixteen	X	X	X							
sixth (ordinal number)	X	X	X							
sixty	X	X	X							
ten	X	X	X							
tens	X	X	X							
tenth (ordinal number)	X	X	X							
third (ordinal number)	X	X	X							
thirteen	X	X	X							
thirty	X	X	X							
three	X	X	X							
twelve	X	X	X							
twenty	X	X	X							
two	X	X	X							
zero	X	X	X							
numeral			X	X	X					
billion				X	X	X				
billionth (ordinal number)				X	X	X				
eighteenth (ordinal number)				X	X	X				

	K	1	2	3	4	5	6	7	8	HS
eightieth (ordinal number)				x	x	x				
eleventh (ordinal number)				x	x	x				
fifteenth (ordinal number)				x	x	x				
fiftieth (ordinal number)				x	x	x				
fortieth (ordinal number)				x	x	x				
fourteenth (ordinal number)				x	x	x				
hundredth (ordinal number)				x	x	x				
million				x	x	x				
millionth (ordinal number)				x	x	x				
nineteenth (ordinal number)				x	x	x				
ninetieth (ordinal number)				x	x	x				
seventeenth (ordinal number)				x	x	x				
seventieth (ordinal number)				x	x	x				
sixteenth (ordinal number)				x	x	x				
sixtieth (ordinal number)				x	x	x				
thirteenth (ordinal number)				x	x	x				
thirtieth (ordinal number)				x	x	x				
thousand				x	x	x				
thousandth (ordinal number)				x	x	x				
trillion				x	x	x				
trillionth (ordinal number)				x	x	x				
twelfth (ordinal number)				x	x	x				
twentieth (ordinal number)				x	x	x				
Roman numeral					x	x	x			

39. Counting

	K	1	2	3	4	5	6	7	8	HS
how many	x	x								
count	x	x	x							

continued →

	K	1	2	3	4	5	6	7	8	HS
number	X	X	X							
number name	X	X	X							
number order	X	X	X							
pair	X	X	X							
count by 2s		X	X	X						
count by 5s		X	X	X						
tallies		X	X	X						
cardinal number							X	X	X	
ordinal number							X	X	X	
counting procedure							X	X	X	
combination										X
permutation										X

40. Compare Numbers

	K	1	2	3	4	5	6	7	8	HS
large/larger	X									
small/smaller	X									
group/grouping	X	X								
less	X	X								
match	X	X								
more	X	X								
compare	X	X	X							
equal	X	X	X							
number	X	X	X							
even number		X	X	X						
greater than (>)		X	X	X						
less than (<)		X	X	X						
odd number		X	X	X						
relationship			X	X	X					

	K	1	2	3	4	5	6	7	8	HS
comparison				X	X	X				
equivalent				X	X	X				
inequality				X	X	X				
random number				X	X	X				
relative size				X	X	X				
relative magnitude							X	X	X	

41. Place Value

	K	1	2	3	4	5	6	7	8	HS
number	X	X	X							
number name	X	X	X							
ones	X	X	X							
place	X	X	X							
tens	X	X	X							
count by 10s		X	X	X						
hundreds		X	X	X						
place value		X	X	X						
represent		X	X	X						
symbol		X	X	X						
amount			X	X	X					
compose			X	X	X					
count by 100s			X	X	X					
decompose/decomposition			X	X	X					
digit			X	X	X					
expanded form			X	X	X					
one-digit number			X	X	X					
rounding			X	X	X					
skip-count			X	X	X					
three-digit number			X	X	X					

continued →

	K	1	2	3	4	5	6	7	8	HS
two-digit number			X	X	X					
value			X	X	X					
whole number			X	X	X					
base-ten numeral				X	X	X				
comparison				X	X	X				
expanded notation				X	X	X				
front-end digit				X	X	X				
multidigit number				X	X	X				
decimal					X	X	X			
place holder					X	X	X			
base 10							X	X	X	
base 60							X	X	X	
nondecimal numeration system							X	X	X	
number system							X	X	X	
reference set							X	X	X	
base e										X
binary system										X
natural number										X

42. Foundations of Fractions

	K	1	2	3	4	5	6	7	8	HS
equal	X	X	X							
number line	X	X	X							
part	X	X	X							
share	X	X	X							
size	X	X	X							
whole	X	X	X							
represent		X	X	X						
fraction			X	X	X					

	K	1	2	3	4	5	6	7	8	HS
relationship			X	X	X					
quantity				X	X	X				
partition					X	X	X			

43. Fractions

	K	1	2	3	4	5	6	7	8	HS
compare	X	X	X							
equal	X	X	X							
number line	X	X	X							
part	X	X	X							
share	X	X	X							
size	X	X	X							
whole	X	X	X							
represent		X	X	X						
symbol		X	X	X						
fraction			X	X	X					
fraction strip			X	X	X					
relationship			X	X	X					
visual fraction model			X	X	X					
whole number			X	X	X					
common fraction				X	X	X				
comparison				X	X	X				
denominator				X	X	X				
equivalent				X	X	X				
estimation				X	X	X				
improper fraction				X	X	X				
numerator				X	X	X				
quantity				X	X	X				
reduced form				X	X	X				

continued →

	K	1	2	3	4	5	6	7	8	HS
simple fraction				x	x	x				
common denominator					x	x	x			
common numerator					x	x	x			
partition					x	x	x			
convert						x	x	x		
reciprocal						x	x	x		
complex fraction							x	x	x	
magnitude							x	x	x	
fraction inversion										x

44. Adding and Subtracting Fractions

	K	1	2	3	4	5	6	7	8	HS
addition	x	x	x							
part	x	x	x							
size	x	x	x							
subtraction	x	x	x							
whole	x	x	x							
sum		x	x	x						
word problem		x	x	x						
compose			x	x	x					
decompose/decomposition			x	x	x					
fraction			x	x	x					
visual fraction model			x	x	x					
benchmark fraction				x	x	x				
denominator				x	x	x				
equation				x	x	x				
equivalent				x	x	x				
estimation				x	x	x				
mathematical problem				x	x	x				
numerator				x	x	x				

	K	1	2	3	4	5	6	7	8	HS
real-world problem				X	X	X				
common denominator					X	X	X			
mixed number					X	X	X			
reasonable					X	X	X			
unlike denominators					X	X	X			
properties of operations							X	X	X	

45. Multiplying and Dividing Fractions

	K	1	2	3	4	5	6	7	8	HS
word problem		X	X	X						
fraction			X	X	X					
multiplication			X	X	X					
visual fraction model			X	X	X					
denominator				X	X	X				
division				X	X	X				
equation				X	X	X				
estimation				X	X	X				
mathematical problem				X	X	X				
multiple				X	X	X				
numerator				X	X	X				
quotient				X	X	X				
real-world problem				X	X	X				
mixed number					X	X	X			
reasonable					X	X	X			
unit fraction					X	X	X			
non-zero						X	X	X		
resize						X	X	X		
properties of operations							X	X	X	

46. Decimal Concepts

	K	1	2	3	4	5	6	7	8	HS
pattern	X	X	X							
whole	X	X	X							
place value		X	X	X						
symbol		X	X	X						
decimal point			X	X	X					
digit			X	X	X					
expanded form			X	X	X					
base-ten numeral				X	X	X				
expanded notation				X	X	X				
multidigit number				X	X	X				
visual model				X	X	X				
decimal					X	X	X			
decimal form					X	X	X			
hundredths					X	X	X			
multidigit decimal					X	X	X			
tenths					X	X	X			
thousandths					X	X	X			
convert						X	X	X		
base 10							X	X	X	
base 60							X	X	X	
decimal notation							X	X	X	
power of 10							X	X	X	
significant digits							X	X	X	
base e										X

47. Ratios and Unit Rates

	K	1	2	3	4	5	6	7	8	HS
relationship			X	X	X					
constant				X	X	X				

	K	1	2	3	4	5	6	7	8	HS
equivalent				X	X	X				
graph				X	X	X				
mathematical problem				X	X	X				
quantity				X	X	X				
real-world problem				X	X	X				
table				X	X	X				
diagram					X	X	X			
multistep problem					X	X	X			
point					X	X	X			
coordinate plane						X	X	X		
origin						X	X	X		
percent						X	X	X		
constant difference							X	X	X	
double number line diagram							X	X	X	
equal ratios							X	X	X	
percents above 100							X	X	X	
percents below 1							X	X	X	
proportion							X	X	X	
proportional gain							X	X	X	
rate							X	X	X	
rate of change							X	X	X	
ratio							X	X	X	
strip diagram							X	X	X	
tape diagram							X	X	X	
unit rate							X	X	X	
constant of proportionality								X	X	X
proportional relationship								X	X	X
common ratio										X

48. Rational and Irrational Numbers

	K	1	2	3	4	5	6	7	8	HS
number line	X	X	X							
value			X	X	X					
constant				X	X	X				
direction				X	X	X				
negative				X	X	X				
positive				X	X	X				
quantity				X	X	X				
real-world problem				X	X	X				
expression					X	X	X			
convert						X	X	X		
coordinate plane						X	X	X		
repeating decimal						X	X	X		
absolute value							X	X	X	
horizontal number line diagram							X	X	X	
integer							X	X	X	
magnitude							X	X	X	
rational number							X	X	X	
rational number system							X	X	X	
real-world context							X	X	X	
signed number							X	X	X	
statement of inequality							X	X	X	
statement of order							X	X	X	
vertical number line diagram							X	X	X	
repeating digit								X	X	X
decimal expansion									X	X
irrational number									X	X
rational approximation									X	X

49. Exponents and Roots

	K	1	2	3	4	5	6	7	8	HS
solution			X	X	X					
value			X	X	X					
whole number			X	X	X					
negative				X	X	X				
operation				X	X	X				
positive				X	X	X				
square number				X	X	X				
exponent					X	X	X			
expression					X	X	X			
numerical expression						X	X	X		
square root						X	X	X		
square root symbol						X	X	X		
cube number							X	X	X	
decimal notation							X	X	X	
exponential notation							X	X	X	
integer							X	X	X	
power of 10							X	X	X	
property							X	X	X	
rational number							X	X	X	
root							X	X	X	
negative exponent								X	X	X
cube root									X	X
cube root symbol									X	X
irrational number									X	X
perfect cube									X	X
perfect square									X	X
scientific notation									X	X

continued →

	K	1	2	3	4	5	6	7	8	HS
cost										X
exponential function										X
profit										X
radical										X
real number										X
revenue										X

50. Quantities

	K	1	2	3	4	5	6	7	8	HS
solution			X	X	X					
formula				X	X	X				
quantity				X	X	X				
scale					X	X	X			
absolute error										X
compound interest										X
data display										X
descriptive modeling										X
level of accuracy										X
limitation										X
relative error										X
scalar										X
vector										X

51. Operations With Complex Numbers

	K	1	2	3	4	5	6	7	8	HS
operation				X	X	X				
number system							X	X	X	
number theory							X	X	X	
complex number										X

	K	1	2	3	4	5	6	7	8	HS
complex number system										X
conjugate complex number										X
imaginary number										X
number subsystems										X
real number										X
real number system										X
relation										X

52. Polynomial Identities and Equations

	K	1	2	3	4	5	6	7	8	HS
equation				X	X	X				
coefficient							X	X	X	
polynomial									X	X
complex solution										X
continuity										X
monomial										X
polynomial identity										X
quadratic equation										X
real number										X

Operations and Algebra

53. Addition and Subtraction

	K	1	2	3	4	5	6	7	8	HS
compose a ten	X	X								
count on	X	X								
group/grouping	X	X								
make ten	X	X								
add	X	X	X							

continued →

	K	1	2	3	4	5	6	7	8	HS
addition	X	X	X							
calculator	X	X	X							
equal	X	X	X							
guess and check	X	X	X							
number	X	X	X							
number line	X	X	X							
ones	X	X	X							
subtract	X	X	X							
subtraction	X	X	X							
tens	X	X	X							
count by 10s		X	X	X						
difference		X	X	X						
false		X	X	X						
hundreds		X	X	X						
greater than (>)		X	X	X						
less than (<)		X	X	X						
model		X	X	X						
place value		X	X	X						
put together		X	X	X						
represent		X	X	X						
strategy		X	X	X						
sum		X	X	X						
symbol		X	X	X						
take apart		X	X	X						
take from		X	X	X						
true		X	X	X						
word problem		X	X	X						
addend			X	X	X					
compose			X	X	X					

	K	1	2	3	4	5	6	7	8	HS
decompose/decomposition			X	X	X					
digit			X	X	X					
mental math			X	X	X					
minuend			X	X	X					
number sentence			X	X	X					
one-digit number			X	X	X					
one-step problem			X	X	X					
relationship			X	X	X					
three-digit number			X	X	X					
two-digit number			X	X	X					
unknown			X	X	X					
whole number			X	X	X					
algorithm				X	X	X				
computation strategy				X	X	X				
equation				X	X	X				
fixed order				X	X	X				
front-end estimation				X	X	X				
irrelevant information				X	X	X				
mathematical problem				X	X	X				
multidigit number				X	X	X				
multiple of ten				X	X	X				
negative				X	X	X				
numerical value				X	X	X				
operation				X	X	X				
positive				X	X	X				
two-step problem				X	X	X				
unit				X	X	X				
abstract					X	X	X			
concrete					X	X	X			

continued →

	K	1	2	3	4	5	6	7	8	HS
multistep problem					X	X	X			
reasonable					X	X	X			
associative property						X	X	X		
commutative property						X	X	X		
distributive property						X	X	X		
open sentence						X	X	X		
standard algorithm						X	X	X		
absolute value							X	X	X	
additive inverse							X	X	X	
horizontal number line diagram							X	X	X	
property							X	X	X	
rational number							X	X	X	
real-world context							X	X	X	
vertical number line diagram							X	X	X	

54. Multiplication and Division

	K	1	2	3	4	5	6	7	8	HS
group/grouping	X	X								
calculator	X	X	X							
equal	X	X	X							
number	X	X	X							
share	X	X	X							
even number		X	X	X						
odd number		X	X	X						
place value		X	X	X						
represent		X	X	X						
strategy		X	X	X						
symbol		X	X	X						
total		X	X	X						
word problem		X	X	X						

	K	1	2	3	4	5	6	7	8	HS
column			X	X	X					
digit			X	X	X					
mental math			X	X	X					
multiplication			X	X	X					
multiply			X	X	X					
one-digit number			X	X	X					
rectangular array			X	X	X					
relationship			X	X	X					
row			X	X	X					
three-digit number			X	X	X					
two-digit number			X	X	X					
unknown			X	X	X					
whole number			X	X	X					
algorithm				X	X	X				
area model				X	X	X				
array				X	X	X				
computation strategy				X	X	X				
divide				X	X	X				
division				X	X	X				
equation				X	X	X				
fixed order				X	X	X				
four-digit number				X	X	X				
irrelevant information				X	X	X				
mathematical problem				X	X	X				
multidigit number				X	X	X				
multiple				X	X	X				
multiple of ten				X	X	X				
operation				X	X	X				
product				X	X	X				

continued →

	K	1	2	3	4	5	6	7	8	HS
quotient				X	X	X				
remainder				X	X	X				
unknown-factor problem				X	X	X				
decimal					X	X	X			
decimal form					X	X	X			
dividend					X	X	X			
divisibility					X	X	X			
divisor					X	X	X			
long division					X	X	X			
multistep problem					X	X	X			
partition					X	X	X			
reasonable					X	X	X			
associative property						X	X	X		
commutative property						X	X	X		
conversion						X	X	X		
distributive property						X	X	X		
non-zero						X	X	X		
open sentence						X	X	X		
reciprocal						X	X	X		
repeating decimal						X	X	X		
rule						X	X	X		
standard algorithm						X	X	X		
integer							X	X	X	
multiplicative inverse							X	X	X	
property							X	X	X	
rational number							X	X	X	
real-world context							X	X	X	
signed number							X	X	X	
terminating decimal								X	X	X

55. Properties of Operations

	K	1	2	3	4	5	6	7	8	HS
add	X	X	X							
addition	X	X	X							
identity property of zero	X	X	X							
pattern	X	X	X							
subtract	X	X	X							
subtraction	X	X	X							
addition table		X	X	X						
multiplication			X	X	X					
multiply			X	X	X					
unknown-number problem			X	X	X					
divide				X	X	X				
division				X	X	X				
identity property of one				X	X	X				
multiplication table				X	X	X				
operation				X	X	X				
associative property						X	X	X		
commutative property						X	X	X		
distributive property						X	X	X		
order of operations						X	X	X		
addition property of equality							X	X	X	
division property of equality							X	X	X	
multiplication property of equality							X	X	X	
property							X	X	X	
subtraction property of equality							X	X	X	

56. Expressions and Equations

	K	1	2	3	4	5	6	7	8	HS
represent		X	X	X						
strategy		X	X	X						

continued →

	K	1	2	3	4	5	6	7	8	HS
word problem		X	X	X						
solution			X	X	X					
unknown			X	X	X					
value			X	X	X					
equation				X	X	X				
equivalent				X	X	X				
estimation				X	X	X				
formula				X	X	X				
operation				X	X	X				
real-world problem				X	X	X				
two-step problem				X	X	X				
exponent					X	X	X			
expression					X	X	X			
place holder					X	X	X			
braces						X	X	X		
brackets						X	X	X		
numerical expression						X	X	X		
open sentence						X	X	X		
order of operations						X	X	X		
parentheses						X	X	X		
simple expression						X	X	X		
algebraic expression							X	X	X	
coefficient							X	X	X	
collect like terms							X	X	X	
combine like terms							X	X	X	
expansion							X	X	X	
linear equation							X	X	X	
linear expression							X	X	X	
nonlinear equation							X	X	X	

	K	1	2	3	4	5	6	7	8	HS
problem context							X	X	X	
problem formulation							X	X	X	
problem space							X	X	X	
rational number							X	X	X	
term							X	X	X	
variable							X	X	X	

57. Factors and Multiples

	K	1	2	3	4	5	6	7	8	HS
whole number			X	X	X					
factor				X	X	X				
factor pair				X	X	X				
multiple				X	X	X				
common factor					X	X	X			
composite number					X	X	X			
greatest common factor					X	X	X			
least common multiple					X	X	X			
prime number					X	X	X			
relatively prime							X	X	X	
prime factorization										X

58. Patterns

	K	1	2	3	4	5	6	7	8	HS
pair	X	X	X							
pattern	X	X	X							
decreasing pattern		X	X	X						
increasing pattern		X	X	X						
pattern		X	X	X						
relationship			X	X	X					

continued →

	K	1	2	3	4	5	6	7	8	HS
geometric pattern				X	X	X				
graph				X	X	X				
growing pattern				X	X	X				
pattern addition				X	X	X				
pattern extension				X	X	X				
pattern subtraction				X	X	X				
repeating pattern				X	X	X				
series				X	X	X				
shrinking pattern				X	X	X				
coordinate plane						X	X	X		
corresponding terms						X	X	X		
ordered pair						X	X	X		
rule						X	X	X		
linear arithmetic sequence							X	X	X	
linear geometric sequence							X	X	X	
linear pattern							X	X	X	
pattern division							X	X	X	
pattern multiplication							X	X	X	
pattern recognition							X	X	X	
tessellation							X	X	X	
sigma notation										X

59. Equations and Inequalities

	K	1	2	3	4	5	6	7	8	HS
false		X	X	X						
true		X	X	X						
solution			X	X	X					
value			X	X	X					
equation				X	X	X				

	K	1	2	3	4	5	6	7	8	HS
equivalent				X	X	X				
graph				X	X	X				
inequality				X	X	X				
mathematical problem				X	X	X				
negative				X	X	X				
operation				X	X	X				
positive				X	X	X				
real-world problem				X	X	X				
sequence				X	X	X				
expression					X	X	X			
multistep problem					X	X	X			
reasonable					X	X	X			
convert					X	X	X			
simpler form					X	X	X			
coefficient							X	X	X	
collect like terms							X	X	X	
combine like terms							X	X	X	
constraint							X	X	X	
infinitely many							X	X	X	
linear equation							X	X	X	
properties of equality							X	X	X	
properties of inequality							X	X	X	
rational number							X	X	X	
set							X	X	X	
simplification							X	X	X	
variable							X	X	X	
solution set								X	X	X
possible value									X	X
reflexive property of equality									X	X

continued →

	K	1	2	3	4	5	6	7	8	HS
substitution property of equality									X	X
symmetric property of equality									X	X
transitive property of equality									X	X

60. Dependent and Independent Variables

	K	1	2	3	4	5	6	7	8	HS
relationship			X	X	X					
graph				X	X	X				
quantity				X	X	X				
real-world problem				X	X	X				
table				X	X	X				
dependent variable							X	X	X	
independent variable							X	X	X	
variable							X	X	X	
random variable								X	X	X
dependent event										X
independent event										X
independent trial										X

61. Slope

	K	1	2	3	4	5	6	7	8	HS
line			X	X	X					
graph				X	X	X				
horizontal axis					X	X	X			
vertical axis					X	X	X			
coordinate plane						X	X	X		
origin						X	X	X		
intercept							X	X	X	
similar							X	X	X	

	K	1	2	3	4	5	6	7	8	HS
slope							X	X	X	
slope intercept formula							X	X	X	
unit rate							X	X	X	
proportional relationship								X	X	X
regression coefficient										X
regression line										X

62. Systems of Equations

	K	1	2	3	4	5	6	7	8	HS
solution			X	X	X					
graph				X	X	X				
algebra						X	X	X		
ordered pair						X	X	X		
graphic representation							X	X	X	
linear equation							X	X	X	
system of equations							X	X	X	
variable							X	X	X	
inspection									X	X
ordered triple									X	X
point of intersection									X	X
quadratic equation										X
system of linear equations										X

63. Structure of Expressions

	K	1	2	3	4	5	6	7	8	HS
structure				X	X	X				
expression					X	X	X			
coefficient							X	X	X	
term							X	X	X	

64. Equivalent Expressions

	K	1	2	3	4	5	6	7	8	HS
equation				X	X	X				
equivalent				X	X	X				
formula				X	X	X				
inequality				X	X	X				
expression					X	X	X			
property							X	X	X	
function									X	X
common ratio										X
complete the square										X
exponential function										X
finite geometric series										X
maximum value										X
minimum value										X
quadratic expression										X
zero of a function										X

65. Arithmetic Operations on Polynomials

	K	1	2	3	4	5	6	7	8	HS
system						X	X	X		
integer							X	X	X	
analogous									X	X
polynomial									X	X
polynomial addition									X	X
polynomial division									X	X
polynomial multiplication									X	X
polynomial subtraction									X	X

66. Zeroes and Factors of Polynomials

	K	1	2	3	4	5	6	7	8	HS
function									X	X
polynomial									X	X
factoring/factorization										X
polynomial solution by bisection										X
polynomial solution by sign change										X
polynomial solution successive approximation										X
remainder theorem										X
zero of a polynomial										X

67. Polynomial Identities

	K	1	2	3	4	5	6	7	8	HS
relationship			X	X	X					
polynomial									X	X
polynomial identity										X

68. Rational Expressions

	K	1	2	3	4	5	6	7	8	HS
expression					X	X	X			
long division					X	X	X			
rational number							X	X	X	
inspection									X	X
polynomial									X	X
computer algebra system										X
rational expression										X

69. Creating Equations

	K	1	2	3	4	5	6	7	8	HS
model		X	X	X						
solution			X	X	X					
formula				X	X	X				
inequality				X	X	X				
label					X	X	X			
scale					X	X	X			
coordinate axes						X	X	X		
constraint							X	X	X	
system of equations							X	X	X	
variable							X	X	X	
quantity of interest										X
system of inequalities										X

70. Reasoning to Solve Equations

	K	1	2	3	4	5	6	7	8	HS
prediction			X	X	X					
solution			X	X	X					
work backward			X	X	X					
equality				X	X	X				
trial and error				X	X	X				
counter example							X	X	X	
deductive reasoning							X	X	X	
inductive reasoning							X	X	X	
logic ALL							X	X	X	
logic AND							X	X	X	
logic IF/THEN							X	X	X	
logic NONE							X	X	X	
logic NOT							X	X	X	
logic OR							X	X	X	

	K	1	2	3	4	5	6	7	8	HS
logic SOME							X	X	X	
nonroutine problem							X	X	X	
solution algorithm							X	X	X	
solution probabilities							X	X	X	
variable							X	X	X	
verification							X	X	X	
simple equation								X	X	X
argument									X	X
assumption										X
extraneous solution										X
formal mathematical induction										X
mathematical theory										X
nature of deduction										X
radical expression										X
rational equation										X
strategy efficiency										X
strategy generation technique										X
viable argument										X

71. Solving Quadratic Equations

	K	1	2	3	4	5	6	7	8	HS
solution			X	X	X					
inspection									X	X
complete the square										X
complex solution										X
derivation										X
factoring/factorization										X
quadratic equation										X
quadratic formula										X
real number										X

72. Graphs of Equations and Inequalities

	K	1	2	3	4	5	6	7	8	HS
solution			x	x	x					
graph				x	x	x				
coordinate plane						x	x	x		
intersection/intersecting						x	x	x		
plot						x	x	x		
set							x	x	x	
variable							x	x	x	
solution set								x	x	x
function									x	x
linear function									x	x
table of values									x	x
absolute value function										x
boundary										x
curve										x
exponential function										x
half-plane										x
line equation										x
linear inequality										x
logarithmic function / log function										x
polynomial function										x
rational function										x
strict inequality										x
successive approximations										x
system of inequalities										x
system of linear inequalities										x

Functions

73. Functions

	K	1	2	3	4	5	6	7	8	HS
line			X	X	X					
graph				X	X	X				
sequence				X	X	X				
table				X	X	X				
algebra							X	X	X	
ordered pair							X	X	X	
rule							X	X	X	
algebraic step function							X	X	X	
integer							X	X	X	
iterative sequence							X	X	X	
linear							X	X	X	
property							X	X	X	
recursive process/sequence							X	X	X	
set							X	X	X	
variable							X	X	X	
Fibonacci sequence									X	X
function									X	X
input									X	X
linear function									X	X
nonlinear function									X	X
output									X	X
algebraic function										X
asymptote of function										X
circular function										X
direct function										X

continued →

	K	1	2	3	4	5	6	7	8	HS
domain										X
element										X
factorial										X
factorial notation										X
function composition										X
function notation										X
geometric function										X
limit										X
periodic function										X
radical function										X
range (of a function)										X
real-world function										X
sinusoidal function										X
subset										X

74. Interpret Functions

	K	1	2	3	4	5	6	7	8	HS
model		X	X	X						
value			X	X	X					
graph				X	X	X				
sketch				X	X	X				
table				X	X	X				
average							X	X	X	
rate of change							X	X	X	
decreasing function									X	X
function									X	X
increasing function									X	X
initial value									X	X
linear function									X	X
linear relationship									X	X

	K	1	2	3	4	5	6	7	8	HS
nonlinear function									X	X
qualitative									X	X
table of values									X	X
domain										X
functional relationship										X
interval										X
local/global behavior										X
minimum/maximum of function										X
quantitative										X
symbolic representation										X

75. Graph Functions

	K	1	2	3	4	5	6	7	8	HS
intercept							X	X	X	
function									X	X
linear function									X	X
absolute value function										X
amplitude										X
area under curve										X
cube root function										X
end behavior										X
exponential function										X
factoring/factorization										X
finite graph										X
inflection										X
logarithmic function / log function										X
midline										X
minimum										X
period										X
piecewise-defined function										X

continued →

	K	1	2	3	4	5	6	7	8	HS
polynomial function										X
quadratic function										X
square root function										X
step function										X
symbolic representation										X
trigonometric function										X
zero of a function										X

76. Properties of Functions

	K	1	2	3	4	5	6	7	8	HS
symmetry				X	X	X				
table				X	X	X				
algebra					X	X	X			
property							X	X	X	
function									X	X
complete the square										X
exponential function										X
extreme value										X
quadratic function										X
zero of a function										X

77. Model Relationships

	K	1	2	3	4	5	6	7	8	HS
model		X	X	X						
relationship			X	X	X					
operation				X	X	X				
formula				X	X	X				
calculation							X	X	X	
network							X	X	X	
recursive process/sequence							X	X	X	
function									X	X

	K	1	2	3	4	5	6	7	8	HS
arithmetic sequence										X
geometric sequence										X
recurrence equation										X
recurrence relationship										X
recursive equation										X
standard function type										X

78. Building New Functions

	K	1	2	3	4	5	6	7	8	HS
value		X	X	X						
graph				X	X	X				
negative				X	X	X				
positive				X	X	X				
expression					X	X	X			
inverse function										X
simple function										X

79. Linear and Exponential Models

	K	1	2	3	4	5	6	7	8	HS
model		X	X	X						
solution			X	X	X					
table				X	X	X				
exponential notation							X	X	X	
growth rate							X	X	X	
input/output table									X	X
linear function									X	X
arithmetic sequence										X
constant percent rate										X
constant rate										X
decay										X

continued →

	K	1	2	3	4	5	6	7	8	HS
exponential function										X
exponential model										X
geometric sequence										X
input-output pair										X
interval										X
logarithm										X
natural log										X
polynomial function										X
unit interval										X

80. Interpret Linear and Exponential Functions

	K	1	2	3	4	5	6	7	8	HS
linear function									X	X
exponential function										X
parameter										X
parameter estimate										X
parametric equation										X

81. Trigonometric Functions

	K	1	2	3	4	5	6	7	8	HS
arc					X	X	X			
coordinate plane						X	X	X		
cosine function										X
extension										X
radian measure										X
real number										X
subtend										X
traverse										X
trigonometric function										X
unit circle										X

82. Periodic Phenomena

	K	1	2	3	4	5	6	7	8	HS
model		x	x	x						
frequency							x	x	x	
amplitude										x
midline										x
periodic phenomena										x
trigonometric function										x

83. Trigonometric Identities

	K	1	2	3	4	5	6	7	8	HS
quadrant							x	x	x	
cosine (cos θ)										x
cosine function										x
phase shift										x
point of tangency										x
Pythagorean identity										x
sine (sin θ)										x
sine function										x
tangent (tan θ)										x
tangent function										x

Geometry

84. Shapes

	K	1	2	3	4	5	6	7	8	HS
corner	x									
shape	x									
side	x									
circle	x	x	x							
rectangle	x	x	x							

continued →

	K	1	2	3	4	5	6	7	8	HS
size	X	X	X							
triangle	X	X	X							
cone		X	X	X						
cube		X	X	X						
cylinder		X	X	X						
open shape		X	X	X						
pyramid		X	X	X						
sphere		X	X	X						
square		X	X	X						
attribute			X	X	X					
face			X	X	X					
hexagon			X	X	X					
pentagon			X	X	X					
solid			X	X	X					
trapezoid			X	X	X					
angle				X	X	X				
parallel lines				X	X	X				
perpendicular lines				X	X	X				
polygon				X	X	X				
quadrilateral				X	X	X				
rhombus				X	X	X				
special quadrilateral				X	X	X				
three-dimensional				X	X	X				
two-dimensional				X	X	X				
angle measure					X	X	X			
cross-section					X	X	X			
geometric					X	X	X			
plane					X	X	X			
prism					X	X	X			

	K	1	2	3	4	5	6	7	8	HS
protractor					X	X	X			
right triangle					X	X	X			
rotation					X	X	X			
equilateral triangle						X	X	X		
intersection/intersecting						X	X	X		
isosceles triangle						X	X	X		
parallelogram						X	X	X		
rectangular prism						X	X	X		
space						X	X	X		
vertex/vertices						X	X	X		
irregular polygon							X	X	X	
orientation							X	X	X	
planar cross section							X	X	X	
property							X	X	X	
slice							X	X	X	
tetrahedron							X	X	X	
plane section								X	X	X
rectilinear figure										X
vertex edge graph										X

85. Compose and Decompose Shapes

	K	1	2	3	4	5	6	7	8	HS
large/larger	X									
shape	X									
small/smaller	X									
equal	X	X	X							
part	X	X	X							
share	X	X	X							
whole	X	X	X							

continued →

	K	1	2	3	4	5	6	7	8	HS
half		X	X	X						
half-circle		X	X	X						
column			X	X	X					
compose			X	X	X					
decompose/decomposition			X	X	X					
fourth (fraction)			X	X	X					
horizontal line			X	X	X					
identical			X	X	X					
quarter-circle			X	X	X					
quarter (one-fourth)			X	X	X					
row			X	X	X					
third (fraction)			X	X	X					
area				X	X	X				
component				X	X	X				
three-dimensional				X	X	X				
two-dimensional				X	X	X				
unit				X	X	X				
composite shape					X	X	X			
partition					X	X	X			
unit fraction					X	X	X			

86. Lines and Symmetry

	K	1	2	3	4	5	6	7	8	HS
line			X	X	X					
line of symmetry			X	X	X					
angle				X	X	X				
line segment				X	X	X				
midpoint				X	X	X				
parallel lines				X	X	X				
perpendicular lines				X	X	X				

	K	1	2	3	4	5	6	7	8	HS
reflection				X	X	X				
right angle				X	X	X				
symmetry				X	X	X				
acute angle					X	X	X			
obtuse angle					X	X	X			
point					X	X	X			
ray					X	X	X			
rotation symmetry					X	X	X			
intersection/intersecting						X	X	X		
axis of symmetry							X	X	X	
line symmetry							X	X	X	
parallel figures							X	X	X	
perpendicular bisector							X	X	X	

87. Coordinate System

	K	1	2	3	4	5	6	7	8	HS
number line	X	X	X							
line			X	X	X					
axis/axes				X	X	X				
direction				X	X	X				
graph				X	X	X				
line segment				X	X	X				
mathematical problem				X	X	X				
parallel lines				X	X	X				
perpendicular lines				X	X	X				
real-world problem				X	X	X				
reflection				X	X	X				
horizontal axis					X	X	X			
plane					X	X	X			
point					X	X	X			

continued →

	K	1	2	3	4	5	6	7	8	HS
vertical axis					X	X	X			
algebra						X	X	X		
coordinate						X	X	X		
coordinate axes						X	X	X		
coordinate plane						X	X	X		
coordinate system						X	X	X		
first quadrant						X	X	X		
intersection/intersecting						X	X	X		
ordered pair						X	X	X		
origin						X	X	X		
travel						X	X	X		
vertex/vertices						X	X	X		
x-axis						X	X	X		
x-coordinate						X	X	X		
y-axis						X	X	X		
y-coordinate						X	X	X		
absolute value							X	X	X	
coordinate geometry							X	X	X	
first coordinate							X	X	X	
quadrant							X	X	X	
ratio							X	X	X	
rectangular coordinates							X	X	X	
second coordinate							X	X	X	
signed number							X	X	X	
slope intercept formula							X	X	X	
Cartesian coordinates										X
directed line segment										X
distance formula										X
geometric problem										X
polar coordinates										X

	K	1	2	3	4	5	6	7	8	HS
simple geometric theorem										X
slope criteria										X

88. Area

	K	1	2	3	4	5	6	7	8	HS
part	X	X	X							
measurement		X	X	X						
model		X	X	X						
attribute			X	X	X					
multiply			X	X	X					
rectangular array			X	X	X					
additive				X	X	X				
area				X	X	X				
area formula				X	X	X				
area model				X	X	X				
formula				X	X	X				
mathematical problem				X	X	X				
real-world problem				X	X	X				
rectangle formula				X	X	X				
side length				X	X	X				
square centimeter (cm²)				X	X	X				
square foot (ft²)				X	X	X				
square inch (in²)				X	X	X				
square meter (m²)				X	X	X				
square unit				X	X	X				
triangle formula				X	X	X				
two-dimensional				X	X	X				
unit				X	X	X				
trapezoid formula					X	X	X			
conservation of area						X	X	X		

continued →

	K	1	2	3	4	5	6	7	8	HS
circle formula							x	x	x	
circumference							x	x	x	
circumference formula							x	x	x	
pi (π)							x	x	x	
plane figure							x	x	x	

89. Perimeter

	K	1	2	3	4	5	6	7	8	HS
area				x	x	x				
mathematical problem				x	x	x				
perimeter				x	x	x				
perimeter formula				x	x	x				
real-world problem				x	x	x				
side length				x	x	x				

90. Surface Area

	K	1	2	3	4	5	6	7	8	HS
formula				x	x	x				
mathematical problem				x	x	x				
real-world problem				x	x	x				
square unit				x	x	x				
three-dimensional				x	x	x				
two-dimensional				x	x	x				
net						x	x	x		
surface area						x	x	x		

91. Volume

	K	1	2	3	4	5	6	7	8	HS
height			x	x	x					
volume			x	x	x					
base				x	x	x				

	K	1	2	3	4	5	6	7	8	HS
cubic unit				X	X	X				
equivalent				X	X	X				
formula				X	X	X				
mathematical problem				X	X	X				
real-world problem				X	X	X				
three-dimensional				X	X	X				
unit				X	X	X				
cubic centimeter (cm³)					X	X	X			
cubic foot (ft³)					X	X	X			
cubic inch (in³)					X	X	X			
cubic meter (m³)					X	X	X			
edge length					X	X	X			
unit cube					X	X	X			
rectangular prism						X	X	X		
volume formula						X	X	X		

92. Scale Drawings

	K	1	2	3	4	5	6	7	8	HS
grid				X	X	X				
scale					X	X	X			
scale drawing					X	X	X			
scale map					X	X	X			
reproduction						X	X	X		
perspective							X	X	X	

93. Angles

	K	1	2	3	4	5	6	7	8	HS
angle				X	X	X				
angle measurement tool				X	X	X				

continued →

	K	1	2	3	4	5	6	7	8	HS
mathematical problem				X	X	X				
real-world problem				X	X	X				
right angle				X	X	X				
acute angle					X	X	X			
angle measure					X	X	X			
center					X	X	X			
circular arc					X	X	X			
corresponding angles					X	X	X			
corresponding sides					X	X	X			
degree					X	X	X			
endpoint					X	X	X			
multistep problem					X	X	X			
obtuse angle					X	X	X			
one-degree angle					X	X	X			
point					X	X	X			
protractor					X	X	X			
ray					X	X	X			
intersection/intersecting						X	X	X		
adjacent angle							X	X	X	
alternate interior angle							X	X	X	
angle bisector							X	X	X	
complementary angle							X	X	X	
exterior angle							X	X	X	
inscribed angle							X	X	X	
interior angle							X	X	X	
similarity							X	X	X	
supplementary angle							X	X	X	
vertical angle							X	X	X	
angle sum									X	X

	K	1	2	3	4	5	6	7	8	HS
angle-angle (AA) criterion									X	X
transversal									X	X
angle of depression										X
central angle										X

94. Pythagorean Theorem

	K	1	2	3	4	5	6	7	8	HS
right triangle					X	X	X			
converse									X	X
dimension									X	X
proof									X	X
Pythagorean theorem									X	X

95. Congruence and Similarity

	K	1	2	3	4	5	6	7	8	HS
equality				X	X	X				
geometric figure				X	X	X				
reflection				X	X	X				
sequence				X	X	X				
rotation					X	X	X			
congruence/congruent							X	X	X	
line segment congruence							X	X	X	
line segment similarity							X	X	X	
similar							X	X	X	
similarity							X	X	X	
angle-angle (AA) criterion									X	X
criteria for triangle congruence									X	X
dilation									X	X
translation									X	X

continued →

	K	1	2	3	4	5	6	7	8	HS
angle-side-angle (ASA) postulate										X
isometry										X
properties of similarity transformations										X
proportion										X
rigid motion										X
side-angle-side (SAS) postulate										X
side-side-side (SSS) postulate										X
similarity transformation										X

96. Transformations

	K	1	2	3	4	5	6	7	8	HS
geometric figure				X	X	X				
flip				X	X	X				
line segment				X	X	X				
parallel lines				X	X	X				
perpendicular lines				X	X	X				
reflection				X	X	X				
plane					X	X	X			
rotation					X	X	X			
coordinate						X	X	X		
graph paper						X	X	X		
parallelogram						X	X	X		
tracing paper						X	X	X		
enlarging transformation							X	X	X	
property							X	X	X	
proportion							X	X	X	
reflection transformation							X	X	X	
scale transformation							X	X	X	

	K	1	2	3	4	5	6	7	8	HS
shape transformation							X	X	X	
shrinking transformation							X	X	X	
slide transformation							X	X	X	
transformation							X	X	X	
dilation									X	X
function									X	X
input									X	X
output									X	X
translation									X	X
carry (a figure onto another figure)										X
geometric description										X
geometry software										X
horizontal stretch										X
rigid motion										X
sequence of transformations										X
undefined notion										X

97. Geometric Theorems

	K	1	2	3	4	5	6	7	8	HS
multiple strategies for proofs							X	X	X	
empirical verification										X
postulate										X
proof paragraph										X
prove										X
theorem										X
theorem direct proof										X
theorem indirect proof										X
truth table proof										X

98. Geometric Constructions

	K	1	2	3	4	5	6	7	8	HS
line			x	x	x					
three-dimensional				x	x	x				
two-dimensional				x	x	x				
point					x	x	x			
compass							x	x	x	
inscribe							x	x	x	
straightedge							x	x	x	
tessellation							x	x	x	
dynamic geometric software										x
formal geometric construction										x
right triangle geometry										x
synthetic geometry										x

99. Dilations

	K	1	2	3	4	5	6	7	8	HS
line segment				x	x	x				
parallel lines				x	x	x				
center					x	x	x			
plane					x	x	x			
ratio							x	x	x	
dilation									x	x
common scale factor										x
fixed center										x
scale factor										x

100. Theorems Involving Similarity

	K	1	2	3	4	5	6	7	8	HS
geometric figure				x	x	x				
congruence criteria										x
prove										x

	K	1	2	3	4	5	6	7	8	HS
similarity criteria										X
theorem										X

101. Trigonometric Ratios

	K	1	2	3	4	5	6	7	8	HS
right triangle					X	X	X			
complementary angle							X	X	X	
property							X	X	X	
similarity							X	X	X	
Pythagorean theorem									X	X
applied problem										X
cosine (cos θ)										X
side ratio										X
sine (sin θ)										X
trigonometric ratio										X
trigonometric relation										X

102. Geometric Trigonometry

	K	1	2	3	4	5	6	7	8	HS
non-right triangle					X	X	X			
right triangle					X	X	X			
Law of Cosines										X
Law of Sines										X
prove										X
resultant force										X

103. Circle Theorems

	K	1	2	3	4	5	6	7	8	HS
center					X	X	X			
circumference							X	X	X	

continued →

	K	1	2	3	4	5	6	7	8	HS
diameter							X	X	X	
inscribe							X	X	X	
inscribed angle							X	X	X	
pi (π)							X	X	X	
radius							X	X	X	
similar							X	X	X	
chord										X
circumscribed circle of a triangle										X
inscribed circle of a triangle										X
prove										X

104. Arc Length and Sectors

	K	1	2	3	4	5	6	7	8	HS
formula				X	X	X				
arc					X	X	X			
intercept							X	X	X	
radius							X	X	X	
similarity							X	X	X	
constant of proportionality								X	X	X
radian measure										X
sector										X

105. Conic Sections

	K	1	2	3	4	5	6	7	8	HS
radius							X	X	X	
focus								X	X	X
Pythagorean theorem									X	X
complete the square										X
directrix										X
parabola										X

106. Geometric Modeling

	K	1	2	3	4	5	6	7	8	HS
cylinder		X	X	X						
model		X	X	X						
structure				X	X	X				
property							X	X	X	
ratio							X	X	X	
density										X
design problem										X
geometric method										X
minimize cost										X
modeling situation										X
physical constraint										X
typographic grid system										X

Measurement, Data, Statistics, and Probability

107. Measurement

	K	1	2	3	4	5	6	7	8	HS
large/larger	X									
small/smaller	X									
longer	X	X								
shorter	X	X								
distance	X	X	X							
length	X	X	X							
number line	X	X	X							
size	X	X	X							
temperature	X	X	X							
weight	X	X	X							
width	X	X	X							
hour (hr)		X	X	X						

continued →

	K	1	2	3	4	5	6	7	8	HS
measurement		x	x	x						
measuring cup		x	x	x						
ruler		x	x	x						
centimeter (cm)			x	x	x					
English system of measurement			x	x	x					
foot (ft)			x	x	x					
gram (g)			x	x	x					
height			x	x	x					
inch (in)			x	x	x					
kilogram (kg)			x	x	x					
mass			x	x	x					
mean			x	x	x					
measuring tape			x	x	x					
median			x	x	x					
meter (m)			x	x	x					
meter stick			x	x	x					
metric system			x	x	x					
millimeter (mm)			x	x	x					
minute (min)			x	x	x					
mode			x	x	x					
money			x	x	x					
second (sec)			x	x	x					
thermometer			x	x	x					
U.S. customary system			x	x	x					
volume			x	x	x					
yardstick			x	x	x					
beaker				x	x	x				
capacity				x	x	x				
cubic unit				x	x	x				
elapsed time				x	x	x				

	K	1	2	3	4	5	6	7	8	HS
equivalent				X	X	X				
estimation				X	X	X				
kilometer (km)				X	X	X				
liter (l)				X	X	X				
measurement scale				X	X	X				
mile (mi)				X	X	X				
milliliter (ml)				X	X	X				
nonstandard unit				X	X	X				
ounce (oz)				X	X	X				
pound (lb)				X	X	X				
quantity				X	X	X				
relative distance				X	X	X				
square unit				X	X	X				
standard unit				X	X	X				
time interval				X	X	X				
truncation				X	X	X				
unit				X	X	X				
ounce (oz)					X	X	X			
two-column table					X	X	X			
conversion						X	X	X		
benchmarking							X	X	X	
linear unit							X	X	X	
measure of center/central tendency							X	X	X	
overestimation							X	X	X	
precision							X	X	X	
underestimation							X	X	X	
Richter scale									X	X
speed									X	X
velocity									X	X

continued →

	K	1	2	3	4	5	6	7	8	HS
acceleration										X
critical paths method										X
decibel										X
direct measure										X
force										X
indirect measure										X
series circuit										X
transitivity principle for indirect measurement										X
unit analysis										X
upper/lower bounds										X

108. Represent and Interpret Data

	K	1	2	3	4	5	6	7	8	HS
sort	X									
less	X	X								
more	X	X								
category		X	X	X						
picture graph		X	X	X						
represent		X	X	X						
total		X	X	X						
bar graph			X	X	X					
horizontal scale			X	X	X					
information			X	X	X					
line plot			X	X	X					
tallies			X	X	X					
data				X	X	X				
data collection method				X	X	X				
equivalent representation				X	X	X				
line graph				X	X	X				
pie chart				X	X	X				

	K	1	2	3	4	5	6	7	8	HS
unit				X	X	X				
Venn diagram				X	X	X				
display					X	X	X			
scale					X	X	X			
scaled graph					X	X	X			
cluster						X	X	X		
data cluster						X	X	X		
data value						X	X	X		
blueprint							X	X	X	
pictorial representation							X	X	X	
table representation of functions							X	X	X	
table representation of probability							X	X	X	
written representation							X	X	X	

109. Time

	K	1	2	3	4	5	6	7	8	HS
calendar	X	X	X							
clock	X	X	X							
day	X	X	X							
week	X	X	X							
year	X	X	X							
analog clock		X	X	X						
digital clock		X	X	X						
half-hour		X	X	X						
hour (hr)		X	X	X						
timc		X	X	X						
a.m.			X	X	X					
minute (min)			X	X	X					
p.m.			X	X	X					

continued →

	K	1	2	3	4	5	6	7	8	HS
second (sec)			x	x	x					
time interval				x	x	x				
time zone				x	x	x				

110. Money

	K	1	2	3	4	5	6	7	8	HS
coin	x	x	x							
dime		x	x	x						
nickel		x	x	x						
penny		x	x	x						
quarter (coin)		x	x	x						
symbol		x	x	x						
decimal point			x	x	x					
dollar bill			x	x	x					

111. Data Distributions

	K	1	2	3	4	5	6	7	8	HS
number line	x	x	x							
pattern	x	x	x							
attribute			x	x	x					
mean			x	x	x					
median			x	x	x					
mode			x	x	x					
observation			x	x	x					
value			x	x	x					
data				x	x	x				
measurement unit				x	x	x				
table				x	x	x				
center					x	x	x			
display					x	x	x			

	K	1	2	3	4	5	6	7	8	HS
range (of numbers or data)					X	X	X			
data value						X	X	X		
plot						X	X	X		
quartile						X	X	X		
box and whisker plot							X	X	X	
box plot							X	X	X	
central value							X	X	X	
data distribution							X	X	X	
data extreme							X	X	X	
data gap							X	X	X	
data set							X	X	X	
deviation							X	X	X	
dispersion							X	X	X	
distribution							X	X	X	
dot plot							X	X	X	
first quartile							X	X	X	
histogram							X	X	X	
interquartile range							X	X	X	
list of values							X	X	X	
mean absolute deviation							X	X	X	
measure of center/central tendency							X	X	X	
outlier							X	X	X	
quantitative							X	X	X	
set							X	X	X	
spread							X	X	X	
statistical question							X	X	X	
statistics							X	X	X	
stem and leaf plot							X	X	X	
striking deviation							X	X	X	

continued →

	K	1	2	3	4	5	6	7	8	HS
third quartile							x	x	x	
variability							x	x	x	
variable							x	x	x	
variable change							x	x	x	
comparative inference								x	x	x
informal								x	x	x
population								x	x	x
random sample								x	x	x
visual overlap								x	x	x
fit									x	x
area under curve										x
confidence interval										x
data display error										x
extreme data point										x
normal curve										x
normal distribution										x
parallel box plot										x
population percentage										x
quartile deviation										x
real number line										x
spreadsheet										x
standard deviation										x
summary statistic										x
univariate data										x
univariate distribution										x

112. Random Sampling

	K	1	2	3	4	5	6	7	8	HS
experiment		x	x	x						
model		x	x	x						

	K	1	2	3	4	5	6	7	8	HS
inference			X	X	X					
information			X	X	X					
prediction			X	X	X					
data				X	X	X				
random				X	X	X				
survey				X	X	X				
valid					X	X	X			
sample						X	X	X		
biased sample							X	X	X	
consistency							X	X	X	
control group							X	X	X	
experimental design							X	X	X	
gain							X	X	X	
generalization							X	X	X	
limited sample							X	X	X	
multiple samples							X	X	X	
reliability							X	X	X	
representative sample							X	X	X	
sample selection techniques							X	X	X	
sampling error							X	X	X	
simulated samples							X	X	X	
statistics							X	X	X	
treatment							X	X	X	
treatment group							X	X	X	
tree diagram							X	X	X	
variation							X	X	X	
population								X	X	X
random sample								X	X	X
random variable								X	X	X

continued →

	K	1	2	3	4	5	6	7	8	HS
simulation								X	X	X
simulation model								X	X	X
data-generating process										X
experimental probability										X
margin of error										X
Monte Carlo simulation										X
observational study										X
parameter										X
parameter estimate										X
parametric equation										X
population mean										X
population parameter										X
population proportion										X
randomization										X
randomized experiment										X
random sampling technique										X
representativeness of sample										X
sample statistic										X
sample survey										X
sampling distribution										X
significant difference										X
validity										X

113. Probability

	K	1	2	3	4	5	6	7	8	HS
chance	X	X	X							
model		X	X	X						
likely			X	X	X					
prediction			X	X	X					
unlikely			X	X	X					

	K	1	2	3	4	5	6	7	8	HS
certainty				X	X	X				
data				X	X	X				
fair chance				X	X	X				
improbability				X	X	X				
source				X	X	X				
equal probability					X	X	X			
likelihood					X	X	X			
probability					X	X	X			
intersection/intersecting					X	X	X	X		
long-run					X	X	X	X		
odds						X	X	X		
associate							X	X	X	
chance event							X	X	X	
chance process							X	X	X	
complementary event							X	X	X	
compound event							X	X	X	
conjecture							X	X	X	
discrepancy							X	X	X	
event							X	X	X	
mutually exclusive events							X	X	X	
outcome							X	X	X	
theoretical probability							X	X	X	
tree diagram							X	X	X	
approximate								X	X	X
characteristic								X	X	X
characteristic of interest								X	X	X
observed frequency								X	X	X
probability model								X	X	X
random process								X	X	X

continued →

	K	1	2	3	4	5	6	7	8	HS
simulation								X	X	X
two-way frequency table									X	X
area under curve										X
central limit theorem										X
characterization										X
combined model										X
complement										X
conditional probability										X
continuous probability distribution										X
discrete probability										X
discrete probability distribution										X
expected value										X
independence										X
probability distribution										X
sample space										X
set of outcomes										X
subset										X
uncertain outcome										X
union										X
weighted average										X

114. Multivariable Data Distributions

	K	1	2	3	4	5	6	7	8	HS
pattern	X	X	X							
model		X	X	X						
data				X	X	X				
data value						X	X	X		
plot						X	X	X		
clustering							X	X	X	

	K	1	2	3	4	5	6	7	8	HS
data point							X	X	X	
frequency							X	X	X	
frequency distribution							X	X	X	
intercept							X	X	X	
nominal data							X	X	X	
outlier							X	X	X	
quantitative							X	X	X	
slope							X	X	X	
trend							X	X	X	
variable							X	X	X	
informal								X	X	X
relative frequency								X	X	X
association									X	X
bivariate data									X	X
bivariate measurement data									X	X
categorical data									X	X
categorical variable									X	X
closeness									X	X
fit									X	X
function									X	X
linear association									X	X
linear function									X	X
linear model									X	X
model fit									X	X
negative association									X	X
nonlinear association									X	X
pattern of association									X	X
positive association									X	X
scatter plot									X	X

continued →

	K	1	2	3	4	5	6	7	8	HS
two-way frequency table									X	X
bivariate data transformation										X
bivariate distribution										X
conditional relative frequency										X
curve fitting										X
curve fitting median method										X
joint relative frequency										X
marginal relative frequency										X
residual										X

115. Linear Models

	K	1	2	3	4	5	6	7	8	HS
data				X	X	X				
projection							X	X	X	
intercept							X	X	X	
rate of change							X	X	X	
slope							X	X	X	
linear model									X	X
causation										X
constant term										X
correlation										X
correlation coefficient										X
linear fit										X
percent rate of change										X
spurious correlation										X
statistical regression										X

116. Rules of Probability

	K	1	2	3	4	5	6	7	8	HS
model		x	x	x						
certainty of conclusions							x	x	x	
outcome							x	x	x	
addition rule										x
conditional probability										x
law of large numbers										x
law of probability										x
uniform probability model										x
variance										x

Appendix
Master List of Terms

This appendix lists all of the words from parts II and III in alphabetical order. Teachers looking for a specific word can use this listing to find it quickly. Each term is followed by initials or a number that indicates where the term can be found in the book. If a word is followed by initials such as ADD or ARR, which represent a category, it is found in part II. If a word is followed by a number, which represents a measurement topic, it is found in part III.

Part II Categories

ADD	Add To	EXEC	Execute	REF	Reference
ARR	Arrange	EXP	Explain	SI	Seek Information
COLL	Collaborate	HYP	Hypothesize	SBP	See the Big Picture
C/C	Compare/Contrast	INF	Infer	SYM	Symbolize
CRE	Create	MEAS	Measure	TM	Think Metacognitively
DEC	Decide	PS	Problem Solve		
DEF	Define	P/A	Prove/Argue	TRANS	Transform
ELAB	Elaborate	PULL	Pull Apart		
EVAL	Evaluate	REDO	Redo		

Part III Measurement Topics

English Language Arts

Reading

1. Questioning, Inference, and Interpretation
2. Themes and Central Ideas
3. Story Elements
4. Connections
5. Word Impact and Use
6. Academic Vocabulary
7. Text Structures and Features
8. Point of View / Purpose
9. Visual/Auditory Media and Information Sources

10. Argument and Reasoning

11. Literary Comparisons and Source Material

12. Rhetorical Criticism

13. Fluency

Reading Foundations

14. Print Concepts

15. Phonological Awareness

16. Phonics and Word Analysis

Writing

17. Argumentative

18. Informative/Explanatory

19. Narrative

20. Task, Purpose, and Audience

21. Revise and Edit

22. Technology

23. Research

24. Access and Organize Information

Speaking and Listening

25. Collaborative Discussions

26. Evaluate Presented Information

27. Speech Writing

28. Presentation and Delivery

Language

29. Grammar

30. Sentences

31. Capitalization and Punctuation

32. Spelling

33. Language Conventions

34. Context Clues

35. Word Origins and Roots

36. Reference Materials

37. Word Relationships

Mathematics

Number and Quantity

38. Number Names

39. Counting

40. Compare Numbers

41. Place Value

42. Foundations of Fractions

43. Fractions

44. Adding and Subtracting Fractions

45. Multiplying and Dividing Fractions

46. Decimal Concepts

47. Ratios and Unit Rates

48. Rational and Irrational Numbers

49. Exponents and Roots

50. Quantities

51. Operations With Complex Numbers

52. Polynomial Identities and Equations

Operations and Algebra

53. Addition and Subtraction
54. Multiplication and Division
55. Properties of Operations
56. Expressions and Equations
57. Factors and Multiples
58. Patterns
59. Equations and Inequalities
60. Dependent and Independent Variables
61. Slope
62. Systems of Equations

63. Structure of Expressions
64. Equivalent Expressions
65. Arithmetic Operations on Polynomials
66. Zeroes and Factors of Polynomials
67. Polynomial Identities
68. Rational Expressions
69. Creating Equations
70. Reasoning to Solve Equations
71. Solving Quadratic Equations
72. Graphs of Equations and Inequalities

Functions

73. Functions
74. Interpret Functions
75. Graph Functions
76. Properties of Functions
77. Model Relationships
78. Building New Functions

79. Linear and Exponential Models
80. Interpret Linear and Exponential Functions
81. Trigonometric Functions
82. Periodic Phenomena
83. Trigonometric Identities

Geometry

84. Shapes
85. Compose and Decompose Shapes
86. Lines and Symmetry
87. Coordinate System
88. Area
89. Perimeter
90. Surface Area
91. Volume
92. Scale Drawings
93. Angles
94. Pythagorean Theorem
95. Congruence and Similarity

96. Transformations
97. Geometric Theorems
98. Geometric Constructions
99. Dilations
100. Theorems Involving Similarity
101. Trigonometric Ratios
102. Geometric Trigonometry
103. Circle Theorems
104. Arc Length and Sectors
105. Conic Sections
106. Geometric Modeling

Measurement, Data, Statistics, and Probability

107.   Measurement

108.   Represent and Interpret Data

109.   Time

110.   Money

111.   Data Distributions

112.   Random Sampling

113.   Probability

114.   Multivariable Data Distributions

115.   Linear Models

116.   Rules of Probability

Terms

A

abbreviation, 33

absolute error, 50

absolute phrase, 30

absolute value, 48, 53, 87

absolute value function, 72, 75

abstract, 29, 53

academic vocabulary, 6

acceleration, 107

accentuate, TRANS

accomplish, CRE

account (version of a story), 8, 11

accuracy, 17, 18, 24, 26

achieve, CRE

acknowledge, REF

acquire, SI

acronym, 31

action, 3, 6, 19

action verb, 29

action word, 29

active listening, 25

active voice, 29

actor, 9

act out, SYM

acute angle, 86, 93

adage, 5

adapt, TRANS

add, 53, 55

addend, 53

addition, 44, 53, 55

addition property of equality, 55

addition relationship, 6

addition rule, 116

addition table, 55

additive, 88

additive inverse, 53

address (street address), 31

adjacent angle, 93

adjectival clause, 30

adjectival phrase, 30

adjective, 29

adjust, TRANS

advance, EXEC

advanced search, 24

adventure, 11

adverb, 29

adverbial clause, 30

adverbial phrase, 30

advertisement, 9

advertising code, 9

advertising copy, 9

advocacy, 10

aesthetic impact, 5

affix, 16, 35

algebra, 62, 73, 76, 87

algebraic expression, 56

algebraic function, 73

algebraic step function, 73

algorithm, 53, 54

allegory, 4, 11

alliteration, 5

allusion, 5

almanac, 9, 11

alphabet, 14

alter, TRANS

alternate claim, 17

alternate interior angle, 93

a.m., 109

ambience, 5

ambiguity, 5

American literature, 11

American Psychological Association, 33

amount, 41

amplitude, 75, 82

analog clock, 109

analogous, 65

analogy, 4, 5, 37

analysis, 1, 18

analyze, PULL

ancient literature, 11

anecdotal scripting, 24

anecdote, 4

angle, 84, 86, 93

angle-angle (AA) criterion, 93, 95

angle bisector, 93

angle measure, 84, 93

angle measurement tool, 93

angle of depression, 93

angle-side-angle (ASA) postulate, 95

angle sum, 93

Anglo-Saxon affix, 35

Anglo-Saxon root, 35

animation, 9

annotated bibliography, 24

answer, EXP, 1

antecedent, 29

anticipate, HYP

antonym, 37

apology, 20

apostrophe, 31

appeal to authority, 10, 17, 26

appeal to emotion, 10, 17, 26

appeal to logic, 10, 17, 26

appendix, 7

applied problem, 101

apply, TRANS

appreciate, TM

approximate, HYP, 113

arc, 81, 104

archetype, 3

area, 85, 88, 89

area formula, 88

area model, 54, 88

area under curve, 75, 111, 113

argue, P/A

argument, 10, 12, 17, 26, 70

arithmetic sequence, 77, 79

arrange, ARR

array, 54

article (part of speech), 29

articulate, EXP

articulation, 28

artifact, 23

ask, SI, 1, 25, 26

assert, P/A

assess, EVAL

associate, C/C, 113

association, 5, 114

associative property, 53, 54, 55

assonance, 33

assumption, 70

asymptote of function, 73

atlas, 9

attack ad hominem, 10, 17

attend (pay attention to), TM, 17

attribute, 84, 88, 111

audible, 28

audience, 20, 21, 27, 33

audio element, 28

audio recording, 9, 28

audio version, 9

author, 8

authoritative, 24

author's bias, 8

author's purpose, 8

autobiographical narrative, 19

autobiography, 11

average, 74

axis/axes, 87

axis of symmetry, 86

B

back cover, 7

ballad, 7

bandwagon, 10

bar graph, 108

base, 91

base 10, 41, 46

base 60, 41, 46

base e, 41, 46

base-ten numeral, 41, 46

beaker, 107

beginning, 7

beginning consonant, 15

beginning sound, 15

belief system, 8

benchmark fraction, 44

benchmarking, 107

bias, 17

biased sample, 112

Bible, 11

biblical allusion, 5

bibliography, 24

billion, 38

billionth (ordinal number), 38

binary system, 41

biographical narrative, 19

biographical sketch, 11

biography, 11

bivariate data, 114

bivariate data transformation, 114

bivariate distribution, 114

bivariate measurement data, 114

blend (sounds together), 16

blog, 22

blueprint, 108

blurring of genres, 7

body language, 28

body (of a text), 7

bold print, 24

book, 7

boundary, 72

box and whisker plot, 111

box plot, 111

braces, 56

brackets, 56

brainstorm, 25

British literature, 11

broadcast, 9

broadcast advertising, 9

broaden, ELAB

build, CRE

business letter, 33

bylaw, 33

C

calculate, EXEC

calculation, 77

calculator, 53, 54

calendar, 109

camera angle, 9

camera focus, 9

camera shot, 9

capacity, 107

capitalization, 14, 31

caption, 7, 24

capture, SI

cardinal number, 39

carry (a figure onto another figure), 96

Cartesian coordinates, 87

cartoon, 9

cast of characters, 7

catalog, 9

categorical data, 114

categorical variable, 114

categorize, C/C

category, 4, 6, 24, 37, 108

causation, 115

cause/effect, 4, 7, 18, 37

CD/DVD, 22

celebrity endorsement, 9

censorship, 12

center, 93, 99, 103, 111

centimeter (cm), 107

central angle, 93

central idea, 2

central limit theorem, 113

central message, 2

central value, 111

certainty, 113

certainty of conclusions, 116

challenge, P/A, 3

chance, 113

chance event, 113

chance process, 113

chapter, 7

chapter title, 7

character, 3, 8, 19

character development, 3

characteristic, 113

characteristic of interest, 113

characterization, 3, 113

character trait, 3

chart, SYM, 9, 18

check, EVAL

checklist, 9

check understanding, 25

children's literature, 11

children's program, 9

choose, DEC

chord, 103

chronological order, 7, 19

chronology, 7

cinematographer, 9

circle, 84

circle formula, 88

circular arc, 93

circular function, 73

circumference, 88, 103

circumference formula, 88

circumlocution, 10, 17, 27

circumscribed circle of a triangle, 103

citation, 11, 22, 23

cite, REF, 1

claim, P/A, 10, 12, 17, 26, 27

clarification, 17, 18, 25, 26, 28

clarify, EXP

clarity of purpose, 8, 21

classification, 18

classify, C/C

clause, 30

climax, 3

clincher sentence, 3

clock, 109

closeness, 114

closing, 31

closing sentence, 17, 18, 19

cloud, 22

clue, 34

cluster, 108

clustering, 114

coefficient, 52, 56, 59, 63

cognate, 35

cohesion, 20

coin, 110

collaborate, COLL

collaboration, 22, 25

collective noun, 29

collect like terms, 56, 59

collegial discussion, 25

colon, 31

column, 54, 85

combination, 39

combine, ADD

combined model, 113

combine like terms, 56, 59

comedy, 7

comma, 31

command, 30

comment, 25

commercial, 9

commercialization, 12

commercial motive, 26

common denominator, 43, 44

common factor, 57

common fraction, 43

common noun, 29

common numerator, 43

common ratio, 47, 64

common scale factor, 99

communicate, EXP

commutative property, 53, 54, 55

comparative, 29

comparative inference, 111

compare, C/C, 40, 43

compare/contrast, 6, 37

comparison, 4, 7, 34, 40, 41, 43

comparison/contrast, 18

compass, 98

compile, SI

complement, 113

complementary angle, 93, 101

complementary event, 113

complete sentence, 28, 30

complete the square, 64, 71, 76, 105

complex fraction, 43

complex number, 51

complex number system, 51

complex sentence, 30

complex solution, 52, 71

component, 85

compose, CRE, 41, 44, 53, 85

compose a ten, 53

composite number, 57

composite shape, 85

composition, 21

composition structure, 21

compound-complex sentence, 30

compound event, 113

compound interest, 50

compound sentence, 30

compound word, 35

comprehend, SBP

computation strategy, 53, 54

compute, EXEC

computer algebra system, 68

computer-generated imagery (CGI), 9

concept, 12, 18

conceptualize, SYM

conceptual map, 24

concise, 27

conclude, INF

conclusion (ending), 3, 7, 17, 18, 19

conclusions (in an argument), 10, 23, 24, 25

concrete, 29, 53

conditional mood, 29

conditional probability, 113, 116

conditional relative frequency, 114

conduct, EXEC

cone, 84

confidence interval, 111

confirm, P/A, 34

conflict, 3

conflicting evidence, 8

conflicting information, 12

conflicting viewpoints, 8

conform, TRANS

confused, 25

congruence/congruent, 95

congruence criteria, 100

conjecture, HYP, 113

conjugate complex number, 51

conjunction, 29

conjunctive adverb, 29

connect, C/C

connection, 4, 25

connotation, 5

connotative meaning, 5

consensus, 25

conservation of area, 88

consider, HYP

consistency, 112

consonance, 33

consonant, 15, 16, 32

consonant blend, 15, 16

constant, 47, 48

constant difference, 47

constant of proportionality, 47, 104

constant percent rate, 79

constant rate, 79

constant term, 115

constraint, 59, 69

construct, CRE

consult, REF

consumer document, 9

content-area vocabulary, 6

context, 5, 6, 19, 33, 34

context clue, 34

contextualize, SBP

continuity, 52

continuous probability distribution, 113

contract, 11

contraction, 29

contradiction, 25

contrast, C/C, 7

contrasting expressions, 5

contribute, COLL

control group, 112

controlling idea, 12

convention, 33

conversation, 25

converse, 94

conversion, 54, 107

convert, TRANS, 43, 46, 48, 59

convey, EXP, 2, 8

coordinate, 87, 96

coordinate adjective, 29

coordinate axes, 69, 87

coordinate geometry, 87

coordinate plane, 47, 48, 58, 61, 72, 81, 87

coordinate system, 87

coordinating conjunction, 29

copyright law, 11

corner, 84

correlation, 115

correlation coefficient, 115

correlative conjunction, 29

correspondence, 16

corresponding angles, 93

corresponding sides, 93

corresponding terms, 58

cosine (cos θ), 83, 101

cosine function, 81, 83

cost, 49

count, 38, 39

count by 2s, 39

count by 5s, 39

count by 10s, 41, 53

count by 100s, 41

counter argument, 10, 17

counter example, 70

counterclaim, 17

counting procedure, 39

count on, 53

couplet, 7

court opinion, 9

create, CRE

creative, 25

credible/credibility, 17, 24, 26

credit, 11

criteria, 21

criteria for triangle congruence, 95

critical paths method, 107

critical standard, 12

criticism, 12

critique, EVAL

cross-reference, 11

cross-section, 84

cube, 84

cube number, 49

cube root, 49

cube root function, 75

cube root symbol, 49

cubic centimeter (cm^3), 91

cubic foot (ft^3), 91

cubic inch (in^3), 91

cubic meter (m^3), 91

cubic unit, 91, 107

cue, 28

cultural experience, 8

cultural expression, 5

cultural influence, 5

cultural nuance, 5

cultural theme, 2

culture, 11

cumulative impact, 5

current affairs, 9

cursive, 33

cursor, 22

curve, 72

curve fitting, 114

curve fitting median method, 114

custom, 8

cylinder, 84, 106

D

dangling modifier, 29

dash, 31

data, 24, 26, 108, 111, 112, 113, 114, 115

data cluster, 108

data collection method, 108

data display, 50

data display error, 111

data distribution, 111

data extreme, 111

data gap, 111

data-generating process, 112

data point, 114

data set, 111

data value, 108, 111, 114

date, 31

day, 109

deadline, 20

debate, 26

decay, 79

decibel, 107

decide, DEC

decimal, 41, 46, 54

decimal expansion, 48

decimal form, 46, 54

decimal notation, 46, 49

decimal point, 46, 110

decision, 3

declarative sentence, 30

decompose, PULL

decompose/decomposition, 41, 44, 53, 85

deconstruct, 12

decontextualize, PULL

decreasing function, 74

decreasing pattern, 58

deduce, INF

deductive reasoning, 70

deepen, ADD

defend, P/A

define, DEF

definition, 5, 6, 18, 34

degree, 93

degree of certainty, 5

delineate, DEF

delivery, 28

democratic, 25

demonstrate, SYM

demonstrative pronoun, 29

denominator, 43, 44, 45

denotation, 5

denotative meaning, 5

density, 106

dependent clause, 30

dependent event, 60

dependent variable, 60

depict, SYM

derivation, 35, 71

derivational suffix, 35

derive, ELAB

describe, EXP

description, 6, 19, 27

descriptive detail, 19, 27

descriptive language, 5

descriptive modeling, 50

design, TM

design problem, 106

desktop, 22

detail, 1, 2, 3, 7, 17, 18, 19, 21, 27

detect, SI

determine, DEF

determiner, 29

develop, CRE

development, 3

deviation, 111

diagnose, PULL

diagram, SYM, 9, 47

dialect, 33

dialogue, 3, 7, 8, 19

diameter, 103

diary, 11

dictation, 9

diction, 28

dictionary, 6, 32, 36

difference, 53

differentiate, C/C

digit, 41, 46, 53, 54

digital clock, 109

digital media, 28

digital source, 24

digital text, 9

digital tool, 22

digressive time, 7

dilation, 95, 96, 99

dime, 110

dimension, 94

direct address, 7

directed line segment, 87

direct function, 73

direction, 48, 87

directionality, 28

directions, 9, 18

direct measure, 107

direct quote, 7

directrix, 105

disagree, P/A

discern, DEF

discipline, 17, 18, 33

discourse, 25, 27

discrepancy, 26, 113

discrete probability, 113

discrete probability distribution, 113

discriminate, C/C

discussion, 25

discussion leader, 25

dispersion, 111

display, 22, 108, 111

distance, 107

distance formula, 87

distinction, 4

distinguish, C/C

distort, 26

distribution, 111

distributive property, 53, 54, 55

divergent, 25

diverse, 25

divide, 54, 55

divided quotation, 7

dividend, 54

divisibility, 54

division, 45, 54, 55

division property of equality, 55

divisor, 54

document, 12

documentary, 9

dollar bill, 110

domain, 73, 74

domain-specific vocabulary, 18

dot plot, 111

double negative, 33

double number line diagram, 47

draft, CRE, 21

drama, 2, 3, 9, 13

drama-documentary, 9

dramatic dialogue, 7

dramatic element, 3

dramatic irony, 8

drastic mood change, 8

dynamic, 22

dynamic geometric software, 98

E

edge length, 91

edit, TRANS, 21

editorial, 11

effect, 5, 8

efficient, 22, 24

eight, 38

eighteen, 38

eighteenth (ordinal number), 38

eighth (ordinal number), 38

eightieth (ordinal number), 38

eighty, 38

elaborate, ELAB

elaboration, 25

elapsed time, 107

electronic media, 9

electronic menu, 24

element, 73

eleven, 38

eleventh (ordinal number), 38

elicit, SI

ellipsis, 31

email, 22

emerge, 2

emotion, 6

emotional appeal, 5

emphasis, 5, 12, 27

emphasize, TRANS

empirical verification, 97

employ, EXEC

encounter, SI

encyclopedia, 36

end behavior, 75

ending, 7

ending consonant, 15

ending sound, 15

endpoint, 93

end punctuation, 14

engage, COLL

English, 33

English system of measurement, 107

enhance, ELAB

enlarging transformation, 96

enunciation, 28

epic, 11

episode, 3

equal, 40, 42, 43, 53, 54, 85

equality, 70, 95

equal probability, 113

equal ratios, 47

equation, 44, 45, 52, 53, 54, 56, 59, 64

equilateral triangle, 84

equivalent, 40, 43, 44, 47, 56, 59, 64, 91, 107

equivalent representation, 108

essay, 11

establish, DEF

estimate, HYP

estimation, 43, 44, 45, 56, 107

ethics, 20

etiquette, 25

etymology, 36

euphemism, 5

evaluate, EVAL

even number, 40, 54

event, 3, 4, 7, 8, 19, 27, 113

everyday language, 33

evidence, 1, 10, 12, 17, 24, 25, 26, 27

evoke, SI, 5

exaggerate, 26

exaggerated claim, 10

examine, PULL

example, 1, 4, 18, 27, 34

excerpt, 11

exchange of ideas, 27

exclamation mark, 31

exclamatory sentence, 30

execute, EXEC

exemplify, DEF

expand, ELAB

expanded form, 41, 46

expanded notation, 41, 46

expansion, 56

expected value, 113

experience, 19, 24, 27

experiment, HYP, 112

experimental design, 112

experimental probability, 112

explain, EXP

explanation, 18, 25

explicit, 1, 25

exploration, 23

explore, HYP

exponent, 49, 56

exponential function, 49, 64, 72, 75, 76, 79, 80

exponential model, 79

exponential notation, 49, 79

exposition, 7

express, EXP

expression, 13, 28, 48, 49, 56, 59, 63, 64, 68, 78

expressive writing, 20

extended quotation, 7

extension, 81

exterior angle, 93

external/internal conflict, 3

extraneous information, 26

extraneous solution, 70

extreme data point, 111

extreme value, 76

eye contact, 28

F

fable, 11

face, 84

facial expression, 28

facilitator, 25

fact, 17, 18, 24, 27

factor, 57

factorial, 73

factorial notation, 73

factoring/factorization, 66, 71, 75

factor pair, 57

fair, 17

fair chance, 113

fairy tale, 11

faithful representation, 9

fallacious reasoning, 10, 26

false, 53, 59

false causality, 10, 26

false statement, 10

fantasy, 11

faulty mode of persuasion, 10, 12, 26

FCC regulation, 9

feature article, 11

feature story, 11

feedback, 22

feeling, 5, 19

Fibonacci sequence, 73

fiction, 9, 11

field study, 23

fifteen, 38

fifteenth (ordinal number), 38

fifth (ordinal number), 38

fiftieth (ordinal number), 38

fifty, 38

figurative language, 5

figurative meaning, 5

figure, 18

figure of speech, 5

figure out, PS

film, 9

film director, 9

filmed production, 9

film producer, 9

film review, 9

filter (in photography), 9

final -e, 16

find out, SI

finite geometric series, 64

finite graph, 75

first, 38

first coordinate, 87

firsthand, 8

first name, 31

first person, 8

first quadrant, 87

first quartile, 111

fit, 111, 114

five, 38

fixed center, 99

fixed order, 53, 54

flashback, 7

flip, 96

flow of ideas, 24

focus, 21, 23, 105

folktale, 9, 11

foot (ft), 107

footnote, 7

force, 107

foreign word, 35

foreshadowing, 5

form, CRE

formal, 5, 25, 27

formal English, 28, 33

formal geometric construction, 98

formal language, 28

formal mathematical induction, 70

format, 9, 18

formula, 50, 56, 64, 69, 77, 88, 90, 91, 104

fortieth (ordinal number), 38

forty, 38

four, 38

four-digit number, 54

fourteen, 38

fourteenth (ordinal number), 38

fourth (fraction), 85

fourth (ordinal number), 38

fraction, 42, 43, 44, 45

fraction inversion, 43

fraction strip, 43

frequency, 82, 114

frequency distribution, 114

friendly audience, 20

friendly letter, 20

front cover, 7

front-end digit, 41

front-end estimation, 53

function, 64, 66, 72, 73, 74, 75, 76, 77, 96, 114

function composition, 73

function notation, 73

functional relationship, 74

future tense, 29

G

gain, 112

gain the floor, 25

gather, SI

gauge, MEAS

gender, 29

generalization, 32, 112

generalize, INF

generate, CRE

genre, 11

geographic name, 31

geometric, 84

geometric description, 96

geometric figure, 95, 96, 100

geometric function, 73

geometric method, 106

geometric pattern, 58

geometric problem, 87

geometric sequence, 77, 79

geometry software, 96

gerund, 29

gesture, 28

glittering generality, 10, 26

glossary, 24, 36

goal, 20

gram (g), 107

grammar, 29

graph, SYM, 9, 47, 58, 59, 60, 61, 62, 72, 73, 74, 78, 87

graphic, 18

graphic artist, 9

graphic novel, 9

graphic organizer, 24

graphic representation, 62

graphics, 9, 28

graph paper, 96

grapple, PULL

greater than (>), 40, 53

greatest common factor, 57

Greek affix, 35

Greek root, 35

greeting, 31

grid, 92

group/grouping, 40, 53, 54

growing pattern, 58

growth rate, 79

guess and check, 53

guest speaker, 9

guide words, 36

H

half, 85

half-circle, 85

half-hour, 109

half-plane, 72

hardware, 22

heading, 18, 24

headline, 7

height, 91, 107

helping verb, 29

hexagon, 84

hierarchic structure, 7

histogram, 111

historical event, 4

historical fiction, 11

historical novel, 11

historical significance, 11

historical theme, 2

holiday, 31

Homeric Greek literature, 11

homograph, 37

homonym, 37

homophone, 37

horizontal axis, 61, 87

horizontal line, 85

horizontal number line diagram, 48, 53

horizontal scale, 108

horizontal stretch, 96

host, 9

hostess, 9

hostile audience, 20

hour (hr), 107, 109

how, 1

how many, 39

humor, 5, 8

hundred, 38

hundreds, 41, 53

hundredth (ordinal number), 38

hundredths, 46

hyperbole, 5

hyperlink, 22, 24

hyphen, 31

hypothesize, HYP

I

icon, 24

identical, 85

identify, DEF

identity property of one, 55

identity property of zero, 55

idiom, 5

illustrate, SYM

illustration, 8, 9, 18

illustrator, 8, 9

image, 9, 28

imagery, 5

imaginary number, 51

imagine, SYM

impact, 5

imperative mood, 29

imperative sentence, 30

implication, 18

implicit, 1, 25

improbability, 113

improper fraction, 43

improve, ADD

inch (in), 107

incident, 3

incongruity, 26

inconsistency, 26

incorporate, ADD

increasing function, 74

increasing pattern, 58

indefinite pronoun, 29

indentation, 33

independence, 113

independent clause, 30

independent event, 60

independent trial, 60

independent variable, 60

index, 24, 36

indicative mood, 29

indirect measure, 107

inductive reasoning, 70

inequality, 40, 59, 64, 69

infer, INF

inference, 1, 112

inferred meaning, 6

infinitely many, 59

infinitive, 29, 35

inflection, 35, 75

influence, 4, 8

inform, EXP

informal, 5, 25, 111, 114

informal English, 33

informal language, 28

information, 4, 8, 9, 12, 17, 18, 22, 24, 25, 26, 108, 112

informational text, 13

informative/explanatory, 18

initial value, 74

initiate, CRE

input, 73, 96

input-output pair, 79

input/output table, 79

inquiry, 23

inscribe, 98, 103

inscribed angle, 93, 103

inscribed circle of a triangle, 103

inspection, 62, 68, 71

integer, 48, 49, 54, 65, 73

integrate, ADD

intensive pronoun, 29

interact, COLL

interaction, 4

interactive element, 28

intercept, 61, 75, 104, 114, 115

interior angle, 93

interior monologue, 7

interjection, 29

Internet, 22

interpret, DEF

interpretation, 12

interquartile range, 111

interrogative mood, 29

interrogative sentence, 30

intersection/intersecting, 72, 84, 86, 87, 93, 113

interval, 74, 79

interview, 9

intonation, 28

introduce, ADD

introduction, 3, 7, 17, 18, 19

inverse function, 78

investigate, PULL

investigation, 23

invitation, 20

irony, 5, 8

irrational number, 48, 49

irregular noun, 29

irregular polygon, 84

irregular spelling, 16, 32

irregular verb, 29

irrelevant, 10, 26

irrelevant information, 53, 54

isometry, 95

isosceles triangle, 84

issue, 25, 26

italics, 31

item/category relationship, 37

iterative sequence, 73

J

jargon, 26, 27

job application, 20

job interview, 20

joint relative frequency, 114

journal, 11

judge, EVAL

judgment, 2

justify, P/A

juxtaposition, 7

K

keyboarding, 22

keyword, 24

kilogram (kg), 107

kilometer (km), 107

knowledge base, 23

L

label, DEF, 69

language, 5, 33

large/larger, 40, 85, 107

last name, 31

Latin affix, 35

Latin root, 35

Law of Cosines, 102

law of large numbers, 116

law of probability, 116

Law of Sines, 102

layout, 28

learning log, 23

least common multiple, 57

lecture, 9

left to right, 14

legal reasoning, 10

legend, 11

length, 107

less, 40, 108

lesson, 2

less than (<), 40, 53

letter (of the alphabet), 14, 16, 32

letter (sent to someone), 31

level of accuracy, 50

library catalog, 23

life story, 11

lighting, 9

likelihood, 113

likely, 113

limit, 73

limitation, 17, 24, 50

limited point of view, 8

limited sample, 112

line, 61, 73, 86, 87, 98

linear, 73

linear arithmetic sequence, 58

linear association, 114

linear equation, 56, 59, 62

linear expression, 56

linear fit, 115

linear function, 72, 73, 74, 75, 79, 80, 114

linear geometric sequence, 58

linear inequality, 72

linear model, 114, 115

linear pattern, 58

linear relationship, 74

linear unit, 107

line equation, 72

line graph, 108

line (in a script), 3

line of reasoning, 27

line of symmetry, 86

line plot, 108

line segment, 86, 87, 96, 99

line segment congruence, 95

line segment similarity, 95

line symmetry, 86

link, C/C

linking phrase, 30

linking verb, 29

linking word, 29

list, ARR

listen, SI, 25

listener, 27

list of values, 111

liter (l), 107

literal language, 5

literal meaning, 5

literary allusion, 5

literary criticism, 12

literary device, 5

literary nonfiction, 13

literary significance, 12

literature, 13

literature review, 23

live production, 9

local/global behavior, 74

locate, DEF

log, 23

logarithm, 79

logarithmic function / log function, 72, 75

logical argument, 10, 12, 17, 26

logical fallacy, 10, 17, 26

logic ALL, 70

logical relationship, 6

logic AND, 70

logic IF/THEN, 70

logic/logical, 10, 12, 17, 18, 26, 27

logic NONE, 70

logic NOT, 70

logic OR, 70

logic SOME, 70

logo, 9

logographic system, 37

long division, 54, 68

longer, 107

long-run, 113

long vowel sound, 15, 16, 32

lowercase, 14

lyric poem, 7

M

magazine, 11

magnitude, 43, 48

main character, 3

main idea, 2, 26, 27

make ten, 53

manipulate, TRANS

manner of speech, 28

map, SYM, 9

margin, 7

marginal relative frequency, 114

margin of error, 112

marketing, 20

mass, 107

mass media, 9

match, C/C, 40

mathematical problem, 44, 45, 47, 53, 54, 59, 87, 88, 89, 90, 91, 93

mathematical theory, 70

maximum value, 64

mean, 107, 111

mean absolute deviation, 111

meaning, 5, 6, 34, 35, 37

meaning clue, 34

measure, MEAS

measurement, 88, 107

measurement scale, 107

measurement unit, 111

measure of center/central tendency, 107, 111

measuring cup, 107

measuring tape, 107

mechanics (language), 33

media-generated image, 9

media/medium, 9, 26

median, 107, 111

medieval literature, 11

memoir, 11

memorandum, 7

memory aid, 28

mental image, 5

mental math, 53, 54

message, 20

metaphor, 5

meter (m), 107

meter (of a poem), 7

meter stick, 107

methodology, 23

metric system, 107

microfiche, 23

middle vowel sound, 15

midline, 75, 82

midpoint, 86

mile (mi), 107

milliliter (ml), 107

millimeter (mm), 107

million, 38

millionth (ordinal number), 38

minimize cost, 106

minimum, 75

minimum/maximum of function, 74

minimum value, 64

minor character, 3

minuend, 53

minute (min), 107, 109

miscue, 16

mixed number, 44, 45

modal auxiliary, 29

mode, 107, 111

model, SYM, 53, 69, 74, 77, 79, 82, 88, 106, 112, 113, 114, 116

model fit, 114

modeling situation, 106

Modern Language Association, 33

modern literature, 11

modifier, 29

modify, TRANS

modulation, 28

money, 107

monitor, TM

monomial, 52

Monte Carlo simulation, 112

mood, 5

moral, 2

more, 40, 108

motivation, 3

motive, 26

movie, 9

multidigit decimal, 46

multidigit number, 41, 46, 53, 54

multimeaning word, 37

multimedia, 9, 18, 28

multimedia presentation, 9

multiple, 45, 54, 57

multiple drafts, 21

multiple of ten, 53, 54

multiple samples, 112

multiple sources, 23

multiple strategies for proofs, 97

multiplication, 45, 54, 55

multiplication property of equality, 55

multiplication table, 55

multiplicative inverse, 54

multiply, 54, 55, 88

multistep problem, 47, 53, 54, 59, 93

multisyllable, 16

music, 9

musical, 9

mutually exclusive events, 113

mystery, 11

myth, 11

mythological allusion, 5

mythology, 11

N

name, DEF

narrate, EXP

narration, 8

narrative, 19

narrator, 8, 19

native culture, 8

native speaker, 28

natural log, 79

natural number, 41

nature of deduction, 70

navigate, EXEC

negative, 48, 49, 53, 59, 78

negative association, 114

negative exponent, 49

negotiate, 20

neoclassic literature, 11

net, 90

network, 77

news, 9

news broadcast, 9

news bulletin, 9

newspaper, 11

nickel, 110

nine, 38

nineteen, 38

nineteenth (ordinal number), 38

ninetieth (ordinal number), 38

ninety, 38

ninth (ordinal number), 38

nominal data, 114

nondecimal numeration system, 41

nonfiction, 9, 11

nonlinear association, 114

nonlinear equation, 56

nonlinear function, 73, 74

nonliteral language, 5

nonliteral meaning, 5

nonrestrictive clause, 30

non-right triangle, 102

nonroutine problem, 70

nonstandard unit, 107

nonverbal cue, 28

non-zero, 45, 54

norm, 17, 18

normal curve, 111

normal distribution, 111

note, SI

notes, 24

notice, SI

noun, 29

noun clause/phrase, 29

novel, 11

nuance, 5

number, 29, 38, 39, 40, 41, 53, 54

number line, 42, 43, 48, 53, 87, 107, 111

number name, 38, 39, 41

number order, 39

number sentence, 53

number subsystems, 51

number system, 41, 51

number theory, 51

number word, 37

numeral, 38

numerator, 43, 44, 45

numerical adjective, 29

numerical expression, 49, 56

numerical value, 53

O

object, 30

objective case, 29

objective summary, 2

objective tone, 17, 18

objective view, 8

object pronoun, 29

observation, 18, 19, 25, 111

observational study, 112

observe, SI

observed frequency, 113

obtuse angle, 86, 93

odd number, 40, 54

odds, 113

ode, 7

omniscient point of view, 8

one, 38

one-degree angle, 93

one-digit number, 41, 53, 54

one-on-one discussion, 25

ones, 38, 41, 53

one-step problem, 53

onomatopoeia, 5

opening monologue, 7

open sentence, 53, 54, 56

open shape, 84

operation, 49, 51, 53, 54, 55, 56, 59, 77

opinion, 17

opposing claim, 17

opposite, 37

oral presentation, 9, 28

oral report, 28

oral tradition, 9

ordered pair, 58, 62, 73, 87

ordered triple, 62

order of events, 3, 19

order of operations, 55, 56

ordinal number, 39

organization, 17, 18, 19, 27

organize, ARR

orient, SBP

orientation, 84

origin, 47, 61, 87

ounce (oz), 107, 107

outcome, 19, 113, 116

outlier, 111, 114

outline, 24

output, 73, 96

overcome, PS

overestimation, 107

overgeneralization, 10, 26

overreliance, 24

overstatement, 10, 26

overview, 7

oxymoron, 5

P

pace, 28

pacing, 19

packaging, 9

page, 14

page format, 7

pair, 39, 58

pamphlet, 9

parable, 5

parabola, 105

paradox, 5

paragraph, 7, 18

parallel box plot, 111

parallel figures, 86

parallel lines, 84, 86, 87, 96, 99

parallelogram, 84, 96

parallel plots, 7

parallel structure, 29

parameter, 80, 112

parameter estimate, 80, 112

parametric equation, 80, 112

paraphrase, TRANS, 24, 25, 26

parentheses, 31, 56

parody, 8

part, 42, 43, 44, 85, 88

participate, COLL, 25

participial phrase, 30

participle, 29

partition, PULL, 42, 43, 54, 85

part of speech, 35, 36

part/whole relationship, 37

passage, 7

passive voice, 29

password, 22

pastoral theme, 2

past tense, 29

pattern, 16, 46, 55, 58, 58, 111, 114

pattern addition, 58

pattern division, 58

pattern extension, 58

pattern multiplication, 58

pattern of association, 114

pattern recognition, 58

pattern subtraction, 58

peer, 21, 25

peer-response group, 21

peer review, 21

penny, 110

pen pal, 20

pentagon, 84

percent, 47

percent rate of change, 115

percents above 100, 47

percents below 1, 47

perfect cube, 49

perfect square, 49

perfect tense, 29

performance review, 20

perimeter, 89

perimeter formula, 89

period, 75

periodical, 11

periodic function, 73

periodic phenomena, 82

period (punctuation mark), 31

permutation, 39

perpendicular bisector, 86

perpendicular lines, 84, 86, 87, 96

persevere, TM

person, 29

persona, 8

personal letter, 20

personal narrative, 19

personal opinion, 2

personal pronoun, 29

personal space, 25

personification, 5

perspective, 8, 25, 27, 92

persuade, P/A

persuasion/persuasive, 25

phase shift, 83

philosophical assumption, 10, 26

photograph, 9

photographer, 9

phrase, 5, 6, 30

phrase grouping, 30

physical constraint, 106

physical description, 3

physical gesture, 28

pi (π), 88, 103

pictorial representation, 108

picture book, 7

picture dictionary, 36

picture graph, 108

piecewise-defined function, 75

pie chart, 108

place, 41

place holder, 41, 56

place value, 41, 46, 53, 54

plagiarism, 23, 24

plagiarize, REF

plan, TM, 20

planar cross section, 84

plane, 84, 87, 96, 99

plane figure, 88

plane section, 84

play, 9, 11

plot, 3, 7, 19, 72, 111, 114

plot development, 3

plural, 29

p.m., 109

poem, 5, 11

poetry, 13

point, 47, 86, 87, 93, 98

point (in an argument), 10, 12, 26

point of agreement, 25

point of disagreement, 25

point of emphasis, 26

point of intersection, 62

point of tangency, 83

point of view, 8, 17, 19, 25

poise, 28

polar coordinates, 87

policy statement, 20

polite form, 33

political cartoonist, 9

political motive, 26

political speech, 9

polygon, 84

polynomial, 52, 65, 66, 67, 68

polynomial addition, 65

polynomial division, 65

polynomial function, 72, 75, 79

polynomial identity, 52, 67

polynomial multiplication, 65

polynomial solution by bisection, 66

polynomial solution by sign change, 66

polynomial solution successive approximation, 66

polynomial subtraction, 65

population, 111, 112

population mean, 112

population parameter, 112

population percentage, 111

population proportion, 112

portrayal, 9

pose, HYP

position, 8, 25

positive, 48, 49, 53, 59, 78

positive association, 114

possessive case, 29

possible value, 59

postulate, 97

posture, 28

pound (lb), 107

power of 10, 46, 49

precise, 33

precision, 107

predicate, 29

predict, HYP

prediction, 34, 70, 112, 113

preface, 7

prefix, 32, 35

premise, 10, 26

preparation, 25

prepare, TM

preposition, 29

prepositional phrase, 29

present, EXP

presentation, 9, 12, 25, 28

present tense, 29

preview, 18

prewriting, 20

primary source, 11, 23

prime factorization, 57

prime number, 57

principle, 10

print, 14

print source, 24

prior knowledge, 20

prism, 84

private audience, 20

probability, 113

probability distribution, 113

probability model, 113

probe, PULL

problem, 19, 23

problem context, 56

problem formulation, 56

problem/solution, 7

problem solve, PS

problem space, 56

procedure, 4

produce, CRE

product, 54

production, 9

production cost, 9

product name, 31

profit, 49

programming, 22

progressive tense, 29

projection, 28, 115

promote, P/A

pronominal, 29

pronoun, 29

pronoun-antecedent agreement, 29

pronounce, 15

pronunciation, 28, 36

proof, 94

proof paragraph, 97

proofread, 21

prop, 28

proper adjective, 29

proper noun, 29

properties of equality, 59

properties of inequality, 59

properties of operations, 44, 45

properties of similarity transformations, 95

property, 49, 53, 54, 55, 64, 73, 76, 84, 96, 101, 106

proportion, 47, 95, 96

proportional gain, 47

proportional relationship, 47, 61

proposition of fact speech, 27

proposition of policy speech, 27

proposition of problem speech, 27

proposition of value speech, 27

prose, 11, 13

protractor, 84, 93

prove, P/A, 97, 100, 102, 103

proverb, 5

provoke, 3

public audience, 20

publication date, 11

public opinion trend, 23

publish, CRE, 22

pull-down menu, 22

pun, 5

punctuation, 31

purpose, 8, 13, 20, 21

put together, 53

pyramid, 84

Pythagorean identity, 83

Pythagorean theorem, 94, 101, 105

Q

quadrant, 83, 87

quadratic equation, 52, 62, 71

quadratic expression, 64

quadratic formula, 71

quadratic function, 75, 76

quadrilateral, 84

qualify, P/A

qualitative, 74

quantify, MEAS

quantitative, 74, 111, 114

quantitative format, 9

quantity, 42, 43, 47, 48, 50, 60, 107

quantity of interest, 69

quarter-circle, 85

quarter (coin), 110

quarter (one-fourth), 85

quartile, 111

quartile deviation, 111

quest, 11

question, SI, 1, 21, 23, 25, 26, 30

question mark, 31

questionnaire, 23

quiz show, 9

quotation, 18

quotation marks, 31

quote, 1, 24

quotient, 45, 54

R

radian measure, 81, 104

radical, 49

radical expression, 70

radical function, 73

radio program, 9

radius, 103, 104, 105

random, 112

randomization, 112

randomized experiment, 112

random number, 40

random process, 113

random sample, 111, 112

random sampling technique, 112

random variable, 60, 112

range (of a function), 73

range (of numbers or data), 111

rate, 47

rate of change, 47, 74, 115

rate (speed), 13

rating, 9

ratio, 47, 87, 99, 106

rational approximation, 48

rational equation, 70

rational expression, 68

rational function, 72

rational number, 48, 49, 53, 54, 56, 59, 68

rational number system, 48

ray, 86, 93

r-controlled, 32

reaction shot, 9

reader, 8, 19

Readers' Guide to Periodical Literature, 36

reading strategy, 13

real number, 49, 51, 52, 71, 81

real number line, 111

real number system, 51

real-world context, 48, 53, 54

real-world function, 73

real-world problem, 44, 45, 47, 48, 56, 59, 60, 87, 88, 89, 90, 91, 93

rearrange, TRANS

reason, INF, 1, 10, 17, 26

reasonable, 44, 45, 53, 54, 59

reasoning, 10, 17, 26, 27

recall, DEF

reciprocal, 43, 54

recitation, 28

recognize, DEF

record, CRE

recount, EXP

rectangle, 84

rectangle formula, 88

rectangular array, 54, 88

rectangular coordinates, 87

rectangular prism, 84, 91

rectilinear figure, 84

recurrence equation, 77

recurrence relationship, 77

recurring theme, 2

recursive equation, 77

recursive process/sequence, 73, 77

red herring, 3

redo, REDO

redraft, 21

reduced form, 43

redundancy, 21

refer, REF

reference, REF

reference set, 41

references / reference materials, 36

refine, TRANS

reflect, TM

reflection, 19, 25, 86, 87, 95, 96

reflection transformation, 96

reflexive pronoun, 29

reflexive property of equality, 59

refocus, 23

register, 33

regression coefficient, 61

regression line, 61

relate, C/C

relation, 51

relationship, 4, 37, 40, 42, 43, 47, 53, 54, 58, 60, 67, 77

relative adverb, 29

relative clause, 30

relative distance, 107

relative error, 50

relative frequency, 114

relatively prime, 57

relative magnitude, 40

relative pronoun, 29

relative size, 40

relevant, 10, 24, 27

reliability, 112

religious literature, 11

remainder, 54

remainder theorem, 66

remark, 25

repeat, REDO

repeating decimal, 48, 54

repeating digit, 48

repeating pattern, 58

replace, TRANS

report, EXP, 23, 27

represent, SYM, 41, 42, 43, 53, 54, 56, 108

representativeness of sample, 112

representative sample, 112

reproduction, 92

request, SI

reread, REDO

research, SI, 23

research paper, 23

research project, 23

research question, 23

residual, 114

resize, 45

resolution, 3, 7, 19

resolve, PS

resource material, 23

respond, EXP

response, 19, 25

restatement, 34

restrictive clause, 30

resultant force, 102

résumé, 20

retell, EXP, 2

revenue, 49

review, 25

revise, TRANS, 21

revisit, REDO

rewrite, TRANS, 21

rhetoric, 8, 26

rhetorical device, 12

rhetorical feature, 12

rhetorical question, 12

rhombus, 84

rhyme, 5, 7, 15

rhyming dictionary, 36

rhythm, 5, 7

Richter scale, 107

right angle, 86, 93

right triangle, 84, 94, 101, 102

right triangle geometry, 98

rigid motion, 95, 96

role, 3, 8, 25

role playing, 8

Roman numeral, 38

romantic period literature, 11

root, 16, 32, 35, 49

rotation, 84, 95, 96

rotation symmetry, 86

rounding, 41

row, 54, 85

rule, 54, 58, 73

ruler, 107

rules of conversation, 25

run-on sentence, 30

S

sales technique, 20

salutation, 31

sample, 112

sample selection techniques, 112

sample space, 113

sample statistic, 112

sample survey, 112

sampling distribution, 112

sampling error, 112

sarcasm, 8

satire, 8

scalar, 50

scale, 50, 69, 92, 108

scaled graph, 108

scale drawing, 92

scale factor, 99

scale map, 92

scale transformation, 96

scan, 24

scatter plot, 114

scene, 7

science fiction, 11

scientific concept/idea, 4

scientific notation, 49

script, 9

scriptwriter, 9

search, SI, 23

search term, 24

search tool, 24

secondary source, 11, 23

second coordinate, 87

secondhand, 8

second (ordinal number), 38

second person, 8

second (sec), 107, 109

section, 7, 18

sector, 104

secure site, 22

seek, SI

segment, 15

select, DEC

self-correct, TM, 34

self-generated question, 23

semicolon, 31

sense of place, 5

sense of time, 5

sensory detail/image, 19

sensory language, 5, 19

sentence, 7, 14, 30, 31

sentence combining, 30

sentence fragment, 30

sentence patterns, 33

sentence structure, 30

sequence, 59, 73, 95

sequence of transformations, 96

sequence / sequential order, 3, 4, 7, 19

series, 4, 7, 11, 58

series circuit, 107

set, 59, 72, 73, 111

set design, 9

set of outcomes, 113

setting, 3, 7, 19

seven, 38

seventeen, 38

seventeenth (ordinal number), 38

seventh (ordinal number), 38

seventieth (ordinal number), 38

seventy, 38

shade(s) of meaning, 5

Shakespeare, 11

shape, TRANS, 84, 85

shape transformation, 96

share, COLL, 42, 43, 54, 85

shift, TRANS

shorter, 107

short story, 11

short vowel sound, 15, 16, 32

shrinking pattern, 58

shrinking transformation, 96

side, 84

side-angle-side (SAS) postulate, 95

sidebar, 24

side length, 88, 89

side ratio, 101

side-side-side (SSS) postulate, 95

sight word, 16

sigma notation, 58

sign, 9

signal word/phrase/clause/sentence, 6

signature, 31

signed number, 48, 54, 87

significant difference, 112

significant digits, 46

significant/significance, 17, 18

similar, 61, 95, 103

similarity, 8, 12, 93, 95, 101, 104

similarity criteria, 100

similarity transformation, 95

simile, 5

simple equation, 70

simple expression, 56

simple fraction, 43

simple function, 78

simple geometric theorem, 87

simpler form, 59

simple sentence, 30

simplification, 59

simplify, TRANS

simulated samples, 112

simulation, 112, 113

simulation model, 112

sine function, 83

sine (sin θ), 83, 101

singular, 29

sinusoidal function, 73

sitcom, 9

situation, 28

six, 38

sixteen, 38

sixteenth (ordinal number), 38

sixth (ordinal number), 38

sixtieth (ordinal number), 38

sixty, 38

size, 42, 43, 44, 84, 107

sketch, 74

skim, 24

skip-count, 41

skit, 9

slang, 5

slanted material, 26

slice, 84

slide transformation, 96

slope, 61, 114, 115

slope criteria, 87

slope intercept formula, 61, 87

small-group discussion, 25

small/smaller, 40, 85, 107

small talk, 25

soap opera, 9

social motive, 26

sociocultural context, 34

software, 22

software update, 22

solid, 84

soliloquy, 7

solution, 49, 50, 56, 59, 62, 69, 70, 71, 72, 79

solution algorithm, 70

solution probabilities, 70

solution set, 59, 72

solve, PS

somber lighting, 9

song, 5

sonnet, 7

sort, ARR, 108

sound, 15, 16, 32

sound effect, 9

sound system, 28

source, 9, 10, 11, 17, 22, 23, 24, 26, 113

source list, 24

space, 14, 84

spatial relationship, 6

speaker, 8, 25, 26

special effect, 9

special interests, 20

specialized language, 6

special quadrilateral, 84

specify, P/A

speech, 9, 27, 28

speech action, 28

speech pattern, 28

speed, 107

speed reading, 13

speed writing, 13

spelling pattern, 32

spell/spelling, 32

sphere, 84

spoken text, 9

spread, 111

spreadsheet, 111

spurious correlation, 115

square, 84

square centimeter (cm²), 88

square foot (ft²), 88

square inch (in²), 88

square meter (m²), 88

square number, 49

square root, 49

square root function, 75

square root symbol, 49

square unit, 88, 90, 107

stage direction, 7

staged version, 9

stance, 26

standard algorithm, 53, 54

standard citation format, 24

standard deviation, 111

standard English, 33

standard function type, 77

standard unit, 107

standard usage, 36

stanza, 7

state, EXP

statement, 17, 30

statement of inequality, 48

statement of order, 48

state of being, 6

state of mind, 5

statistical question, 111

statistical regression, 115

statistics, 111, 112

status indicator, 22

stay on topic, 20

stem and leaf plot, 111

step function, 75

stereotype, 8

stimulate, CRE

story, 2, 3, 5, 11, 13, 27

storybook, 7

story element, 3

story map, 19

straightedge, 98

strategy, 53, 54, 56

strategy efficiency, 70

strategy generation technique, 70

stream of consciousness, 7

strengthen, TRANS, 21

stress, 33

strict inequality, 72

striking deviation, 111

strip diagram, 47

structural analysis, 12

structure, 7, 63, 106

study, SI, 26

style, 5, 20, 27, 33

style manual, 33

style sheet format, 33

subheading, 24

subject, 12, 30

subjective case, 29

subjective view, 8

subject pronoun, 29

subject-verb agreement, 29

subjunctive mood, 29

subliminal message, 7

subordinate character, 3

subordinating conjunction, 29

subplot, 7

subset, 73, 113

substantive, 17

substitute, TRANS

substitution property of equality, 59

subtend, 81

subtract, 53, 55

subtraction, 44, 53, 55

subtraction property of equality, 55

subvocalize, 28

successive approximations, 72

suffix, 32, 35

suggestion, 21

sum, 44, 53

summarize, EXP, 2

summary, 2

summary sentence, 7

summary statistic, 111

superlative, 29

supernatural tale, 11

supplementary angle, 93

support, P/A, 1, 10, 17, 26, 27

supporting evidence, 27

supporting idea/detail, 2

surface area, 90

surmount, PS

surprise, 7

survey, 112

suspense, 3, 8, 19

syllabication, 32

syllabic system, 32

syllable, 15, 16

syllable pattern, 32

symbol, 14, 41, 43, 46, 53, 54, 110

symbolic representation, 74, 75

symbolism, 5, 7

symbolize, SYM

symmetric property of equality, 59

symmetry, 76, 86

synonym, 37

syntax, 30, 33

synthesis, 25

synthesize, EXP

synthetic geometry, 98

system, 65

system of equations, 62, 69

system of inequalities, 69, 72

system of linear equations, 62

system of linear inequalities, 72

T

table, 18, 47, 60, 73, 74, 76, 79, 111

table of contents, 24

table of values, 72, 74

table representation of functions, 108

table representation of probability, 108

tabloid newspaper, 11

tag question, 31

tailor, TRANS

take apart, 53

take from, 53

take turns, 25

talk, 25, 28

talk show, 9

tallies, 39, 108

tall tale, 11

tangent function, 83

tangent (tan θ), 83

tape diagram, 47

target audience, 20

task, 20

technical directions, 18

technical language, 18

technical meaning, 6

technical procedure, 4

technology, 22

television program, 9

temperature, 107

tempo, 7

temporal change, 7

temporal relationship, 6

ten, 38

tens, 38, 41, 53

tension, 7

tenth (ordinal number), 38

tenths, 46

term, 56, 63

terminating decimal, 54

tessellation, 58, 98

test, HYP

tetrahedron, 84

text, 1, 2, 5, 7, 8, 9, 13, 24, 34

textbook, 11

text boundary, 22

textual clue, 34

textual element/feature, 28

textual evidence, 1

thank-you letter, 20

theater, 9

theme, 2, 27

theme music, 9

theorem, 97, 100

theorem direct proof, 97

theorem indirect proof, 97

theoretical probability, 113

thermometer, 107

thesaurus, 36

thesis, 17, 23

thesis statement, 17, 23

third (fraction), 85

third (ordinal number), 38

third person, 8

third quartile, 111

thirteen, 38

thirteenth (ordinal number), 38

thirtieth (ordinal number), 38

thirty, 38

thousand, 38

thousandth (ordinal number), 38

thousandths, 46

three, 38

three-digit number, 41, 53, 54

three-dimensional, 84, 85, 90, 91, 98

time, 109

time frame, 19

time interval, 107, 109

time lapse, 9

time line, 9

time zone, 109

title, 31

title page, 7

tone, 5, 20, 27, 33

topic, 6, 8, 12, 17, 18, 21, 23, 25, 27

topic sentence, 18

top to bottom, 14

total, 54, 108

trace, REF

tracing paper, 96

traditional literature, 11

tragedy, 7

transform, TRANS

transformation, 96

transition, 21

transitive property of equality, 59

transitivity principle for indirect measurement, 107

translate, TRANS

translation, 95, 96

transversal, 93

trapezoid, 84

trapezoid formula, 88

travel, 87

traverse, 81

treatment, 112

treatment group, 112

tree diagram, 112, 113

trend, 114

trial and error, 70

triangle, 84

triangle formula, 88

trickster tale, 11

trigonometric function, 75, 81, 82

trigonometric ratio, 101

trigonometric relation, 101

trillion, 38

trillionth (ordinal number), 38

true, 53, 59

truncation, 107

truth in advertising, 5

truth table proof, 97

try a new approach, 21

twelfth (ordinal number), 38

twelve, 38

twentieth (ordinal number), 38

twenty, 38

two, 38

two-column table, 107

two-digit number, 41, 53, 54

two-dimensional, 84, 85, 88, 90, 98

two-step problem, 53, 56

two-way frequency table, 113, 114

typeface, 28

typing, 22

typographic grid system, 106

U

uncertain outcome, 113

undefined notion, 96

underestimation, 107

underline, 31

understand, SBP

understatement, 8

uniform probability model, 116

union, 113

unit, 53, 85, 88, 91, 107, 108

unit analysis, 107

unit circle, 81

unit cube, 91

unit fraction, 45, 85

unit interval, 79

unit rate, 47, 61

univariate data, 111

univariate distribution, 111

universal theme, 2

unknown, 53, 54, 56

unknown-factor problem, 54

unknown-number problem, 55

unlike denominators, 44

unlikely, 113

update, TRANS

uppercase, 14

upper/lower bounds, 107

URL (uniform resource locator), 22

usage, 29

U.S. customary system, 107

username, 22

V

valid, 10, 17, 27, 112

validity, 112

value, 41, 48, 49, 56, 59, 74, 78, 111

variability, 111

variable, 56, 59, 60, 62, 69, 70, 72, 73, 111, 114

variable change, 111

variance, 116

variation, 112

vector, 50

velocity, 107

Venn diagram, 108

verb, 29

verbal cue, 25

verbal irony, 5

verb phrase, 30

verb tense, 29

verification, 70

verify, P/A

vernacular, 33

verse, 7

version, 11

vertex edge graph, 84

vertex/vertices, 87, 84

vertical angle, 93

vertical axis, 61, 87

vertical number line diagram, 48, 53

viable argument, 70

video recording, 9

video version, 9

viewer perception, 20

viewpoint, 8

villain, 3

visual aid, 28

visual display, 28

visual element, 28

visual format, 9

visual fraction model, 43, 44, 45

visualize, SYM

visual model, 46

visual overlap, 111

visual text, 9

vivid, 19

vocabulary, 6

voice, 8

voice inflection, 28

voice level, 28

volume, 28, 91, 107

volume formula, 91

vote, 25

vowel, 15, 16

vowel sound, 16

vowel team/combination, 16

W

warranty, 11

web page, 9

website, 22

week, 109

weight, 107

weighted average, 113

well-reasoned, 25

what, 1

when, 1

where, 1

who, 1

whole, 42, 43, 44, 46, 85

whole number, 41, 43, 49, 53, 54, 57

why, 1

width, 107

word, 5, 6, 14, 15, 16, 32, 34, 35, 37

word borrowing, 35

word change pattern, 35

word choice, 5

word family, 32

word function, 34

wordiness, 21

word origin, 35

word part, 32

word position, 34

word problem, 44, 45, 53, 54, 56

word processing, 22

work backward, 70

world literature, 11

writing product, 22

written exchange, 7

written representation, 108

X

x-axis, 87

x-coordinate, 87

Y

yardstick, 107

y-axis, 87

y-coordinate, 87

year, 109

Z

zero, 38

zero of a function, 64, 75, 76

zero of a polynomial, 66

References and Resources

Adams, M. J. (1990). *Beginning to read: Thinking and learning about print*. Cambridge, MA: MIT Press.

Alexander, P. A., Kulikowich, J. M., & Schulze, S. K. (1994). How subject-matter knowledge affects recall and interest. *American Educational Research Journal, 31*(2), 313–337.

Anderson, R. C., & Nagy, W. E. (1992). The vocabulary conundrum. *American Educator, 16*(4), 14–18, 44–47.

Anderson, R. C., & Nagy, W. E. (1993). *The vocabulary conundrum* (Tech. Rep. No. 570). Champaign: University of Illinois, Center for the Study of Reading.

Anderson, R. C., & Pearson, P. D. (1984). A scheme-theoretic view of basic processes in reading. In P. D. Pearson (Ed.), *Handbook of reading research* (pp. 255–292). New York: Longman.

Angle. (2005). In *Merriam-Webster's collegiate dictionary* (11th ed., p. 48). Springfield, MA: Merriam-Webster.

Baumann, J. F., & Kame'enui, E. J. (1991). Research on vocabulary instruction: Ode to Voltaire. In J. Flood, J. M. Jensen, D. Lapp, & J. R. Squire (Eds.), *Handbook of research on teaching the English language arts* (pp. 604–632). New York: Macmillan.

Beck, I. L., & McKeown, M. G. (1991). Conditions of vocabulary acquisition. In R. Barr, M. L. Kamil, P. Mosenthal, & P. D. Pearson (Eds.), *Handbook of reading research* (Vol. 2, pp. 789–814). New York: Longman.

Beck, I. L., & McKeown, M. G. (2001). Text talk: Capturing the benefits of read-aloud experiences for young children. *Reading Teacher, 55*(1), 10–20.

Beck, I. L., & McKeown, M. G. (2007). Increasing young low-income children's oral vocabulary repertoires through rich and focused instruction. *The Elementary School Journal, 107*(3), 251–273.

Beck, I. L., McKeown, M. G., & Kucan, L. (2002). *Bringing words to life: Robust vocabulary instruction*. New York: Guilford Press.

Beck, I. L., McKeown, M. G., & Kucan, L. (2008). *Creating robust vocabulary: Frequently asked questions and extended examples*. New York: Guilford Press.

Beck, I. L., Perfetti, C. A., & McKeown, M. G. (1982). Effects of long-term vocabulary instruction on lexical access and reading comprehension. *Journal of Educational Psychology, 74*(4), 506–521.

Becker, W. C. (1977). Teaching reading and language to the disadvantaged: What we have learned from field research. *Harvard Educational Review, 47*(4), 518–543, 577.

Bellanca, J. A., Fogarty, R. J., & Pete, B. M. (2012). *How to teach thinking skills within the Common Core: 7 key student proficiencies of the new national standards*. Bloomington, IN: Solution Tree Press.

Berlin, B., & Kay, P. (1999). *Basic color terms: Their universality and evolution*. Stanford, CA: Center for the Study of Language and Information Publications.

Biemiller, A. (1999). *Language and reading success*. Newton Upper Falls, MA: Brookline Books.

Biemiller, A. (2001). Teaching vocabulary: Early, direct, and sequential. *American Educator, 25*(1), 24–28, 47.

Biemiller, A. (2005). Size and sequence in vocabulary development: Implications for choosing words for primary grade vocabulary instruction. In E. H. Hiebert & M. L. Kamil (Eds.), *Teaching and learning vocabulary: Bringing research to practice* (pp. 227–242). Mahwah, NJ: Erlbaum.

Biemiller, A. (2012). Teaching vocabulary in the primary grades: Vocabulary instruction needed. In E. J. Kame'enui & J. F. Baumann (Eds.), *Vocabulary instruction: Research to practice* (2nd ed., pp. 34–50). New York: Guilford Press.

Biemiller, A., & Slonim, N. (2001). Estimating root word vocabulary growth in normative and advantaged populations: Evidence for a common sequence of vocabulary acquisition. *Journal of Educational Psychology, 93*(3), 498–520.

Blachowicz, C. L. Z., & Fisher, P. (2008). Attentional vocabulary instruction: Read-alouds, word play, and other motivating strategies for fostering informal word learning. In A. E. Farstrup & S. J. Samuels (Eds.), *What research has to say about vocabulary instruction* (pp. 32–55). Newark, DE: International Reading Association.

Bloom, B. S. (1976). *Human characteristics and school learning.* New York: McGraw-Hill.

Bos, C. S., & Anders, P. L. (1990). Toward an interactive model: Teaching text-based concepts to learning disabled students. In H. L. Swanson & B. Keogh (Eds.), *Learning disabilities: Theoretical and research issues* (pp. 247–262). Hillsdale, NJ: Erlbaum.

Bos, C. S., Anders, P. L., Filip, D., & Jaffe, L. E. (1989). The effects of an interactive instructional strategy for enhancing reading comprehension and content area learning for students with learning disabilities. *Journal of Learning Disabilities, 22*(6), 384–390.

Boulanger, D. F. (1981). Ability and science learning: A quantitative synthesis. *Journal of Research in Science Teaching, 18*(2), 113–121.

Breland, H. M., Jones, R. J., & Jenkins, L. (1994). *The College Board vocabulary study.* New York: College Entrance Examination Board.

Burris, C. C., & Garrity, D. T. (2012). *Opening the Common Core: How to bring all students to college and career readiness.* Thousand Oaks, CA: Corwin Press.

Calderón, M., Hertz-Lazarowitz, R., & Slavin, R. (1998). Effects of Bilingual Cooperative Integrated Reading and Composition on students making the transition from Spanish to English reading. *The Elementary School Journal, 99*(2), 153–165.

Carleton, L., & Marzano, R. J. (2010). *Vocabulary games for the classroom.* Bloomington, IN: Marzano Research Laboratory.

Carlo, M. S., August, D., McLaughlin, B., Snow, C., Dressler, C., Lippman, D., et al. (2004). Closing the gap: Addressing the vocabulary needs of English-language learners in bilingual and mainstream classrooms. *Reading Research Quarterly, 39*(2), 188–215.

Carroll, J. B. (1971). *Learning from verbal discourse in educational media: A review of the literature.* Princeton, NJ: Educational Testing Service.

Carroll, J. B., Davies, P., & Richman, B. (1971). *The American Heritage word frequency book.* Boston: Houghton Mifflin.

Casale, U. P. (1985). Motor imaging: A reading-vocabulary strategy. *Journal of Reading, 28*(7), 619–621.

Castek, J., Dalton, B., & Grisham, D. L. (2012). Using multimedia to support generative vocabulary learning. In E. J. Kame'enui & J. F. Baumann (Eds.), *Vocabulary instruction: Research to practice* (2nd ed., pp. 303–321). New York: Guilford Press.

Chall, J. S., Jacobs, V. A., & Baldwin, L. E. (1990). *The reading crisis: Why poor children fall behind.* Cambridge, MA: Harvard University Press.

Christinson, J., Wiggs, M. D., Lassiter, C. J., & Cook, L. (2012). *Navigating the mathematics Common Core State Standards: Getting ready for the Common Core handbook series.* Englewood, CO: Lead and Learn Press.

Clark, H. H., & Clark, E. V. (1977). *Psychology and language: An introduction to psycholinguistics.* New York: Harcourt Brace Jovanovich.

Cohen, J. (1988). *Statistical power analysis for the behavioral sciences* (2nd ed.). Hillsdale, NJ: Erlbaum.

Common Core. (2012a). *Common Core curriculum maps in English language arts, grades K–5.* San Francisco: Jossey-Bass.

Common Core. (2012b). *Common Core curriculum maps in English language arts, grades 6–8.* San Francisco: Jossey-Bass.

Common Core. (2012c). *Common Core curriculum maps in English language arts, grades 9–12.* San Francisco: Jossey-Bass.

Covington, M. V. (1992). *Making the grade: A self-worth perspective on motivation and school reform.* Cambridge, England: Cambridge University Press.

Coyne, M. D., Capozzoli-Oldham, A., & Simmons, D. C. (2012). Vocabulary instruction for young children at risk of reading difficulties: Teaching word meanings during shared storybook readings. In E. J. Kame'enui & J. F. Baumann (Eds.), *Vocabulary instruction: Research to practice* (2nd ed., pp. 51–71). New York: Guilford Press.

Crawford, J. (2012). *Aligning your curriculum to the Common Core State Standards.* Thousand Oaks, CA: Corwin Press.

Cromley, J. G., & Azevedo, R. (2007). Testing and refining the direct and inferential mediation model of reading comprehension. *Journal of Educational Psychology, 99*(2), 311–325.

Cunningham, A. E., & Stanovich, K. E. (1997). Early reading acquisition and its relation to reading experience and ability 10 years later. *Developmental Psychology, 33*(6), 934–945.

Cunningham, A. E., & Stanovich, K. E. (1998). What reading does for the mind. *American Educator, 22*(1–2), 8–15.

Curtis, M. E. (1987). Vocabulary testing and vocabulary instruction. In M. G. McKeown & M. E. Curtis (Eds.), *The nature of vocabulary acquisition* (pp. 37–51). Hillsdale, NJ: Erlbaum.

Daggett, W. R., Gendron, S. A., & Heller, D. A. (2010). *Transitioning to the Common Core State Standards and next generation assessments.* Rexford, NY: International Center for Leadership in Education.

Dalton, B., & Grisham, D. L. (2011). eVoc strategies: 10 ways to use technology to build vocabulary. *The Reading Teacher, 64*(5), 306–317.

DK Merriam-Webster children's dictionary. (2008). New York: Dorling Kindersley.

Dochy, F., Segers, M., & Buehl, M. M. (1999). The relation between assessment practices and outcomes of studies: The case of research on prior knowledge. *Review of Educational Research, 69*(2), 145–186.

Dunkle, C. A. (2012). *Leading the Common Core State Standards: From common sense to common practice.* Thousand Oaks, CA: Corwin Press.

Dunn, M., Bonner, B., & Huske, L. (2007). *Developing a systems process for improving instruction in vocabulary: Lessons learned.* Alexandria, VA: Association for Supervision and Curriculum Development.

Durkin, D. (1979). What classroom observations reveal about reading comprehension instruction. *Reading Research Quarterly, 14*(4), 481–533.

Durso, F. T., & Shore, W. J. (1991). Partial knowledge of word meanings. *Journal of Experimental Psychology: General,*
     120(2), 190–202.

Elleman, A. M., Lindo, E. J., Morphy, P., & Compton, D. L. (2009). The impact of vocabulary instruction on pas-
     sage-level comprehension of school-age children: A meta-analysis. *Journal of Research on Educational*
     Effectiveness, 2(1), 1–44.

Elwood, M. I. (1939). A preliminary note on the vocabulary test in the revised Stanford-Binet scale, form L. *Journal*
     of Educational Psychology, 30(8), 632–634.

Fellbaum, C. (Ed.). (1998). *WordNet: An electronic lexical database.* Cambridge, MA: MIT Press.

Fenno, N. L. (2011). *Common Core standards alignment workbook.* Marblehead, MA: Core Learning Resources.

Fisher, D., & Frey, N. (2013a). *Common Core English language arts in a PLC at work, grades K–2.* Bloomington, IN:
     Solution Tree Press.

Fisher, D., & Frey, N. (2013b). *Common Core English language arts in a PLC at work, grades 3–5.* Bloomington, IN:
     Solution Tree Press.

Fry, E. B., Kress, J. E., & Fountoukidis, D. L. (2000). *The reading teacher's book of lists* (4th ed.). San Francisco:
     Jossey-Bass.

Gifford, M., & Gore, S. (2008). *The effects of focused academic vocabulary instruction on underperforming math stu-
     dents.* Alexandria, VA: Association for Supervision and Curriculum Development.

Graves, M. F. (2008). Instruction on individual words: One size does not fit all. In A. E. Farstrup & S. J. Samuels
     (Eds.), *What research has to say about vocabulary instruction* (pp. 56–79). Newark, DE: International
     Reading Association.

Graves, M. F., & Slater, W. H. (1987, April). *The development of reading vocabularies in rural disadvantaged students,
     inner-city disadvantaged students, and middle-class suburban students.* Paper presented at the annual
     meeting of the American Educational Research Association, Washington, DC.

Hart, B., & Risley, T. R. (1995). *Meaningful differences in the everyday experience of young American children.*
     Baltimore: Brookes.

Hart, B., & Risley, T. R. (2003). The early catastrophe: The 30 million word gap by age 3. *American Educator, 27*(1),
     4–9.

Hattie, J. A. C. (2009). *Visible learning: A synthesis of over 800 meta-analyses relating to achievement.* New York:
     Routledge.

Haystead, M. W., & Marzano, R. J. (2009). *Meta-analytic synthesis of studies conducted at Marzano Research
     Laboratory on instructional strategies.* Englewood, CO: Marzano Research Laboratory. Accessed at http://
     files.solution-tree.com/MRL/documents/Instructional_Strategies_Report_9_2_09.pdf on December 17,
     2012.

Hoff, E. (2003). The specificity of environmental influence: Socioeconomic status affects early vocabulary develop-
     ment via maternal speech. *Child Development, 74*(5), 1368–1378.

Jenkins, J. R., Stein, M. L., & Wysocki, K. (1984). Learning vocabulary through reading. *American Educational
     Research Journal, 21*(4), 767–787.

Kagan, S., & Kagan, M. (2009). *Kagan cooperative learning* (2nd ed.). San Clemente, CA: Kagan.

Kamil, M. L., & Hiebert, E. H. (2005). Teaching and learning vocabulary: Perspectives and persistent issues. In E.
     H. Hiebert & M. L. Kamil (Eds.), *Teaching and learning vocabulary: Bringing research to practice* (pp. 1–23).
     Mahwah, NJ: Erlbaum.

Kanold, T. D. (Ed.). (2012a). *Common Core mathematics in a PLC at work, grades K–2*. Bloomington, IN: Solution Tree Press.

Kanold, T. D. (Ed.). (2012b). *Common Core mathematics in a PLC at work, grades 3–5*. Bloomington, IN: Solution Tree Press.

Kanold, T. D. (Ed.). (2012c). *Common Core mathematics in a PLC at work, high school*. Bloomington, IN: Solution Tree Press.

Kanold, T. D. (Ed.). (2012d). *Common Core mathematics in a PLC at work, leader's guide*. Bloomington, IN: Solution Tree Press.

Kanold, T. D. (Ed.). (2013). *Common Core mathematics in a PLC at work, grades 6–8*. Bloomington, IN: Solution Tree Press.

Kendall, J. (2011). *Understanding Common Core State Standards*. Alexandria, VA: Association for Supervision and Curriculum Development.

Kendall, J. (Ed.). (2012a). *Common Core standards for high school English language arts: A quick-start guide*. Alexandria, VA: Association for Supervision and Curriculum Development.

Kendall, J. (Ed.). (2012b). *Common Core standards for high school mathematics: A quick-start guide*. Alexandria, VA: Association for Supervision and Curriculum Development.

Kendall, J. (Ed.). (2012c). *Common Core standards for middle school English language arts: A quick-start guide*. Alexandria, VA: Association for Supervision and Curriculum Development.

Kendall, J. (Ed.). (2013). *Common Core standards for middle school mathematics: A quick-start guide*. Alexandria, VA: Association for Supervision and Curriculum Development.

Kendall, J. S., & Marzano, R. J. (2000). *Content knowledge: A compendium of standards and benchmarks for K–12 education* (3rd ed.). Aurora, CO: Mid-continent Research for Education and Learning.

Kintsch, W. (1974). *The representation of meaning in memory*. Hillsdale, NJ: Erlbaum.

Kintsch, W. (1979). On modeling comprehension. *Educational Psychologist, 14*(1), 3–14.

Kintsch, W. (1998). *Comprehension: A paradigm for cognition*. New York: Cambridge University Press.

Kintsch, W., & van Dijk, T. A. (1978). Toward a model of text comprehension and production. *Psychological Review, 85*(5), 363–394.

Klesius, J. P., & Searls, E. F. (1990). A meta-analysis of recent research in meaning vocabulary instruction. *Journal of Research and Development in Education, 23*(4), 226–235.

Landau, S. I. (1984). *Dictionaries: The art and craft of lexicography*. New York: Scribner.

Lesaux, N. K., & Kieffer, M. J. (2010). Exploring sources of reading comprehension difficulties among language minority learners and their classmates in early adolescence. *American Educational Research Journal, 47*(3), 596–632.

Lesaux, N. K., Kieffer, M. J., Faller, S. E., & Kelley, J. G. (2010). The effectiveness and ease of implementation of an academic English vocabulary intervention for linguistically diverse students in urban middle schools. *Reading Research Quarterly, 45*(2), 196–228.

Lewinski, R. J. (1948). Vocabulary and mental measurement: A quantitative investigation and review of research. *Journal of Genetic Psychology, 72*, 247–281.

Lipsey, M. W. (1990). *Design sensitivity: Statistical power for experimental research*. Newbury Park, CA: SAGE.

Lipsey, M. W., & Wilson, D. B. (2001). *Practical meta-analysis.* Thousand Oaks, CA: SAGE.

Mahan, H. C., & Witmer, L. A. (1936). A note on the Stanford-Binet vocabulary test. *Journal of Applied Psychology, 20,* 258–263.

Malone, T. W. (1981a). Toward a theory of intrinsically motivating instruction. *Cognitive Science, 5*(4), 333–367.

Malone, T. W. (1981b). *What makes things fun to learn? A study of intrinsically motivating computer games.* Paper presented at the annual meeting of the American Educational Research Association, Los Angeles.

Manzo, U. C., & Manzo, A. V. (2008). Teaching vocabulary-learning strategies: Word consciousness, word connection, and word prediction. In A. E. Farstrup & S. J. Samuels (Eds.), *What research has to say about vocabulary instruction* (pp. 80–105). Newark, DE: International Reading Association.

Marmolejo, A. (1990). *The effects of vocabulary instruction with poor readers: A meta-analysis.* Unpublished master's thesis, Columbia University Teachers College, New York.

Marmolejo, A. (1991, April). *The effects of vocabulary instruction with poor readers.* Paper presented at the annual meeting of the American Educational Research Association, Chicago.

Martinez, M., & Roser, N. L. (2003). Children's response to literature. In J. Flood, D. Lapp, J. R. Squires, & J. M. Jensen (Eds.), *Handbook of research on teaching the English language arts* (2nd ed., pp. 799–813). Mahwah, NJ: Erlbaum.

Marulis, L. M., & Neuman, S. B. (2010). The effects of vocabulary intervention on young children's word learning: A meta-analysis. *Review of Educational Research, 80*(3), 300–335.

Marzano, R. J. (2002). *Identifying the primary instructional concepts in mathematics: A linguistic approach.* Centennial, CO: Marzano Research Laboratory.

Marzano, R. J. (2004). *Building background knowledge for academic achievement: Research on what works in schools.* Alexandria, VA: Association for Supervision and Curriculum Development.

Marzano, R. J. (2005). *Marzano program for building academic vocabulary: Preliminary report of the 2004–2005 evaluation study.* Centennial, CO: Marzano Research Laboratory. Accessed at www.marzanoresearch.com /documents/BuildingAcademicVocabulary-PreliminaryReport.pdf on December 17, 2012.

Marzano, R. J. (2006). *Marzano program for building academic vocabulary: Supplemental report of effects on specific subgroups (FRL & ELL students).* Centennial, CO: Marzano Research Laboratory. Accessed at www .marzanoresearch.com/documents/BuildingAcademicVocabulary-SupplementalReport.pdf on December 17, 2012.

Marzano, R. J. (2007). *The art and science of teaching: A comprehensive framework for effective instruction.* Alexandria, VA: Association for Supervision and Curriculum Development.

Marzano, R. J. (2009). *Designing & teaching learning goals & objectives.* Bloomington, IN: Marzano Research Laboratory.

Marzano, R. J. (2010). *Teaching basic and advanced vocabulary: A framework for direct instruction.* Boston: Cengage ELT.

Marzano, R. J. (with Boogren, T., Heflebower, T., Kanold-McIntyre, J., & Pickering, D.) (2012) . *Becoming a reflective teacher.* Bloomington, IN: Marzano Research Laboratory.

Marzano, R. J., Brandt, R. S., Hughes, C. S., Jones, B. F., Presseisen, B. Z., Rankin, S. C., et al. (1988). *Dimensions of thinking: A framework for curriculum and instruction.* Alexandria, VA: Association for Supervision and Curriculum Development.

Marzano, R. J., & Marzano, J. S. (1988). *A cluster approach to elementary vocabulary instruction.* Newark, DE: International Reading Association.

Marzano, R. J., & Pickering, D. J. (2005). *Building academic vocabulary: Teacher's manual.* Alexandria, VA: Association for Supervision and Curriculum Development.

Marzano, R. J., Pickering, D. J., & Pollock, J. E. (2001). *Classroom instruction that works: Research-based strategies for increasing student achievement.* Alexandria, VA: Association for Supervision and Curriculum Development.

Marzano, R. J., Yanoski, D. C., Hoegh, J. K., & Simms, J. A. (with Heflebower, T., & Warrick, P.). (2013). *Using Common Core standards to enhance classroom instruction and assessment.* Bloomington, IN: Marzano Research Laboratory.

McCoid, J. (2011). *Common Core State Standards: Building a solid foundation.* Charleston, NC: CreateSpace.

McEwan-Adkins, E. K., & Burnett, A. J. (2013). *20 literacy strategies to meet the Common Core: Increasing rigor in middle & high school classrooms.* Bloomington, IN: Solution Tree Press.

McKeown, M. G., Beck, I. L., & Apthorp, H. S. (2010). *Examining depth of processing in vocabulary lessons.* Unpublished manuscript.

McKeown, M. G., Beck, I. L., Omanson, R. C., & Perfetti, C. A. (1983). The effects of long-term vocabulary instruction on reading comprehension: A replication. *Journal of Reading Behavior, 15*(1), 3–18.

McKeown, M. G., Beck, I. L., Omanson, R. C., & Pople, M. T. (1985). Some effects of the nature and frequency of vocabulary instruction on the knowledge and use of words. *Reading Research Quarterly, 20*(5), 522–535.

McNemar, Q. (1942). *The revision of the Stanford-Binet scale, an analysis of the standardization data.* Boston: Houghton Mifflin.

Miller, G. A. (1995). WordNet: A lexical database for English. *Communications of the ACM, 38*(11), 39–41.

Moats, L. C. (1999). *Teaching reading is rocket science: What expert teachers of reading should know and be able to do.* Washington, DC: American Federation of Teachers.

Mol, S. E., Bus, A. G., & de Jong, M. T. (2009). Interactive book reading in early education: A tool to stimulate print knowledge as well as oral language. *Review of Educational Research, 79*(2), 979–1007.

Mol, S. E., Bus, A. G., de Jong, M. T., & Smeets, D. J. H. (2008). Added value of dialogic parent-child book readings: A meta-analysis. *Early Education and Development, 19*(1), 7–26.

Nagy, W. (2005). Why vocabulary instruction needs to be long-term and comprehensive. In E. H. Hiebert & M. L. Kamil (Eds.), *Teaching and learning vocabulary: Bringing research to practice* (pp. 27–44). Mahwah, NJ: Erlbaum.

Nagy, W. E., Anderson, R. C., & Herman, P. A. (1987). Learning word meanings from context during normal reading. *American Educational Research Journal, 24*(2), 237–270.

Nagy, W., Berninger, V., Abbott, R., Vaughan, K., & Vermeulen, K. (2003). Relationship of morphology and other language skills to literacy skills in at-risk second grade readers and at-risk fourth grade writers. *Journal of Educational Psychology, 95*(4), 730–742.

Nagy, W. E., & Herman, P. A. (1984). *Limitations of vocabulary instruction* (Tech. Rep. No. 326). Champaign: University of Illinois, Center for the Study of Reading.

Nagy, W. E., & Herman, P. A. (1987). Breadth and depth of vocabulary knowledge: Implications for acquisition and instruction. In M. G. McKeown & M. E. Curtis (Eds.), *The nature of vocabulary acquisition* (pp. 19–35). Hillsdale, NJ: Erlbaum.

Nation, I. S. P. (1990). *Teaching and learning vocabulary.* New York: Newbury House.

National Early Literacy Panel. (2008). *Developing early literacy: Report of the National Early Literacy Panel.* Washington, DC: National Institute for Literacy.

National Governors Association Center for Best Practices & Council of Chief State School Officers. (2010a). *Common Core State Standards for English language arts & literacy in history/social studies, science, and technical subjects: Appendix A—Research supporting key elements of the standards and glossary of key terms.* Washington, DC: Authors.

National Governors Association Center for Best Practices & Council of Chief State School Officers. (2010b). *Common Core State Standards for mathematics.* Washington, DC: Authors.

National Reading Panel. (2000). *Teaching children to read: An evidence-based assessment of the scientific research literature on reading and its implications for reading instruction—Reports of the subgroups.* Washington, DC: U.S. National Institutes of Health, National Institute of Child Health and Human Development.

Nye, C., Foster, S. H., & Seaman, D. (1987). Effectiveness of language intervention with the language/learning disabled. *The Journal of Speech and Hearing Disorders, 52*(4), 348–357.

Padak, N., Newton, E., Rasinski, T., & Newton, R. M. (2008). Getting to the root of word study: Teaching Latin and Greek word roots in elementary and middle grades. In A. E. Farstrup & S. J. Samuels (Eds.), *What research has to say about vocabulary instruction* (pp. 6–31). Newark, DE: International Reading Association.

Peery, A., Wiggs, M. D., Piercy, T. D., Lassiter, C. J., & Cebelak, L. (2011). *Navigating the English language arts Common Core State Standards.* Englewood, CO: Lead and Learn Press.

Petty, W., Herold, C., & Stoll, E. (1967). *The state of the knowledge about the teaching of vocabulary.* Sacramento, CA: Sacramento State College.

Poirier, B. M. (1989). *The effectiveness of language intervention with preschool handicapped children: An integrative review.* Unpublished doctoral dissertation, Utah State University, Logan, UT.

Rasinski, T., Padak, N., Newton, R. M., & Newton, E. (2007). *Building vocabulary from word roots.* Huntington Beach, CA: Teacher Created Materials.

Raven, J. C. (1948). The comparative assessment of intellectual ability. *British Journal of Psychology, 39*(12), 12–19.

Reeves, D. B., Wiggs, M. D., Lassiter, C. J., Piercy, T. D., Ventura, S., & Bell, B. (2011). *Navigating implementation of the Common Core State Standards.* Englewood, CO: Lead and Learn Press.

Roehr, S., & Carroll, K. (Eds.). (2010). *Collins COBUILD illustrated basic dictionary of American English.* Boston: Heinle Cengage Learning.

Roser, N., & Juel, C. (1982). Effects of vocabulary instruction on reading comprehension. In J. Niles & L. Harris (Eds.), *New inquiries in reading research and instruction* (pp. 110–118). Rochester, NY: National Reading Conference.

Rothman, R. (2011). *Something in common: The Common Core standards and the next chapter in American education.* Cambridge, MA: Harvard Education Press.

Sadoski, M., & Paivio, A. (2001). *Imagery and text: A dual coding theory of reading and writing.* Mahwah, NJ: Erlbaum.

Scarborough, H. S. (2001). Connecting early language and literacy to later reading (dis)abilities: Evidence, theory, and practice. In S. B. Neuman & D. K. Dickinson (Eds.), *Handbook of early literacy research* (pp. 97–110). New York: Guilford Press.

Schiefele, U., & Krapp, A. (1996). Topic interest and free recall of expository text. *Learning and Individual Differences, 8*(2), 141–160.

Scott, J. A., Jamieson-Noel, D., & Asselin, M. (2003). Vocabulary instruction throughout the day in twenty-three Canadian upper-elementary classrooms. *The Elementary School Journal, 103*(3), 269–286.

Scott, J. A., Miller, T. F., & Flinspach, S. L. (2012). Developing word consciousness: Lessons from highly diverse fourth-grade classrooms. In E. J. Kame'enui & J. F. Baumann (Eds.), *Vocabulary instruction: Research to practice* (2nd ed., pp. 169–188). New York: Guilford Press.

Scott, J., & Nagy, W. E. (1997). Understanding the definitions of unfamiliar verbs. *Reading Research Quarterly, 32*(2), 184–200.

Shapiro, B. J. (1969). The subjective estimation of relative word frequency. *Journal of Verbal Learning and Verbal Behavior, 8*(2), 248–251.

Silver, H. F., Dewing, R. T., & Perini, M. J. (2012). *The core six: Essential strategies for achieving excellence with the Common Core.* Alexandria, VA: Association for Supervision and Curriculum Development.

Smith, M. K. (1941). Measurement of the size of general English vocabulary through the elementary grades and high school. *Genetic Psychology Monographs, 24*, 311–345.

Snow, C. E. (1990). The development of definitional skill. *Journal of Child Language, 17*(3), 697–710.

Snow, C. E. (2002). *Reading for understanding: Toward an R&D program in reading comprehension.* Santa Monica, CA: RAND.

Spache, G. (1943). The vocabulary tests of the revised Stanford-Binet as independent measures of intelligence. *Journal of Educational Research, 36*(7), 512–516.

Stahl, K. A. D., & Stahl, S. A. (2012). Young word wizards! Fostering vocabulary development in preschool and primary education. In E. J. Kame'enui & J. F. Baumann (Eds.), *Vocabulary instruction: Research to practice* (2nd ed., pp. 72–92). New York: Guilford Press.

Stahl, S. A. (1999). *Vocabulary development.* Cambridge, MA: Brookline Books.

Stahl, S. A. (2005). Four problems with teaching word meanings (and what to do to make vocabulary an integral part of instruction). In E. H. Hiebert & M. L. Kamil (Eds.), *Teaching and learning vocabulary: Bringing research to practice* (pp. 95–114). Mahwah, NJ: Erlbaum.

Stahl, S. A., & Clark, C. H. (1987). The effects of participatory expectations in classroom discussion on the learning of science vocabulary. *American Educational Research Journal, 24*(4), 541–555.

Stahl, S. A., & Fairbanks, M. M. (1986). The effects of vocabulary instruction: A model-based meta-analysis. *Review of Educational Research, 56*(1), 72–110.

Stahl, S. A., & Nagy, W. E. (2006). *Teaching word meanings.* Mahwah, NJ: Erlbaum.

Stanovich, K. E. (1986). Matthew effects in reading: Some consequences of individual differences in the acquisition of literacy. *Reading Research Quarterly, 21*(4), 360–407.

Sternberg, R. J. (1987). Most words are learned from context. In M. G. McKeown & M. E. Curtis (Eds.), *The acquisition of word meanings* (pp. 89–106). Hillsdale, NJ: Lawrence Erlbaum Associates.

Tamir, P. (1996). Science assessment. In M. Birenbaum & F. J. R. C. Dochy (Eds.), *Alternatives in assessment of achievements, learning processes, and prior knowledge* (pp. 93–129). Boston: Kluwer Academic.

Terman, L. M. (1918). The vocabulary test as a measure of intelligence. *Journal of Educational Psychology, 9*(8), 452–466.

Tobias, S. (1994). Interest, prior knowledge, and learning. *Review of Educational Research, 64*(1), 37–54.

Tulving, E. (1972). Episodic and semantic memory. In E. Tulving & W. Donaldson (Eds.), *Organization of memory* (pp. 185–191). New York: Academic Press.

van Dijk, T. A. (1977). *Text and context: Explorations in the semantics and pragmatics of discourse.* London: Longman.

van Dijk, T. A. (1980). *Macrostructures: An interdisciplinary study of global structures in discourse, interaction, and cognition.* Hillsdale, NJ: Erlbaum.

van Dijk, T. A., & Kintsch, W. (1983). *Strategies of discourse comprehension.* New York: Academic Press.

Wechsler, D. (1949). *Manual, Wechsler intelligence scale for children.* New York: Psychological Corporation.

White, T. G., Sowell, J., & Yanagihara, A. (1989). Teaching elementary students to use word-part clues. *The Reading Teacher, 42*(4), 302–308.

Index

A

affixes, 30–31

Alphabet Antonyms, 37

analogies, creating, 24, 28–29

assessing vocabulary

knowledge, 52–54

multiple-choice items, weak versus strong, 52–53

tracking chart, 53

B

background knowledge, 5

BAV (Building Academic Vocabulary), 14

Beck, I., 11, 15, 34–35, 36–37, 41, 42, 44, 52

Berlin, B., 9

Biemiller, A., 7

Bos, C., 42

Building Background Knowledge for Academic Achievement (Marzano), 44

C

Castek, J., 6, 7

CCSS (Common Core State Standards)

formation of, 1

vocabulary development and, 5, 7

vocabulary instruction and, 9

Clark, C., 34

classifying, 24, 27

Classroom Feud, 37

Collins COBUILD Illustrated Basic Dictionary, 15–16

Common Core State Standards Initiative, 1

comparing and contrasting, 24, 25–27

comparison matrix, 26–27

correlations, 6, 8–9, 10

Council of Chief State School Officers, 1

Covington, M., 36

Create a Category, 37

cumulative disadvantage, 7

Curtis, M., 13

D

Dalton, B., 6

Definition, Shmefinition, 37

definitions versus descriptions, 15–16

dictionary definitions, problem with, 15

differences, identifying similarities and, 24–29

Digital Vocabulary Field Trip, 37

discussions of terms, student, 34–36

DK Merriam-Webster Children's Dictionary, 15, 16

Draw Me, 37

dual coding theory, 19

Durso, F., 13

E

"Early Catastrophe: The 30 Million Word Gap by Age 3, The" (Hart and Risley), 6

effect size, 10–11

ELA (English Language Arts), measurement topics, 44, 45, 47

etymonline.com, 33

examples, providing, 18–19

F

Fairbanks, M., 10, 41

features of words, 16–18

G

games, use of, 36–40

give-one-get-one, 36

Grisham, D., 6

H

Hart, B., 6, 7, 14

Haystead, M. W., 14

Herman, P. A., 13

Hiebert, E., 7

Hoegh, J. K., 1

Hoff, E., 6

I

imagens, 19, 22–24

independent reading, vocabulary development and, 8

inside-outside circle, 36

IQ scores

    influence of socioeconomic status and, 6

    vocabulary development and, 8–9

J

Jenkins, J., 8

K

Kamil, M., 7

Kay, P., 9

knowledge

    background, 5

    prior, 5

    vocabulary and, 7–9

Kucan, L., 15

L

Landau, S., 15

linguistic representations, 19–20

logogens, 19, 20

M

Magic Letter, Magic Word, 37

Malone, T., 36

Marmolejo, A., 42

Marulis, L., 7

Marzano, R. J., 1, 8, 9, 13, 14, 16, 22, 24, 43, 44, 51, 52

Marzano Research Laboratory, 1, 44

mathematics, measurement topics, 44, 45, 47

McKeown, M., 11, 15, 36–37

measurement topics, 44, 45, 47, 89

mental processes, vocabulary development and, 8–9

Merriam-Webster Online, 33

meta-analysis, 10–11

metaphors, creating, 24, 28

Motor Imaging, 37

N

Nagy, W. E., 9, 13, 34

Name It!, 37

Name That Category, 38

National Governors Association (NGA), Center for Best Practices, 1

National Reading Panel (NRP), 7

Neuman, S., 7

nonlinguistic representations, 19–20, 22–24

notebooks, vocabulary, 20–22

O

Opposites Attract, 38

oral conversations, role of, 5–6

P

paired thinking, 35–36

Paivio, A., 19

percentile gain, 10–11

Perfetti, C., 36–37

Pickering, D. J., 22, 24, 51, 52

Pollock, J. E., 24

Possible Sentences, 38

prefixes. *See* affixes

prior knowledge, 5

propositional networks, 19–20

Puzzle Stories, 38

R

Rasinski, T., 32

reading ability, vocabulary development and, 7

Risley, T., 6, 7, 14

role cards, 35

Root Relay, 38

root words, 32–34

S

Sadoski, M., 19

Secret Language, 38

Semantic Feature Analysis, 38–39

semantic networks, 19–20

Sentence Stems, 39

Shore, W., 13

Silly Questions, 39

similarities and differences, identifying, 24–29

Simms, J. A., 1

Slonim, N., 7

Snow, C. E., 15

socioeconomic status, influence of, 6, 11

Sowell, J., 30

Stahl, K., 8

Stahl, S., 8, 9, 10, 11, 15, 29–30, 33, 34, 41, 42

Stein, M., 8

Sternberg, R. J., 9

student interest, vocabulary development and, 6–7

suffixes. *See* affixes

T

Talk a Mile a Minute, 39

Teaching Children to Read: An Evidence-Based Assessment of the Scientific Research Literature on Reading and Its Implications for Reading Instruction (NRP), 7

terms, selecting. *See* vocabulary terms, selecting

think-pair-share, 35

Tier 1 vocabulary, 41

Tier 2 vocabulary, 41, 42–44, 55–88

Tier 3 vocabulary, 41, 44–47, 89–213

Two of a Kind, 39

U

Using Common Core Standards to Enhance Classroom Instruction and Assessment (Marzano, Yanoski, Hoegh, and Simms), 1

V

Venn diagrams, 25–26

visual analogy diagrams, 29

vocabulary

    acquisition rates, 7

    development, 5–7, 13

    importance of, 5

    independent reading and, 8

    knowledge, 7–9

    knowledge, assessing, 52–54

    mental processes and, 8–9

    notebooks, 20–22

    reading ability and, 7

Tier 1, 41

Tier 2, 41, 42–44, 55–88

Tier 3, 41, 44–47, 89–213

See also vocabulary terms, selecting

Vocabulary Charades, 39

vocabulary instruction

effects of, 9–11

goal of, 13

vocabulary instruction, steps for

description, explanation, example of term, provide, 14–19

description, explanation, example of term, student restatement of, 19–22

games, use of, 36–40

picture, symbol, graphic representation of term, student provided, 22–24

reinforcement activities, 24–34

student discussions of terms, 34–36

vocabulary size, influence of socioeconomic status and, 6

vocabulary terms, selecting

assessing students' vocabulary knowledge, 52–54

individual teacher, 49–50

multiple-choice items, weak versus strong, 52–53

rating scale for, 51

school or district teams, 51–52

vocabulary terms, self-evaluation of knowledge of, 21, 22

Vocab Vids, 39

W

websites, for word roots and affixes, 33

What Is the Question?, 39

Where Am I?, 39

Which One Doesn't Belong?, 40

White, T., 30–31

Who Am I?, 40

Word Associations, 40

word features, 16–18

Word Harvest, 40

wordinfo.info, 33

Wordle, 40

word parts, understanding, 29–34

word walls, 36–37

Word Wizzle, 40

Wysocki, K., 8

Y

Yanagihara, A., 30

Yanoski, D. C., 1